# The Lost Haven of Sharon Taylor:

## Casualties in the Battle for Gender Equality in Sports

## By C. Terry Walters

i

Terremoto Grande Publishing

Cover design by Josh Lane

Library of Congress Control Number 2015912458

ISBN 978-0-9833285-2-0

# Dedications

Dedicated to all the women who contributed to the creation of Title IX and to those who paid a price to fight for the civil rights contained therein.

And to

My granddaughters, Mia and Isabella

And to

Pat Bethea Bell
1931-2015

# Table of Contents

Foreword................................................................viii

Introduction.............................................................1

Chapter One -The First 60 Years........................9

Chapter Two – Troubled Waters........................38

Chapter Three – A Flurry of Litigation..............56

Chapter Four – Taylor Fights Back....................73

Chapter Five - The Day of Reckoning................90

Chapter Six - The Brock Parker Saga................104

Chapter Seven – A Slap in the Face...................128

Chapter Eight - A Tale of Four Presidents.........142

Chapter Nine - Not the Only One......................166

Chapter Ten – Worse Than Fresno State?..........189

Chapter Eleven - The Price They Paid...............205

Chapter Twelve - Lessons Learned (Or Not)......216

Chapter Thirteen – Most Proud.........................227

Chapter Fourteen - Perspective.........................238

Appendices...................................................241

Notes............................................................270

# Acknowledgments

I would like to thank everyone who generously agreed to share their memories, comments, opinions, and observations via telephone, email or face-to-face interviews:

Bernice Sandler ... "Godmother of Title IX" for her work w/ Edith Green and others in Congress

Pat Bethea Bell ... Taylor's 4th grade teacher and lifelong friend

President Craig Dean Willis ... LHU 1982 - 2004

Jim Swistock ... LHU alumnus, entrepreneur, and former LHU Trustee

Virginia Roth ... LHU alumna, business executive, and former LHU Trustee

Bruce Baumgartner ... Superheavyweight Gold-medal Olympian, and Dir. of Athletics at Edinboro University of PA

Anthony "Rocky" Bonomo ... collegiate wrestling champion; Head Coach of Wrestling at LHU, 2004-2009

Barbara B. Dixon ... Interim President of LHU, 2010-2011

Peter A. Campbell ... Assoc. Dir. of Athletics with ST, 2001-2012; briefly, Interim AD 2012-2013

Dr. Gayatri S. Devi ... Professor of English, and advocate for students and women's issues

Tom Justice ... Asst. Men's Wrestling coach, turned Women's Swimming Coach, and very successful Volleyball Coach

Prof. Virginia "Bridget" Roun ... physical educator/sports studies faculty member; former Asst. FH Coach (with ST) and Head Lacrosse Coach, 1987-1996

Terry Fike ... Head Coach of Women's Wrestling Club

Dr. Betty Baird Schantz ... Former Dean of Education, Temple University, and Assoc. Dean of Education at LHU; owner, Partnership House B&B

Dr. Zak Hossain ... Professor of Sociology, Anthropology and Social Work, and former Provost at LHU

Diane Milutinovich ... Sr. Associate AD at Fresno State University

Merrily Dean Baker ... Assoc. AD at Princeton University; Director of Athletics at Michigan State U. (first woman AD in the Big Ten); Vice President at the NCAA; 11th and last President of the AIAW

Dr. Donna A. Lopiano ... Women's Dir. of Athletics at Univ. of Texas, Austin; Executive Director of the Women's Sports Foundation; and the 10th President of the AIAW

Judith Sweet ... Director of Athletics at the U. of California, San Diego; first woman (elected) President of the NCAA; later, Vice President (staff position) of the NCAA

Nancy-Hogshead-Makar, J.D....Three-time Olympic champion swimmer, 1984 and CEO of Champion Women

Karen Weaver...Filed Hockey All-American LHU 1980

Pat Rudy ... LHU Head Field Hockey Coach since 1996

Brock Parker ... Former LHU wrestler

Lori Baker ... Mother of Brock Parker

Aaron Fry ... Former LHU wrestler

Robbin Fry ... Mother of Aaron Fry

Joey Rivera. Wrestling coach at East Stroudsburg U.

Lindy Vivas ... Former Head Volleyball Coach at Fresno State

Melissa Heinz ... Former Head Women's Soccer Coach at Winthrop and Valdosta U.

Jaye Flood ... Former Head Volleyball Coach Florida Gulf Coast U.

Holly Vaughn ... Former LPGA golfer and Head Women's Golf Coach FGCU

Dennis Therrell—Former head football coach LHU 1990-95, D.C. 1987-89

Josh Lane... for book cover and photo design (joshlane.stet@gmail.com).

I am grateful to Roxanne Gustitis (LHU '82) for permission to use her letter to the Lock Haven Express.

Special thanks to Christine H. B. Grant ...Director of Women's Athletics U. of Iowa, founding member of AIAW, U. of Iowa Athletics Hall of Fame

Linda D. Koch ... Vice President for Student Affairs (only one ever) at LHU, 1987-2013; had oversight for Office of Law Enforcement on campus for her invaluable contributions, not the least of which was her insight into the workings of a state university.

I would like to acknowledge the indispensible proofreading and editing performed by Carolyn Perry who also opened up her home to me during my visit to New Orleans and gave me important tips to more enjoy the Jazz Fest.

Thanks to Jay Penica of Penica Associates for suggesting to Sharon Taylor that I could write a book about her life.

I would additionally like to recognize the contributions of attorney Kathleen Yurchak (Goodall & Yurchak Attorneys At Law) for legal guidance.

While I visited Lock Haven, Betty Schantz provided me the use of her Bed and Breakfast for interviews.

Lastly and most importantly, I thank Sharon E. Taylor for sharing both the happy and bitter events that make up her life story.

# Foreword

# By Dr. Christine H. B. Grant

## The Lost Haven of Sharon Taylor:
## Casualties in the Battle for Gender Equality in Sports

When I was asked to write a foreword to this book, I decided that I would try to look at the content from a larger perspective. I hope this will help readers to understand the significance of Sharon Taylor's story.

A few years ago, I watched the movie "Iron Jawed Angels" that documented the battle in the early 20th century to achieve the rights of women to vote in the U.S.A. Recently, I viewed the film "Suffragette" that portrayed a similar battle that occurred in Great Britain around the same time period. Both accounts were simultaneously depressing and inspiring; depressing because of the brutal and relentless reaction of many men as their domination of women was being threatened, and inspiring because of the inordinate strength of many women to endure the cruel treatment since they believed that the cause was worthy of any personal sacrifice, including incarceration, multiple forced feedings and, for Emily Davison, death. Emily Davison was jailed nine times and force-fed 49 times before deliberately entering the race track and being fatally injured by the King's horse at the Epson Derby in 1913. The incident immediately brought national media attention and public support to the cause.

In the U.S.A., the first public demand for suffrage for women had come at the 1848 conference in Seneca Falls. It took 72 years to achieve these rights.

In Britain, suffrage was first advocated by Mary Wollstonecraft in 1792. It was then demanded by the Chartist Movement in the 1840s. The enfranchisement of women over the age of 30 passed in 1918; then, in 1928 the age for women was lowered to the same age as men, i.e., 21 years.

In both countries, it took decades to achieve the desired results because of the fierce opposition to women's rights. Opposition to full equality continues today but the extent of it is difficult to gauge since it is less overt. In the opinion of many, the two most important pieces of legislation for women's equality in the U.S.A. in the 20th century were suffrage in 1920 and Title IX of the Education Amendments of 1972.

Title IX mandated the elimination of all gender-based discriminatory practices in educational institutions. Almost immediately, admission standards and access to all academic offerings were changed, as were the criteria for the awarding of financial aid. These revolutionary actions were implemented almost without resistance, but when it was discovered that Title IX also required educational institutions to provide equal opportunity to, and equal treatment of, students in interscholastic and intercollegiate athletic programs, "all hell broke loose".

For many, the intrusion of women into the sacred realm of competitive sport was unacceptable, in the same way it was unacceptable for women to fight for the right to vote. Sport, like politics, was viewed strictly as a male domain.

Resistance to Title IX came in many forms. In the 1970's, attempts were made to exclude from coverage: all of athletics, "revenue producing" sports and, the true objects of concern, football and men's basketball. Unsuccessful in those attempts, institutions were left with no option but to expand opportunities for girls and women at the high school and college/university levels. Reluctantly, they did so and thus began the athletic revolution in the U.S.A. that continues to this day, 43 years after the passage of Title IX.

Surely four decades would seem to be long enough to reach a semblance of equity; sadly, this is not the case. In every measure at the high school or college level, playing slots for boys and men exceed those for girls and women; budgets are similarly skewed; provision of uniforms, travel expenses, facilities, and recruiting expenses (college level) all favor male participants over female participants, even when girls and women are the dominant gender in enrollment and they compete against the same opponents in conferences and leagues. And, at NCAA member institutions the disparities are greater in divisions and subdivisions where institutions have the most lavish budgets.

Throughout higher education, personnel decisions, often made in the name of equity, disadvantaged women professionals: the male "Dean of Students" replaced gender-identified Deans of Men and Deans of Women; a male department head in the Physical Education Department took the place of the Men's Chair and the Women's Chair in formerly separate departments. In the vast majority of cases when gender-separated entities were combined, women were placed in subordinate positions to men even though both had the same academic preparation and qualifications.

Perhaps the most egregious example of the loss of ground for women in higher education occurred in the coaching ranks. The rapid decline in the number of female collegiate coaches began in the late 1970s when money started to be allocated to women's athletics. Prior to that time, when there was almost no money spent on women's sports, more than 90% of all head coaches were female and most received no compensation. However, as coaches began to be compensated, more men became interested in these head coaching positions. Today, only 40% of women's teams are coached by women, yet women have been essentially locked out of coaching men's teams with only 4% of men's teams coached by women. When the data of head coaches of all men's and women's teams in the NCAA are combined, 80% of all teams are coached by men.

Female administrators fared no better than female coaches after the late '70s; when women's athletic departments were merged with men's, in almost all instances, a man was chosen as "the" athletic director and the woman may have been retained in a subordinate position.

At the national level, female administrators enjoyed an entire decade of decision- making in the organization named the Association for Intercollegiate Athletics for Women (AIAW) that was founded in 1971 to create and govern national championships for college and university women. However, after a highly successful decade, the AIAW was put out of business by the NCAA initiating women's championships and, in 1982, most of the women's programs were put under the jurisdiction of the men's organization by the almost exclusively male-dominated faculty representatives' group in the NCAA. The result was that women, who had for a decade enjoyed the leadership opportunities in the AIAW and who had built a different type of organization, were forced to live, without vote, in an organization for which they did not vote and under a structure and a value system with which many did not agree. Almost simultaneously, women's programs were incorporated into existing men's conferences.

Thus, in a few short years, women's athletic programs had been merged at the institutional level, at the conference level, and at the national level. In these mergers, many women were demoted from their decision-making positions, were fired, or decided to "voluntarily" leave the athletic environment.

While female coaches and administrators in intercollegiate athletics have never felt particularly welcomed in many athletic departments over the decades, in recent years, the number of women being fired or forced to resign appears to be on the increase. This trend truly deserves to be researched more thoroughly than it has ever been.

This preamble brings me to the topic of this book: Sharon Taylor. She was a tremendously successful coach, a greatly respected administrator and a national and international leader who helped forge unprecedented opportunities for women in intercollegiate athletics in the U.S.A. Her commitment and dedication have earned her accolades from her peers across the nation as well as an uncommonly long list of awards that pay tribute to her accomplishments.

Given her achievements and her national reputation, one could have anticipated a well-deserved celebration of Taylor's more than 40 years' tenure at Lock Haven University. Instead, for several years in the latter part of her career, she was subjected to unsubstantiated claims of bias and lack of support for the men's athletic teams. She was then removed from her position as Director of Athletics.

Throughout the decades, those in women's athletics have often been scapegoated for the decline in the number of teams in men's so-called "minor sports", or blamed for any decline in the performances of some men's teams regardless of the reality of the situation.

Although it is a great relief to realize that the physical brutality of the suffrage movement has not been a characteristic of the athletic revolution, the results of emotionally abusive and hostile environments cannot be ignored or condoned. These tactics are alternate forms of emotional violence designed to destroy the soul of even the strongest women. The culture on some campuses that demeans women and devalues their careers must be changed. That is the challenge to today's university officials and athletic administrators who believe in and are committed to true fairness for all.

Like generations of other strong women before her, Sharon Taylor challenged the status quo on behalf of female student-athletes in the pursuit of justice and equality for all students…men, as well as women. She, like her forbearers, also paid a price.

This is her story.


**Christine H.B. Grant, PhD**
**Athletics Director Emerita, and Associate Professor Emerita**
**The University of Iowa**
**9th President of the AIAW**

Dr. Christine H. B. Grant

# Introduction

*Lost Haven* was written to tell the story of Sharon E. Taylor, former Director of Athletics at Lock Haven University in Pennsylvania. Taylor was, and certainly still is, a strong advocate for gender equity in athletics. As a youth, she had many more athletic options than her parents' generation, but girls' and women's sports still lagged light years behind men's programs. Prior to the 1970s, high school girls and collegiate women had no legal right to engage in organized sports activities. Some schools offered more female sports teams than others. More often than not, the coaches were women, although few were compensated for their efforts.

Title IX of the Education Amendments of 1972 became part of the pantheon of important pieces of civil rights legislation to emerge in the decade following the assassination of John F. Kennedy. One cannot point to the passage of Title IX and declare that it changed everything. It did not; at least not immediately. Another decade went by before the regulations would be ironed out, and the major attempts to kill or weaken the law would be defeated.

An understanding of Title IX is a prerequisite to be able to appreciate the life force that drove Sharon Taylor and countless other women to fight for gender equity in athletics. Thus, Lost Haven begins with the story of Bernice "Bunny" Sandler, called the "Godmother of Title IX." Sandler was not an athlete, nor was her goal to strike down the dominance that men held over sports. But, she did just that.

## Too Strong For a Woman

The impetus for the creation of Title IX can be attributed to a woman named Bernice Sandler. Sandler was not an athlete like Katherine Switzer, who wanted the right to participate in long-distance running along with the men. Switzer signed up for the Boston Marathon in 1967 as K. V. Switzer. Marathon officials had no reason to suspect that K. V. was a woman because the race was officially for men only. Despite the fact that a race official "caught her" in mid race, she ignored his command to stop and completed the course.

Sandler was not an Olympic swimming medalist like Lynn Colella who competed at the collegiate level but had no opportunity to earn a scholarship, unlike her brother Rick. Nor was Sandler a college or university coach struggling to field a women's sports team without a budget for transportation, equipment or recruiting.

Bernice Sandler was, in fact, not an athlete at all. In the late 1960s she was teaching at the University of Maryland's College of Education while finishing her doctorate degree. Her goal was obtaining a professorship at that same institution. Several positions were available and she felt confident in her qualifications. Upon learning that she had not been selected, she turned to a faculty member to seek the reasons for her exclusion. Quite candidly, her friend told her she had not really been considered for any of the openings. What he said next totally blew her mind. "You come on too strong for a woman."

"Too strong for a woman." Those words initially stunned Sandler, and sent her home crying. Upon reflection, those same words lit a fire that hasn't been extinguished to this day. Sandler calls them "the five words that created Title IX."

Sandler never viewed herself as "that kind of woman." Her nickname, Bunny, projects an image that lies 180 degrees from the dominant personality implied by her faculty friend's assessment. Forty-plus years later, she still wonders about that comment. "I was certainly much sweeter and ladylike, much more demure than I am now. God knows, I did want to be more ladylike. It was one of my goals then. It certainly isn't now."

Sandler later applied for a research position with a Washington firm that had been awarded a federal contract. The interviewer very bluntly told her that he did not hire women because they take off from work when their kids are sick. She responded that her kids were in high school and did not require her to stay home with them when illness struck. She thought that her comeback was very logical, but the balance of the interview did not include a discussion of her credentials, which she deemed as perfect. Instead it became a screed on the folly of hiring women.

She next scheduled an interview with an employment agency specializing in professional job openings. Sandler was surprised to learn that she was not actually a professional. Said the interviewer, "Oh, you're not a professional. You're a housewife who went back to school." [1]

Sandler surmised, "It's immoral to discriminate like that. It must be illegal." To her surprise, she soon learned that it was not illegal to discriminate against women. Surely, Title VII of the Civil Rights Act provided some provisions for women in the workplace. The act prohibited discrimination in employment on the basis of race, color, religion, national origin and sex. There it was. But wait, the act included an exemption for "educational institutions in their educational activities." So, if you were a woman administrator or faculty member at the University of Maryland, or any other school, you were on your own. No equal rights protection for you.

Turning to Title VI of the same act, she discovered that the educational workplace was covered but that sex discrimination was missing from the protections. [2]

Finally, she learned that the Equal Pay Act prohibited sex discrimination in pay scale except for professional and administrative employees. This exemption included faculty members. [3]

In essence, federal civil rights legislation possessed a tiny crack, which Sandler and other women like her could slip silently through.

**The Footnote**

Sandler decided not to give up. She posed the questions, "What did the Blacks do? How did they break down segregation and workplace discrimination? Were there any strategies that women could use?" Her research led her to a report issued by the U.S. Commission on Civil Rights, which discussed the presidential Executive Order prohibiting federal contractors from discriminating on the basis of race, color, religion or national origin.

At first, this report seemed to offer no relief, but then Sandler spotted a footnote. She followed it to the rear of the report and read it once, then again, after which she let out a loud shriek. It appeared to her that she had found a way to legally fight sex discrimination. Just as the words "too strong for a woman" launched her mission to seek gender equity in the workplace, this footnote moved her closer to her goal.

The footnote said simply that Executive Order 11246, signed by President Lyndon B. Johnson in 1965, added sex discrimination to the law pertaining to U.S. government contractors. Most colleges and universities benefited from federal contracts and were subject to the provisions of this executive order. [4]

Sandler admits, "My next thought was that I had read it wrong. The self-confidence of women, even now, is less than men in general. I thought, I must have read it wrong or must have misunderstood it."

She did have enough confidence to call the Office of Federal Contract Compliance and ask them about the footnote. They put her in touch with a man that she thought was the director, but turned out to be the assistant director. Vincent Macaluso was his name. What he said next, took Sandler by surprise. He told her that he had been waiting for several years for someone to deploy Executive Order 11246 in the battle against sex discrimination.

Sandler and Macaluso combined talents and mapped out the first ever complaint against universities for engaging in sex discrimination. Sandler uncovered data showing the number of female employees decreasing each year at the University of Maryland. This was due to the systematic dismissal of women who were frequently replaced by men. She also determined that women were discriminated against in pay scale and opportunities for advancement. The latter charges blatantly violated the law set down by Executive Order 11246.

As the word began to spread of her efforts, information from women all over the country began to arrive in her mailbox. Before Sandler, the term sex discrimination essentially did not exist. Many women accepted this as status quo until they realized that they were actually victims of discrimination. Sandler's experience at Maryland was being duplicated at educational institutions everywhere. Before long, Sandler had filed similar complaints against hundreds of other schools.

## Congress Gets Involved

Many sources cite Hawaii congresswoman Patsy Mink as the co-author of Title IX. Senator Birch Bayh also gets credit as a co-author. According to Bunny Sandler, Representative Edith Green from Oregon deserves the honors for getting things moving in the House. Mink had introduced a bill called the Women's Educational Equity Act. Mink's goal was to add sex discrimination to Title VI and remove the educational exemption from Title VII. But Edith Green had something that Mink did not. She had the power that comes with heading a committee. Mink's bill would go nowhere until the head of a committee took up the cause.

A coalition of Black civil rights leaders warned Mink and Green that opening Title VI for a sex discrimination amendment might invite other more damaging changes as well. The opponents of racial equality had not folded their tents and gone home. The curse of unintended consequences had to be considered.

Green then introduced a similar bill, formed a sub-committee, and scheduled hearings. Mink's bill merged with that of Edith Green. Bunny Sandler worked hand-in-hand with Green, including the very important job of lining up women to testify before Green's committee.

## The Power of Women Together

The 1960s in America was an era of great change and unrest. The women's movement was one of the most explosive and divisive social causes taking root. The National Organization for Women formed in 1966 following a June meeting in Betty Friedan's hotel room. The group of 28 women were concerned about the EEOC's inability to enforce Title VII. A conference was scheduled in October to take action. At this conference, 19 women and two men founded NOW and elected Betty Friedan as their first president. [5]

NOW's aggressive approach to activism successfully brought women's issues to the forefront, but the press consistently presented them in a negative light. Sandler is very blunt in her assessment of the media's role in women's rights. "They were showing (these) women as man-hating, castrating bitches; terrible people that do radical things. They have marches and demonstrations."

Elizabeth "Betty" Boyer was an early member and supporter of NOW, but she recognized that most professional women could not relate to the controversial actions of NOW. One issue being pressed by NOW was abortion. Sandler claims that most women had never even heard the word spoken aloud. "If talked about at all, you whispered it." Any connection, whatsoever, with the abortion issue could kill support within Congress. An organization of professional, socially conservative women was needed to garner support throughout the country. Congress would not react well to the thought of "bra-burners" pushing for legislation.

Boyer, also a member of the Women's Equity Action League (WEAL), worked to create a charter declaring that they would lobby for women's rights only in the area of law, education and employment. WEAL recruited a number of Congressional women for their board of directors, including Martha Griffiths and Shirley Chisholm.

Sandler calls the American Council of Education the big elephant in Washington. Almost every college or university president has belonged to the A.C.E. They had the power to become a major obstacle to Edith Green's bill. But an odd thing happened when they were invited to testify. Sandler recalls, "Their lobbyist said that they didn't want to testify because there was no sex discrimination in education. Even if it existed, it was not a problem to them. Because no one testified, they had no idea what was in the bill."

Many women, however, did testify. Sandler had corresponded with many women employees of educational institutions from all over the country. She passed on their names to Green who invited them to come to Washington to share their stories and data.

Representative Shirley Chisholm (NY) recounted how her gender was a far greater handicap during her political career than her skin pigmentation. [6]

After seven days of hearings, Sandler was hired to prepare a written record of the hearings. She also offered to put together a coalition of women to promote and lobby Congressional members for their vote. Green emphatically denied her request. Miraculously, no major opposition to the bill had appeared, so she didn't want to awaken any potential pockets of resistance. The sleeping dogs would not be aroused.

## Two Men Seal the Deal

Senator Birch Bayh not only introduced the sister bill in the Senate, he performed the very important role of deflecting opposition and sculpting very narrow exceptions that prevented the bill from becoming watered down. By the time the bill reached the Senate, various interest groups had begun to wonder how, or if, it would impact them. As an example, national fraternity groups reckoned that they could no longer remain in existence as male-only organizations if Title IX passed. They asked for an exemption. Bayh granted it for admission purposes only. If they presented any kind of educational program, women would be entitled to attend. The fraternity representatives went home relieved and happy.

Sandler enjoys telling the story of how a group of southern senators came to Bayh in a tizzy. They loved to hold beauty pageants with college scholarships going to the winners. This new legislation would end the pageants unless men were allowed to complete. As a group, they asked Bayh, "Are you going to take scholarships away from our beautiful young women?" Bayh sent them home with an exemption as long as each contest had a talent component.

A question arose on the floor of the Senate demanding to know if women were going to be allowed to play on the football team. Bayh said "no" and serious opposition from university athletics never appeared.

In June of 1972, Congress passed Title IX and sent it to President Richard Nixon for his approval or veto. A few days before the bill arrived on Nixon's desk, five burglars had been arrested while breaking into Democratic National Party offices in the Watergate Complex.

The President probably had a distraction or two going on at that point. Allen Barra suggests that Nixon had virtually no idea of the impact Title IX would have on women's athletics. The principals involved in forging and passing the legislation likewise missed the implications for athletics. [7]

Nixon signed the bill into law on July 1, 1972, and joined the list of heroes and heroines in the story of Title IX. Love him or hate him, he deserves partial credit for this game-changing legislation.

Title IX did not mention sports. It did not mention women. Title IX, in fact, consisted of these 37 words:

*No person in the United States shall, on the basis of sex, be excluded from participation in, be denied the benefits of, or be subjected to discrimination under any education program or activity receiving federal financial assistance.*

# Chapter One -The First 60 Years

### Early Years

In 1953, a recent graduate of West Chester State Teachers College accepted an elementary teaching position with the Coatesville School District on the far western fringe of the Philadelphia suburbs. Pat Bethea Bell, a transplant from California, would teach fourth grade at Caln Elementary in Thorndale.

As Bell settled in to her first teaching job, one particular student stuck out almost immediately. Bell, now in her eighties, remembers very clearly, "I thought she was extraordinarily bright. She walked around with her black hair, bangs, black eyes and her little fists clenched all the time like she was going to hit someone. She was kind of bottled up. She swears that I kept her out in the hall most of the year. But I think she's kidding."

The object of Bell's reminiscence is Sharon Taylor. Bell theorizes that Taylor's teeth-grinding personality may have been related to the arrival of a baby brother after nine years of being the only child. Sharon disputes Bell's contention. She really wanted a baby brother and was ecstatic when Geoffrey Garth Taylor was born in February 1954. Taylor adds that she told her mother and father as they left for the hospital, "If it's a girl, leave her there."

Bell continued, "I don't know what made her so charming, but she charmed my whole family. My mother, my aunt and I just loved her; we had her over to the house for dinner. This is odd, but she is the only student that I kept a life-long relationship with."

Bell taught in the public schools for seven years before moving into adult education. She ranks Sharon Taylor as the best student she ever had.

Bell did not observe that Taylor was exceptionally athletic. "I certainly wouldn't have been surprised that she became an athlete, but I never anticipated her career while in fourth grade. All we played was some baseball and dodge ball. She loved that. I actually think that if she were a few years younger she would have been a civil rights lawyer. Why?

She was very brainy and very determined and dedicated. She goes after things, which is probably the quality of a good athlete."

"She got along with the other students fine as long as they didn't cross her. If anybody crossed her it was likely to be a boy. She would "pop 'em", as she used to say. She had a little temper and she would pop 'em. I never saw her fight with any of the girls. I think she got along very well overall."

Sharon Elizabeth Taylor was born on December 18, 1944, in Coatesville to Kathryn Mae Davis Taylor and Clarence Ernest Taylor, Jr. Her father moved to Coatesville from nearby Spring City as a boy. Her mother was born in Philadelphia but likewise moved to Coatesville.

Sharon's parents supported her athletic endeavors, though rarely in person. Her dad's job as a sheet metal specialist at Gindy Manufacturing in Downingtown kept him away from most sporting events. He did play a large part in keeping her interested at a young age by playing outdoors with her. Her mother was a homemaker and seldom found transportation to the games. Most American households in that era owned just one vehicle. Plus, she did not drive at that point in her life.

**Sharon Taylor:** *I couldn't do anything wrong in the eyes of my father. That was just a given. He was my biggest fan.*

*His name was Clarence, but his friends just called him Taylor. The family called him June or Junior, because he was named for his father.*

*I got my athletic genes from my Dad. He probably could have been a good athlete except he was a Depression child. He had to work from the time he reached high school. He worked for the CCC one summer (Civilian Conservation Corps). He was talented but he didn't get to play in any organized sport. He would come outside and play with me any time he could. Sometimes we would go to the park and play football. I remember coming home and complaining to my Mom that Daddy tackled me and made me get "hair" in my mouth. I meant grass, but I told her hair. I was three or four years old at the time.*

*Dad served in the Army Air Corps in World War II and came home to a job driving trucks. An accident cost him his leg. He wore an artificial leg from 1947 on. This never slowed him down and none of my friends even knew about it unless I told them.*

*I thought my father could do anything, because he really could. He built our house, fixed our car, did electrical wiring, everything. When I was about five years old, he turned a perfectly scaled baseball bat on a lathe and gave it to me. The bat even had my initials burned into it. Inside the diamond shape where the words Louisville Slugger might have been, he branded "S.E.T."*

*When I coached at Lock Haven, he traveled to some of the field hockey and softball games. Afterward, he would write up an article summarizing the game and highlighting Chester County student athletes. He would present his write-ups to the Local Daily News in West Chester. They would actually print his stories in the paper.*

*While I thought my father could do everything, I thought my mother knew everything. Her name was Kathryn Mae (Davis) Taylor. Family called her Mae. She was born in the Philadelphia area but moved to Coatesville by the time she entered high school. Her mother was a Quaker from the Main Line. Her father changed his name to Davis from Jablonski to court my grandmother. He was from Milwaukee and was very Polish. He worked on the Reading Railroad when he moved the family to Coatesville.*

*My mother didn't go to college but she was quite intelligent. She would help me spell words when she was in a good humor; make me look them up myself when she wasn't. She once made me carry a note to school to correct a teacher who mispronounced a word.*

*I had a young teacher that I thought the world of. She also served as our Girl Scout leader. I had written a report on Mozart, which I gave to my mother to read aloud. She came to a part where she read that Mozart was a child prodigy. I told her that the word should be pronounced protégée, although I spelled it p-r-o-d-i-g-y. I told her that Miss Dennis says it's pronounced protégée. She sat down and wrote a letter to Miss Dennis explaining the difference between the two words. I had to carry it to school and give it to my teacher.*

*My mother would always tell other people how proud she was of me. Like any other mother-daughter relationship, we had issues. We were both very strong-willed. My aunt, Mom's sister, once said to my dad, "Do you know why Sharon and Mae can't get along? It's because*

11

*Sharon is doing everything Mae would liked to have done when she was young." My aunt recognized that my mother had aspirations for things that just never happened.*

*My mom never drove, although she did get her license when I was in high school. The only thing she ever saw me play was softball. She happened to be in the stands one day when I was pitching. The batter hit the ball back through the box. The ball glanced off my glove and hit me in the face, knocking me down. When I finally became coherent she was standing over me. I started shouting, "Get off the field!" Everyone knew I was all right.*

*When I graduated from high school, I received a transistor radio and a Spalding baseball glove that cost $40, a lot of money in the 1960s. I didn't ask for the radio, but my mom told me why she bought it. She said that she didn't want to tell anybody she got her daughter a baseball glove for high school graduation.*

*But, actually, my parents were decades ahead of their time. As a girl I owned every tea service, bride doll, playhouse, etc., but I also had baseball (not softball) bats, gloves and balls, as well as a football and tennis racket. It took into the 1970s for parents to even consider such things for their daughters.*

Former LHU president Craig Dean Willis recalled a conversation he had with Clarence Taylor on the sidelines of a field hockey game. Willis asked him what Sharon was like as a young girl. The elder Taylor thought about the question for a moment and answered, "We knew early on that she was coordinated. We knew also that she was not easily intimidated. The other thing about her is she always had strategies."

Willis inquired about the use of the plural word "strategies". Taylor continued, "Because that's the way she was. I will give you an example. If you asked her why she didn't take the open shot in a high school basketball game when it was obviously from her spot on the court, she replied, 'First of all, the other team was expecting it. Second, I needed to pass it to Sue because she needed to build up her confidence. If she missed the shot I would be there for the rebound. I could then pass back to Jane who was good at the long shots. Again, I would be there for the rebound.' This could go on for several more steps."

## Early Influences

**Sharon Taylor:** *Babe Zaharias was the first woman that I ever heard about that was really a great athlete. Babe Zaharias taught me that women could be successful in sports, but she didn't serve as a call to gender equity. She was from West Texas; she was very rough like she just stepped off an oilrig. She didn't fit the model approved for female athletes at that time. A woman could only be gymnast, swimmer or tennis player. Team sports were not acceptable for women to play.*

*At a benefit they used to hold in Hershey for cancer research, I remember telling Chuck Bednarik (Philadelphia Eagles Hall of Fame linebacker 1948-1962) that he had been a hero of mine when there were no female role models. I was on the dais with Chuck, who was also one of my Dad's favorites. He signed his nametag and passed it down the table to me. I still have it.*

*A contemporary role model was Joan Joyce, probably the best softball player in the whole world. Today we are good friends. She is now the softball coach at Florida Atlantic. She still probably holds ASA and International records. She was the greatest pitcher in women's softball. I can't remember how many perfect games she pitched. She played for the Brakettes in Stratford, Connecticut. Connecticut was the heart of women's fast pitch softball in the 1960s-70s. Unfortunately, Joan just missed the Olympic years (1996-2008). She was also outstanding in volleyball and basketball. Taking up golf later in life, she joined LPGA tour at about 34 years old; just a great all-around athlete.*

*Another woman role model was Dutch hurdler Fannie Blankers-Koen. As a new mother with two kids she won four gold medals at the 1948 London Olympics. In the late 1960s, it was Donna DeVerona who was everybody's sweetheart after she won gold medals in Tokyo as a fourteen-year-old swimmer. Donna today is a great advocate for equity and Title IX.*

*Eddie Feigner (The King and his Court) was another influence. My father took me to see them play in 1955 or 1956 when I was in grade school. Feigner would pitch behind his back, under his leg, from second base, even blindfolded. Once he pitched to this monster of a guy who swung and missed. The catcher threw the ball over the fence and the batter thought somehow he had hit a home run. Many years later, my summer team, the Pennsburg Shamrocks, played an opener against*

13

*another women's team before the King played (the main attraction). I was in college at that time. I didn't get to play against him though.*

Like many residents of Chester County, the Taylor household favored the Philadelphia sports teams, particularly the Phillies. When playing hardball with the neighborhood boys, young Sharon would pretend she was Richie Ashburn as she walked to the plate to take her turn at bat. On the mound, she saw herself as Phillies great Robin Roberts facing down enemy batters. To this day, she designates Roberts as her favorite baseball player. Both Phillies have been enshrined in the Baseball Hall of Fame.

**High School Sports**

Unlike many high schools during the 1950s and 1960s, Coatesville fielded varsity sports teams for girls, four sports, in fact. Taylor played three of the four: softball, field hockey and basketball. She did not try out for the swim team. The sport she played the most was softball because of the summer leagues that were available. In fact, by her sophomore year, she was participating in adult leagues.

**Sharon Taylor:** *For four summers I worked at Pepperidge Farms, the last three years I worked a shift from midnight to the following morning lidding bread. Pepperidge had square loaves, so you had to put the dough in the bread pan and put a lid on it so when it rises it can't go any higher and it comes out square. I was working on the ovens during the summer, but I was always done by noon or sooner. I would go home and put the fan in the window (because) we had no AC. I would sleep under the fan for four or five hours, get up, get something to eat, and go off to play softball in the evening. I would come home around ten and find out from my dad what time I had to go back in to work. I would catch a quick nap, and start all over again.*

While Coatesville may have been a little ahead of their time with regard to girls' sports, they still exhibited some of the prevailing sexist traditions. In basketball, for example, the boys had almost exclusive use of the gym. The only exceptions occurred when the boys were playing a game in the evening. Once or twice a week, the girls had the gym at 3:00 p.m.

And while the boys' teams had playoffs at the end of the season to crown champions, the girls' teams played out their schedules and called it a season.

**Sharon Taylor:** *We didn't think anything of it in those days. Now looking back on that...well that was just the way it was. At that age, I didn't feel a sense of mission to change the world. You grow up in that setting and you adapt to your surroundings. The boys would come home from their school league games, then I would join them in the back lot. We always played baseball; I never even saw a softball until junior high school.*

Despite the success she had on the diamond, her real love was field hockey. She could never put her finger on the exact reason, but that enthusiasm would serve her well for the next half century.

As Taylor entered the twelfth grade, it was a forgone conclusion that she would attend West Chester State College. West Chester was well known and highly regarded for its physical education curriculum, her chosen field. Suddenly, one of life's serendipitous events happened and changed everything.

**Sharon Taylor:** *I grew up fourteen miles from West Chester and all of my physical education teachers had gone to West Chester State. From 7th grade right into 12th grade I was going to go to West Chester for physical education. Actually, my first love in school was history and politics, but, in 1962, if you were a young woman who wanted to be involved in sports as a career, you went into physical education. So, I applied right away in my senior year and was accepted. Around the beginning of October one of my 10th grade teachers, Bea Hallman, called and said that she was going to Lock Haven for her homecoming. She asked me if I wanted to come to Harrisburg and ride up with her for the day. I said sure. We watched the football game and walked around campus and I went home and told my parents that's where I wanted to go to school. I fell in love with the place. First of all, it was very friendly. You could walk around West Chester bleeding from the head and nobody would have said a word to you. Most of the kids came from Philadelphia, from the big city. Walk across the campus at Lock Haven and everybody said "hi" even though they didn't know you.*

15

## College Athlete

As accomplished as she was at all three sports, Taylor did not receive an athletic scholarship to Lock Haven State College. No one did. They offered no scholarships to men, let alone women. Sharon Taylor would have to pay her own way. Ironically, the first scholarship awarded to a female student athlete at Lock Haven went to Sherry Derr, a field hockey player recruited in 1981 by Coach Taylor. During her career, Derr scored 74 goals, definitely earning the annual scholarship award of $300.

During the early to mid-sixties, Lock Haven offered only two women's sports, field hockey (since 1945) and basketball (since the 1930s). Taylor participated in both. The Lock Haven women were more fortunate than many others. Penn State University, for example, had no varsity sports for women until 1964. Many women athletes had to settle for playing intramural sports, or play on a club team. During Taylor's tenure as a hockey player at Lock Haven, her squad competed against a club team from Penn State, and later, their varsity squad.

Taylor soon fell under the spell of Dr. Charlotte Smith, who coached both basketball and hockey. Many of Smith's attitudes, and coaching techniques would imprint on Taylor. Charlotte Smith recognized that most of her student athletes majored in physical education and were destined to be teachers and coaches. She geared her coaching style to that premise.

**Sharon Taylor:** *Dr. Smith would put us through all kinds of drills, and yet when we played and came off the field at halftime she would let us players talk to each other to try to figure things out for ourselves. If we didn't "get it," she would step in and say, "I suggest that..." She was a master teacher in that regard. Charlotte Smith was a woman of quiet dignity, a gentle soul. As an educator, she was the consummate professional.*

*I had her as a teacher in such disparate subjects as coaching team sports and dance; and, I had her as a student teacher supervisor. She ran the entire women's intramural program and coached both varsity sports. This was pre-contract, and she just worked like a dog.*

As important as Charlotte Smith was to the development of women's sports at Lock Haven, she stood side by side with another pioneering woman, Elizabeth K. Zimmerli. Dr. Zimmerli arrived in Lock Haven in 1946, from West Chester State Teachers College, as it was called until 1960. She had earned her PhD from Stanford University.

She became the first woman in the country to administer a physical education program comprised of both men and women. The standard organizational chart had a man in charge of both programs, or separate programs with a woman in charge of the women's program only. The position required more than just overseeing varsity and intramural sports. As an educator, she created the physical education curriculum, insisting on coed classes in most courses.

The influence of Charlotte Smith and Elizabeth Zimmerli would serve Taylor well as she evolved from player, to teacher and coach, to administrator.

Although Taylor was now playing collegiate varsity sports, her teams still did not vie for a league or conference championship. No women's teams received recognition for finishing with the best record. No women's teams had a chance to meet other successful teams in a play-off. When the last contest on the schedule concluded, the women emptied their lockers, if they had one, and packed their gear away until the following year, or in the case of seniors, packed it away for good.

Field hockey remained without national play-offs into the 1970's. When a championship tournament finally arrived later in that decade, Sharon Taylor would play a major role in its birth.

**Coaching Career**

Approaching her graduation from Lock Haven State College in 1966, Taylor began to look for a position in the physical education realm. At Susquehanna University in Selinsgrove, PA, Physical Education Director Bruce Wagenseller had an opening for a physical education teacher. In addition to teaching, the position would also include a head coaching position in field hockey. Fortunately for Taylor, Wagenseller was also a disciple of Dr. Zimmerli.

**Sharon Taylor:** *Bruce was one of Dr. Zimmerli's "boys." She picked up the phone and said, "Bruce, I have a candidate for you for that* *job." I had an interview the next week and a job the following week. She was very influential. I was hired to coach hockey, which I did for all five years. I started a tennis team the second or third year (I was there) and coached it, as well. During my last year, Ricki Stringfellow, who was the basketball coach, took a maternity leave. I told them I would coach basketball rather than having them go out and find a coach for one year.*

After four years at Susquehanna, Taylor was granted a leave of absence for one year to earn her Master's degree at the University of North Carolina at Greensboro. At one time, the school was known as the Women's College of the University of North Carolina. Although it had become coed in 1963, it retained a star-studded faculty of women educators, and had one of the best graduate programs in the nation.

Taylor had finished her graduate work by April 1971, but opted to stay in Greensboro for the summer to take a course in Russian history and to attend a seminar led by Katherine "Tyke" Ley visiting from Cortland State (now known as SUNY Cortland). The Cortland website features a biography that refers to her as "... a nationally renowned leader in athletics administration who, as the SUNY Cortland's women's physical education department chair from 1966-78, advocated and oversaw the transformation of women's athletics from 'play days' into full-fledged intercollegiate competition."

In 1971, Dr. Ley had just finished chairing the Commission on Intercollegiate Athletics for Women (CIAW) which was about to unveil the first governance organization for women's collegiate athletes: the Association for Intercollegiate Athletics for Women (AIAW). Ley and other women physical educators, committed to the idea of offering programs for the highly skilled woman athlete, had approached the NCAA about sponsoring championships for women. Having been rebuffed by the NCAA, they created their own education-based governance organization.

In her course, Dr. Ley granted each of her attendees a fifteen-minute meeting to present an idea or new concept in athletics. Taylor's topic revolved around a pet peeve that had hounded her as a student athlete and later as a coach. Field hockey, like other women's sports at the collegiate level, offered no national championship to determine the best teams in the country. Taylor wanted to discuss her ideas for a hockey play-off system, perhaps to be sanctioned by the new women's organization just being formed. Taylor suggested that AIAW could sponsor field hockey.

Both Taylor and Ley understood that the USFHA, United States Field Hockey Association, had jurisdiction over field hockey and had run tournaments for decades. The USFHA hosted a series of post-season tournaments, but the object was not to crown a champion. The tournaments were designed to identify and select the best hockey players from each region and bring them together to play at a national venue where the USFHA would ultimately select the members of the national team to represent the USA in international competition. The AIAW would not interfere with the USFHA's structure. Taylor returned to her job at Susquehanna University more determined than ever to find a way to get a national championship tournament for field hockey.

Susquehanna University could only hold her for one more year. She wanted to teach and coach at a school with a professional program (physical education majors) and compete at a higher level. She looked to her alma mater. Lock Haven had an opening for the 1972-73 school year. Five years of coaching field hockey at Susquehanna had garnered her a total of just nine victories. Her record of 9-25-8 did not impress anyone, but Charlotte Smith and Lock Haven knew what kind of person they were getting.

**Sharon Taylor:** *I applied at three places, because I didn't know if I would get the job at Lock Haven. I didn't apply there first because there wasn't an opening. Then they fired the individual who taught and coached tennis. She and Dr. Matthew Maetozo (Dean of the College of Health and Physical Education) did not see eye to eye on education.*

*Knowing that Dr. Smith was going to retire, I took the job at Lock Haven and coached tennis for one season. Dr. Smith retired in 1973. It was understood that I would pick up hockey and lacrosse. I had never played lacrosse, but I had played basketball. Lacrosse is like basketball with a stick and a smaller ball. I took myself to lacrosse camp that summer. There I was at 27 years of age thinking I was a pretty good athlete, and I was in the beginner group with an English woman, Maggie Boyd, who was at the top of the world for teaching lacrosse. But I was a coach, and the concepts of teaching lacrosse are very much like basketball in terms of all the cuts, defense, give-and-go and things like that.*

19

*Everybody thinks lacrosse is like hockey. It has no relationship to hockey except it's played on a field that looks similar. The ball is down here for hockey (points to the floor) and up there for lacrosse (brings her hands above her shoulders). If you have the ball and you're getting pressure, you pass the ball, cut and maybe get it back; "give-and-go" like basketball. Hockey and soccer are very much alike and have borrowed some strategies from each other, but lacrosse, no. If you had to start a lacrosse team (from scratch), you'd first look at your (best) basketball players.*

When her first season as the head coach of the lacrosse team began, Taylor found two important allies among her players, Barbara Collins and Jackie "Jake" Crowell. Barb and Jake would visit Taylor in her office and share their knowledge and advice with the new coach. Taylor would often pass along their observations and strategies during practice sessions. The two players served as unofficial and unrecognized student coaches.

**Sharon Taylor:** *If I had any questions I would talk to them very frankly. I knew coaching but I didn't know lacrosse. They knew I didn't have a lot of background, but they trusted me that we would do all right, and we did. They were the ones I would go to and say, "Look, you know I don't have a lot of background and I'm going to bounce things off you but then I will make the decision." That was how we did things and it worked out very well.*

Taylor must have been a quick study; in 1979 she guided the women's lacrosse team to the first Division II national championship, sponsored by the U.S. Women's Lacrosse Association (USWLA).

During Taylor's first year back at Lock Haven, she decided to take her plea for a hockey championship directly to the USFHA, which had recently elected Phyllis Weikart as president. Weikart, then a professor at the University of Michigan, had once been the goalkeeper for the U.S. national team. After hearing Taylor's rationale and her well-reasoned ideas for the tournament structure, Weikart made a wise decision. She would sanction a committee to study the feasibility of such a tournament. Sharon Taylor would chair the committee.

20

For a whole year the committee studied the matter, attempting to meld together the philosophy inherent in championship competition with the structure of the USFHA sections. At one point, a vacancy occurred on the committee. Phyl Weikart recommended the field hockey coach at James Madison University, Leotus "Lee" Morrison. Morrison was a very experienced hockey coach, but vehemently opposed the championship format. She believed that field hockey "was different."

How could this appointment possibly enhance the chances for a championship? To Taylor's surprise, Morrison took a 180 degree turn in her opinion and by August of 1973, the committee delivered a one sentence recommendation to the USFHA Board of Directors: "The United States Field Hockey Association recognizes the current trend toward championship play at state, regional, and national levels, as a viable means of meeting the competitive needs of girls and women in the sport of field hockey."

The board took its first vote and came away with the decision of sending the proposal back to committee. One particular director, who was opposed to the concept, stepped up and said, "No, it's unfair to send it back to committee. Let's deal with it and make a decision."

Following additional discussion, the board voted again and narrowly passed the resolution. The committee now had the mandate to create a collegiate championship model. Interestingly, the IFWHA, the international body governing women's hockey, announced one month later that their next tournament, in 1975, would be a World Cup Championship.

Sharon Taylor had begun to make a name for herself in the world of women's field hockey, despite the fact that she had never coached a winning team and could count the number of victories on her fingers. The next time she addressed her field hockey players, she could tell them that soon they could test themselves against the best teams in the country.

Taking over for Charlotte Smith in the fall of 1973, Taylor's hockey team finished with six wins and just two losses. She could now present herself as a winning hockey coach. Her first foray into lacrosse netted a three-win three-loss season; not a bad beginning.

As Taylor continued to hone her skills as a coach and teacher, the process of formulating a national play-off system slogged onward through 1973, 1974, and into 1975. Lee Morrison, a convert to a field hockey championship, was very active in the AIAW, becoming the Association's third president. With her help, the committee pressed the AIAW to join the USFHA in a joint championship format. A joint committee was formed and Sharon Taylor again was chosen as chairperson.

**Sharon Taylor:** *The two national women's organizations got the job done and the first USFHA/AIAW National Field Hockey Championship was held in 1975, to be hosted by James Madison University. The two organizations co-sponsored (the tournament) for 4 years, and then in 1978, Donna Lopiano, who was the AIAW commissioner of national championships, came to the tournament held in Washington at Central Washington University. She said, "I want to talk to you and the joint committee about the possibility of AIAW taking over the championship. We talked about it, agreed, and made the proposal to USFHA and they said, "Fine, we will recognize it." That's how field hockey came to have an AIAW championship, starting in 1979, like all the other women's sports.*

*An interesting thing happened in the spring of 1976. I went to a meeting of the EAPECW, the Eastern Association for Physical Education for College Women. We had a banquet and Dr. Ley was there. I went over to "kiss her ring" and pay my respects because she was a giant in the field, a remarkable woman. The first words out of her mouth were, "I see you got your field hockey championship." I was blown away that she remembered that 15-minute conversation that we had back in 1971. But she did, and she was very happy for me and proud of that, as well.*

Meanwhile, back at Lock Haven, Taylor's hockey team turned in a record of 7-2-2 in 1974-75, followed by an astounding 18-2-1 record during the 1975-76 season. This was the turning point where women's programs had a true "season" with more contests, and where Lock Haven became a regional, and soon a national power in women's field hockey. They won the Pennsylvania State Athletic Conference (PSAC) championship in 1979, 1980, 1981 and 1982. Following the PSAC tournament, the 1982 team won the NCAA Division II crown defeating Bloomsburg (PA). They finished with a near perfect 16-1 record. In 1983 they came within a whisker of repeating as national champions when they fell to Bloomsburg 1-0 and settled for the NCAA Division II Runner-Up Trophy.

When the NCAA discontinued the Division II championship in 1984, Taylor took LHU to Division I. Competing there for five years with virtually no scholarship money, the team finished in the top 20 in the nation in all but one year, but had no conference or post-season opportunity. Foregoing the few scholarship dollars, LHU returned to the PSAC and Division III competition. In 1989, LHU won the PSAC, the Regional, and the NCAA Division III crowns.

With the NCAA's reinstatement of Division II in 1992, Lock Haven, with Taylor still at the helm, claimed the national championship three out of the next four years. They were the runner-up the only year (1993) in which they did not wear the crown. Taylor's last year in coaching, her team rewarded her with her first perfect season (21-0) in addition to the national championship.

If pushed to name her most memorable season, Taylor reluctantly concedes that 1995, her final year in coaching, stands out. She had already made the decision to step down as head coach well before the beginning of the 1995 season.

**Sharon Taylor:** *You couldn't make this story up, a perfect 21-0 record and two championships, the conference (PSAC) and the national (NCAA). Two years earlier, when I made up my mind when I would retire, there were a couple of things I wanted to accomplish. I wanted to hit my 300th win, and I got that (the 300th) the previous season and I wanted to go through LHU's 50th anniversary of field hockey in 1995, so that is where I focused. I didn't want to tell the team in the beginning because I didn't want the 50th celebration to be seen as a farewell to me. So, I didn't tell them until we got past that weekend. Then I looked at the schedule and I picked the day before a game against a team I was pretty sure we could beat even if we completely fell apart. That was when I told them. It was a horrible scene. Everybody cried, I cried. I looked to my captain, Caroline Gillich, to say something but she was in tears, bawling, almost sobbing. I said to her, "Well, you're no help!" It was a pretty emotional event.*

Taylor has a little difficulty choosing her most memorable game as a coach. Following an excellent 18-1-2 season, her 1981 hockey team advanced to the national championship tournament, the final one to be sponsored by AIAW. Lock Haven's only loss during the regular season was at the hands of eventual Division I champion, Penn State. Her retelling of the final playoff game provides a very rare example of Taylor staking a claim to the success of the team. She unfailingly allows the players to take the credit for the victories and the championships.

**Sharon Taylor:** *Most memorable game? Well, if it wasn't the final game of 1995, it had to be the 1981 championship game. Everybody anticipated that it would be Lock Haven and Ithaca because Ithaca had won everything in New York. In the semis we played LaSalle. LaSalle was a turf team and we were a grass team but we beat them playing on Cornell's turf field. Ithaca played Syracuse in the semis. Ithaca had beaten Syracuse three times that season.*

*Syracuse upset Ithaca, so we ended up playing Syracuse in the national championship. The first half was scoreless. It was freezing cold and it had started to snow. I have to say that I really have to credit myself for making a difference there. We were in Cornell's stadium, which was a horseshoe design with a building housing offices that overlooked the stadium. It had started to snow in the scoreless first half, and it was freezing cold. When the whistle blew for halftime our team started to head for the bench. I started to run for the end of the field while I motioned to the kids and pointed to the building. We went right off the field into the heated lobby of the building and sat on the floor. We stayed in there for the duration of the halftime break. The Syracuse players stayed out in the cold with their jackets on, standing on the sideline.*

*Our kids were very warm. With 30 seconds left in the halftime my team got up and ran onto the field right into position. The whistle blew and we out shot them 18-1 and scored two goals. It was a combination of the kids really wanting it, and the fact that they never cooled down. They were very warm and they went straight out, and I really credit some of that win to a pretty good idea!*

*It was also memorable because the AIAW structure meant so much to me, and to have finally gotten the Golden Lady (AIAW winner's trophy). It was really something to win the trophy of the organization for which we created the field hockey championship.*

As stellar as Taylor's coaching career appears, disappointments still linger on the fringe of her memory. Two years in a row (1976 and 1977), her Eagles reached the semi-finals of the national championships but lost on tiebreakers. There was no shoot out or sudden death extra period. In the first game against West Chester State, LHU's potential winning goal was incorrectly waved-off by an official. Lock Haven finished third in the nation both years.

More bothersome to Taylor, though, is the recollection of the very strange 1988 season. Why? Because a Sharon Taylor-led team finished with a losing record. Her team ended the season at 7-12-1. An odd decision by the NCAA in 1984 to discontinue the Division II championship forced all schools to choose between Division I and Division III. The middle classification no longer existed. Taylor saw little valor in dropping down to play the smaller programs, so she opted for Division I and encountered a steady stream of very competitive large university opponents for the next five years.

Even the immortal Bear Bryant had one losing season during his 36 years of coaching football at the collegiate level. In 1954 he guided (or misguided) his Texas A&M squad to a 1-9 record. Despite all of her successful campaigns, Taylor felt that she had defiled the legacy passed down by her mentor Charlotte Smith. She used the word "traumatized" to describe how she felt. But then, one day, she looked back over the records and discovered that Smith's 1950 club had finished the season 2-3-3. So, Sharon Taylor had not fashioned Lock Haven's first ever losing season in field hockey. She had something in common with Charlotte Smith and Bear Bryant.

Coach Taylor steadfastly refuses to name her best players during the thirty-year career. She claims that she cannot cite the outstanding performers. What she means is that she WILL not cite them. She had so very many talented players and she does not want to omit anybody. The concept of succeeding as a team still permeates her thinking.

After a bit of cajoling, she made a small concession and conditionally began to mention some players by name.

**Sharon Taylor:** *Don't use these names but there was (name deleted) who left a scholarship at Temple to come here to play. There was (name deleted) who has been coaching at ESU forever. She was a great* *four-sport athlete at LHU. And (name deleted), who still complains nearly 40 years later that if I hadn't moved her to midfield she would still be the school's all-time scoring leader. The important thing is that they all went out and became even better people. I never had a disciplinary problem and I can count on one hand the players who didn't make it academically. In the 23 years I coached (at Lock Haven) that is the most memorable part of my professional life, those young women who came through that program and who went on to make great contributions of their own.*

Although she is reluctant to discuss the individual stars of her teams, she readily talks about the lighter moments involving her athletes. One such story even features a student name that does not have to be redacted. In 1992 LHU hosted the Division II field hockey championship. On the eve of the tournament, players and coaches attended a banquet. Lock Haven's goalkeeper, Allison Brita, showed up in what was described as an "outrageous outfit." Coach Taylor proposed a deal: if her team won their game the next day, she would don Allison's outfit.

**Sharon Taylor:** *The echo from the referee's whistle hadn't stopped when I heard a voice ask, "S.T., when are you going to wear Allison's outfit?" A few weeks later when we had a team meeting, I got all dressed up in those clothes, with a wig and stick-on tattoos. A male coach who must remain unnamed dressed up looking like a pimp and escorted me into the room. Some of them didn't even know who I was. I was pretty proud to even fit into Allison's outfit. I looked like Tina Turner!*

Another story involved LHU's former hockey field and a player named Joan Laird. The playing surface featured very little actual grass. The players dubbed it "Astro-dirt." During a playoff game in which the field became a muddy quagmire, Laird somehow managed to finish the game with her uniform unsullied. She had the reputation of being a very neat young woman. One of her teammates approached Taylor and asked, "S.T., can we throw Joan in the mud?" Without even answering, Taylor approached Laird and asked to see her new team jacket. Once the jacket had been removed, the other players grabbed her and tossed her gently into the mud.

One last anecdote illustrates her relationship to her "kids." One student approached Taylor during her senior year and said to her coach, "I can't believe how afraid of you I was until I was a junior." Taylor concedes that she was a taskmaster on the practice field. She recalls that her father likened her to former Philadelphia Eagles coach Dick Vermeil, himself a perfectionist who was also known as a great motivator.

Taylor sums up her career with a statement that coaching has a very special place in her heart. Sensing that this statement, true as it may be, isn't quite enough to explain how she feels about her life's work, she tells a story about Olympic champion Billy Mills and his young daughter.

**Sharon Taylor:** *Billy Mills came to a conference that I attended at Temple University in 1973. I was later able to bring him to Lock Haven. Mills, the only American to win the 10,000 meters in the Olympics (Tokyo in 1964) was a Native American. There was a movie made about him called "Running Brave." He told a story to the audience about his daughter. She was 8 years old and she wanted to take his gold medal to school for show-and-tell. He decided to let her take it, but he said to her, "I want to tell you that at the Olympics, of all the runners in the world, only a few get a chance."*

*She said, "Yeah I know that."*

*He continued, "Of all the runners in the world at the Olympics there are only 3 medals given in each event."*

*She was very impatient with him and said, "Yeah, Daddy, I know that."*

*She took the gold medal and went off to school to show her classmates and teacher. When Mills came home that night he asked her, "So what did you tell your class?"*

*She said, "I told them that of all the runners in the world, very few get to the Olympics."...He was beaming with pride, as she continued, "Of all the runners at the Olympics there are only three medals. And I told them that this gold medal...is exactly like the one Peggy Fleming won."*

*His moral to the story was, "So, little girls will have their heroes."*

*That's the way I felt about my coaching career. When I was growing up my heroes were men, Robin Roberts of the Phillies and Chuck Bednarik of the Philadelphia Eagles.*

*My whole life's work was to make sure that little girls could have heroes of their own. That was kind of the way I felt about my coaching career.*

*The remarkable thing about Lock Haven University field hockey is that, in 70 years, only three women have been involved in making the program what it is. Dr. Charlotte Smith started the program in 1945 when I was eight months old. I played for her, and then took over when she retired. Pat Rudy played for me, and is now the head coach. I doubt that there is any program in the nation with such a succession.*

### Athletics Administration

Beginning in 1978 and lasting until 1987, Taylor also served as Associate Director of Athletics while coaching hockey each of those years, and lacrosse through 1979. Her final lacrosse team brought home the USWLA Division II National Champion Trophy.

She served one year as Interim Director of Athletics until given the official title in 1988. When Dr. Willis was asked what qualities he saw in Sharon Taylor that led him to consider her for the interim position, he named two. "One, I wanted someone who had been a successful coach. Who could argue with her coaching career? And I wanted somebody that I knew was a team player."

Taylor's predecessor had criticized Willis' stance on a certain issue in the newspaper and was warned not to repeat that mistake or he would be fired. Not long afterward, the soon-to-be-former A.D. told the local press that despite his advice, Willis had voted the wrong way on an NCAA issue. Big mistake. True to his word, Willis reassigned the director of athletics and Sharon Taylor replaced him on an interim basis.

How did Willis know that Taylor would be a team player? They each have different theories about that. Taylor recalls their very first meeting and attributes that conversation to the good working relationship that they enjoyed for 22 years.

**Sharon Taylor:** *Well, maybe it was because of the first time I met the new President at his office in 1982. I introduced myself and welcomed him to Lock Haven. I told him that I liked what he had to say during his campus interview and that I was looking forward to working with him. I also told him that the feminist in me had hoped that Dr. Helen Wise (another candidate) would be selected, but that he was definitely my strong second choice. I guess he figured that if I would tell him that, it was unlikely that I would lie to him about anything else. Also, I think that retiring President Frank Hamblin had said some positive things about me. And, later when I met Craig's wife, Dr. Marilyn Willis, I realized that he was quite used to dealing with strong, independent women.*

Now that Taylor had become one of the country's very few females serving as A.D. for both men's and women's programs, there was some trepidation among the male coaches. Would Taylor turn her back on their programs in favor of the women's teams? Taylor tells an anecdote that makes light of the males' fears.

**Sharon Taylor:** *After I became A.D., my friend Judith Davidson introduced me for a NACWAA award, and she paraphrased a comment I had made, "A lot of the men were very nervous when Sharon became A.D." She continued, "I have sanitized that statement a great deal. If you want to know how Sharon told it to me, you will have to ask her." I am still not saying!*

*They were afraid I was going to do what detractors had accused me of, which was to just take care of the women's programs. I had only worked in women's athletics so the men thought I was going to be very biased against them. They would never have questioned whether a new male A.D. was going to be biased against women. That was just the way it was. But, I think they quickly realized that I would do my best for all of my programs and, over a quarter of a century, some of the male coaches were my closest allies. As I told my friends, I now have sons as well as daughters.*

The promotion of Taylor did not sit well with all of Lock Haven's trustees, but none had the temerity to complain to Dr. Willis. Instead they passed along to the president comments they were hearing from some of the male coaches and faculty members. Said Willis, "Some of those people asked me, 'Why do you want a woman? And why do you want a woman who is Sharon Taylor? Do you know how aggressive she is, and how she can sometimes be a bully?' Yeah, there were some of those things said to me."

Was she a bully? Willis explains, "She's a negotiator. That's one of her chief skills. Yes, (she bullies) in the sense that she could be intimidating. Let me tell you what her father said about her negotiation skills. She only beat up other kids when that (negotiating) failed." Taylor claims that her dad was kidding about that, but growing up in her neighborhood, neither boys nor girls backed down easily. She calls it a good lesson.

Like many other women in positions of authority over men, Taylor went out of her way to not flaunt her power. She asked to remain in her old office where she had served as a coach. One of the university vice presidents insisted that she move into the "big office," suggesting that images are important. She offered to trade the large office for a parking place, but he declined.

Taylor takes a lot of pride in how much effort she put into supporting the men's programs early in her tenure as A.D. At first, she only had four fulltime coaches, all men's teams. The other coaches split their time between teaching and coaching. She went to President Willis and convinced him of the need to hire three more full-time coaches, all for men's teams.

After the new hires had come on board, she went to Willis again and explained that some full-time women coaches were needed to address Title IX discrepancies. Said Taylor, "That simply was my strategy, the way I approached it." When she left the A.D. position LHU had 31 full-time coaches.

When the subject of fairness to men's sports arises, Taylor tells the "Dave Bower story." The story begins around 1989 when the football coach, Tom Jones, received approval from Taylor to add two assistant coaches. Jones then asked for an additional $5,000 in salary for one of them. Taylor refused.

**Sharon Taylor:** *Tom Jones came from the Middle America Conference. He thought he was wonderful and he was going to raise a* *lot of money and turn the program around. He didn't produce any of that. I had gotten him one additional coach the very first year I was A.D. I had gotten him a couple of other things, office space and such. I said, "We've gotten this much and I'm not going back to ask for more. At some point later we can talk about salaries. I'm not going back over there right now, and nickel and dime (the president) for a couple of thousand more."*

*So Jones sent Dave Bower down to try to talk me into it. Dave was working with the football team. A Lock Haven grad, he had been a top-notch quarterback when he was a student. Dave came in to my office and said, "You probably know why I'm here."*

*I said, "As I told Tom, I'm just not going to do it. I get resources from Craig (Willis) because I don't bug him about it every minute." Dave said, "I understand, but he (Jones) told me to do it so I had to ask you."*

*He started out of the door, then stopped in the doorway, turned around and said, "I just want to tell you, you've gotten more for us in the year you've been here than Tod (Eberle, Taylor's predecessor) was able to do in all the time I've been here. I appreciate it."*

*I said, "Thank you. I appreciate that a great deal."*

Taylor continued to coach field hockey through the 1995 season, after which she turned over the reins to her former player, Pat Rudy. Rudy has maintained Taylor's high standards by winning over 500 career games and leading LHU to the national championship game in 1998 (lost to Bloomsburg) and 2000 (defeated Bentley). She remains at the helm of Lock Haven's field hockey team, now successfully competing in Division I in the Atlantic Ten Conference.

Throughout her teaching and coaching career, Taylor was able to undertake other professional activities to advance the cause of women's sports, field hockey in particular, by participating in various regional and national organizations. Below is a partial list of her organizational contributions:

- President of the United Sates Field Hockey Association (USFHA)

- Board of Directors of the United States Olympic Committee (USOC)

- President of the National Association of Collegiate Women Athletics Administrators (NACWAA)

- Vice President of the Association for Intercollegiate Athletes for Women (AIAW)

- U.S. Delegate to International Federation of Women's Hockey Association (IFWHA) and Federation Internationale de Hockey (FIH)

- Consultant to the President's Commission on Olympic Sport, 1976

Each time Taylor made the news for her accomplishments, Lock Haven University benefited from the positive publicity. President Craig Dean Willis was proud of her and what she meant to LHU. She seemed poised to join Elizabeth Zimmerli and Charlotte Smith in Lock Haven's pantheon of storied contributors. That, sadly, would begin to change when Willis retired in 2004.

During the decade following the passage of Title IX, much remained to be done. Nowhere in the language was athletics mentioned. A system for measuring fairness had to be developed. President Nixon tasked the Department of Health, Education and Welfare (HEW) to carry out this undertaking. Committees were formed. Experts were consulted. Hearings were held. Regulations were formulated and amended. Adding to the extreme challenge of creating this landmark civil rights law out of whole cloth, Title IX advocates had to fight off the many powerful forces trying to kill or seriously water it down. Senator John Tower introduced a bill in 1974 that would exempt revenue–producing sports from Title IX regulations. Senator Jacob Javits proposed another plan that allowed for flexibility in dealing with the various sports. The Tower Amendment failed and Javits' Amendment passed.

**Sharon Taylor:** *At that time what Title IX said was you had to have equal expenditures on both sides of the program (men and women). We didn't even ask for that. What we wanted was to have the Javits amendment followed, which is, you spend what it costs. If it costs $300 to fully outfit a football player and only $150 to fully outfit a hockey player, that's equity. We took that position.*

Taylor worked in the trenches to create guidelines that were fair to both the women's programs as well as the men's. One of her most memorable contributions involved a meeting with the Secretary of HEW, Joseph Califano, Jr.

**Sharon Taylor:** *This is 1979 and all the "regs" were written, all the fuss in Congress was largely over. All the attempts to change the law (were over). Califano was responsible for putting out the final policy interpretation.*

*Sara Weddington, President Jimmy Carter's liaison for women's issues, arranged for six of us and our legal counsel, Margot Polivy, to meet with Secretary Califano. We had limited time, so we had carefully scripted our presentation.*

*Kaye Hart, this sweet little Mormon from Utah who had been transplanted to Temple University, cited to Califano how women were being retaliated against for their support of Title IX. She gave the example of a woman at a school in Texas who was happily married, three or four kids, and how the guys started saying that she was a lesbian. They were trying to blacken her reputation because she supported Title IX.*

*Califano listened to her and he said, "That's very hard to believe." There was this pregnant pause because we never expected that he would say he didn't believe us. (Speaking from) my history background, I said to him, "Mr. Secretary, if this were the 1950s instead of the 1970s, they would have been calling us Communists." He thought about it for 5-10 seconds then he said, "I understand." That's all I had to say, he understood that you can hurl accusations and people can't prove a negative. You just do it, and then it's out there. This was a weapon, and only the terms changed.*

To the disappointment of Taylor and her colleagues, Califano did not feel he could side with the women's point of view. That was April of 1979.

In July, President Jimmy Carter fired Califano and named Patricia Harris as the new Secretary of HEW. On December 11, 1979, Harris issued a final Policy Interpretation of Title IX, with the athletics piece consistent with the approach espoused by the leaders in women's athletics.

The three main areas of compliance, the so-called "Three Prong Test, were, and are today:

1. Financial assistance (scholarships) should be proportionate to the number of males and females in an institution's athletic program (which should essentially reflect the institution's enrollment percentages).
2. The "Laundry List" of other program areas requires that equivalent resources be allocated for games and practice times, uniforms and equipment, travel, tutoring, facilities, recruitment, etc.
3. The governing principle is compliance in meeting the athletic interests and abilities of male and female students in an equitable manner. [1]

Educational institutions now had their blueprint for compliance with gender equity in athletics.

Taylor does not claim to be one of the principal initiators of Title IX, but she certainly played a very active role in the grass roots effort to bring this important civil rights act to fruition and, later, to keep it alive. She spoke at rallies, organized letter-writing campaigns on her college campus, contacted educators and organizations around the country to ask for their support, lobbied decision makers like Joseph Califano and her own legislators, and stood with the women and men who stood for the law.

**Sharon Taylor:** *You know, the 1960s and '70s were a period of activism and, for me, a great training ground. I was passionate about political issues. So I went to rallies and marches and supported or opposed actions, policies and principles totally unrelated to athletics and sport. Most of the time, we were in D.C, but also in Philadelphia, Harrisburg, or Baltimore.*

*We marched for civil rights, the Equal Rights Amendment, and against the war in Vietnam. I supported Cesar Chavez and his farm workers, and demonstrated for divestment from South Africa and to free Nelson Mandela. From our campus at Susquehanna University, friends and I*

34

*would regularly travel to Bucknell University for rallies and draft card burnings, which occurred regularly. So later, to work for and demonstrate for Title IX was very natural and important; it was just an extension of civil rights legislation into the areas that I had chosen for my profession.*

*One very memorable event in my political activism occurred in January 1973, on the day of Richard Nixon's second inauguration. I had been visiting grad school friends in Greensboro, NC, and was driving back to Pennsylvania on the day before the event. I was listening to the radio and heard announcers keep talking about the inauguration, and about the large crowds of demonstrators expected in D.C. for the anti-war march that was being billed as "The March Against Death." Halfway up I-81 in Virginia, I turned off the highway and went east toward Washington.*

*I arrived in D.C. around 10 p.m. and found a large crowd at the Lincoln Memorial. Having no hotel reservation before the inauguration was problematic (even if I could have afforded a D.C. hotel in those days!). I found a place to park my bus...yes, I owned a 1967 VW bus!...gathered a couple of blankets that I had in back, and headed for the Memorial. That night, I shared my blankets, and their two sleeping bags, with a young man and woman from the Socialist Workers Party as we huddled together for warmth and tried to sleep on the marble floor of the Lincoln Memorial.*

*The next day we cheered Rep. Bella Abzug (NY) as she gave the "Counter Inauguration" at the Washington Monument; then we marched and chanted and generally tried to disrupt the transportation for "fat cats" headed for the White House after Nixon's swearing–in.*

*So, later that year and for years to come, the work we did for Title IX was much more refined, professional and mainstream, but it was not a whit less important!*

The following is a partial list of honors received by Sharon Taylor for contributions to athletics and sport in the U.S.:

- Inductee, United States Field Hockey Association Hall of Fame, 2014

- Lifetime Achievement Award, given by NACWAA, 2013

- AAUW Gateway to Equity Award (for Title IX Advocacy), 2013

- Presidential Award, National Association for Girls and Women in Sport, 2013

- Inductee, Coatesville High School Hall of Fame, 2011

- National Field Hockey Coaches' Hall of Fame, 2003

- National Administrator of the Year Award, given by NACWAA, 1998

- Jostens' Female Administrator of the Year Award, given by ECAC, 1997

- Pathfinder Award, National Association for Girls and Women in Sport, 1996

- Division II Field Hockey National "Coach of the Year", 1993,1994,1995

- Pennsylvania State Athletic Conference "Coach of the Year", 1989, 1992, 1994, 1995

- The Women's Sports Foundation's 1992 "Coaches Award", sponsored by Budget Rent-a-Car (for excellence and dedication to coaching women athletes)

- Inductee, Clinton County Chapter of PA Sports Hall of Fame, 1991

- Katherine Ley Award (for contributions to women's athletics), given by ECAC, 1988

Each time the bright light of success shone on Sharon Taylor, a reflected glow bathed the Lock Haven campus.

Three times under Taylor's tenure, Lock Haven won the Dixon Trophy, symbolic of overall excellence in collegiate sports, men and women's. Three times Lock Haven stood above the other thirteen universities in the Pennsylvania State System of Higher Education. The third smallest and most rural of schools in the PASSHE, Lock Haven had something to show high school students, and their parents, to help them choose a college.

During Taylor's tenure as coach and/or Director of Athletics, her various teams brought dozens of state, regional, and national championship trophies home to Lock Haven University.

Walking around the Lock Haven University campus, one sees the Zimmerli Gymnasium sitting adjacent to Charlotte Smith Field. One could easily imagine a future addition to the Lock Haven campus that bears the name Taylor Hall. Or, perhaps a new sports facility called the Sharon Taylor Sports Complex. Based on the accomplishments described in this chapter, such an honor would be well deserved. Time and again newspapers and magazines reported the contributions that Sharon Taylor had made to the advancement of women's athletics. Each time, Lock Haven University gained credibility for the foresight of employing such a difference maker on their campus.

Something occurred in 2004 that changed everything. President Willis retired. Willis' departure left a power void that was quickly filled by a small number of trustees. These trustees, in turn, were overly influenced by a group of former Lock Haven athletes with a mission. The next few chapters will describe that mission, and clearly explain why future visitors to the Lock Haven campus are unlikely to see a facility named for Sharon Taylor for years to come.

# Chapter Two – Troubled Waters

In Ernest Hemingway's *The Old Man and the Sea*, Santiago, the unlucky Cuban fisherman, failed to bring home a catch for almost three months. Venturing out into the Gulf Stream to try to break the cursed dry spell, he hooked a monstrously large marlin. Santiago fought the marlin for more than 48 hours from his small skiff before winning the war of attrition and hauling the fish tightly alongside his boat before starting back home with his prize.

Like Santiago, Sharon E. Taylor, struggled to return home with her prize. In Sharon's world, home would be retirement and the joy of looking back over an extremely satisfying career. The great marlin strapped to Santiago's boat could symbolize her outstanding body of work and contributions to Lock Haven University, and to women's athletics in particular.

Premier athlete, successful college coach, U.S. Field Hockey Association President, and passionate advocate for gender equality in sports, she began 2012 in her 24th year as Director of Athletics at Lock Haven University. Seated in the rural and mountainous center of Pennsylvania, the university might well have provided an escort for her triumphant journey into retirement. That did not happen.

Just as a series of shark attacks bedeviled the old fisherman, so did influential trustees and alumni, gullible community members, bitter coaches and weak university administrators conspire to rip the flesh from her reputation during Taylor's final years as Lock Haven's Director of Athletics.

In addition to her manifold duties as head of the athletics department, she had to defend herself and her employer from a barrage of legal challenges. Eventually, she had to defend herself from her employer.

On February 3, 2012, Lock Haven University Sports Information Director Doug Spatafore released this announcement:

*In order to achieve greater efficiency and to meet the needs of a growing department, Lock Haven University will consolidate the athletics faculty and the Department of Sports Studies. This consolidation entails a shift of responsibilities. Effective at the end of the semester, Sharon Taylor will assume teaching duties while Peter Campbell and Danielle Barney's major responsibilities will continue to reside in directing the LHU athletics programs.*

By June, Sharon Taylor would be strictly a faculty member, a professor of Sports Studies. Her erstwhile assistants would temporarily take over the duties of leading Lock Haven's athletics department.

When Santiago reached shore, he had only a carcass to show for his struggles. The most prodigious creature he had ever taken from the sea would have surely defined his life. The repeated shark attacks had decimated his trophy catch. Here the allegory ends. Although her reputation was sullied in the eyes of a few, Sharon Taylor's accomplishments at Lock Haven, and on the world stage, remain unassailable.

In 1987, Lock Haven University President Craig Dean Willis chose Sharon Taylor to be the school's Interim Director of Athletics. She became responsible for coordinating LHU's 18 intercollegiate sports. She retained her position as head coach of the women's field hockey team, a position she had held since 1973, and would hold for another eight years. One year later, the interim tag fell away. The appointment became official.

Today, a female athletics director is not a rare bird. As this book goes to press, Penn State, North Carolina State, Rutgers, University of Chicago, Northern Arizona, Denver, Loyola (Illinois), Mount Saint Mary's (MD), Western Michigan, Colgate, Monmouth, California (PA), Lewis and Clark, Elizabethtown and Columbia all currently employ females to lead their athletics departments.

Looking strictly at Division I schools, men still hold sway. In 2011, only five of 120 A.D.s were women. [1] As women gain experience at the smaller universities, many will move into similar positions within the bigger programs.

In 1988, a woman in charge of men's sports (as well as women's) found herself in a small exclusive club. There was no map to guide her through the narrow pathway she needed to follow. Women's sports had to be grown to nearly equal status without hurting men's programs.

In addition to the basic principle that a woman could do the job as well as a man, LHU president Willis understood that Title IX was not going away, despite repeated attempts to weaken or destroy it. Many athletics directors held a very tenuous grasp of how Title IX worked and how it should be administered and reported. But Sharon Taylor knew, because she had worked in the trenches to defend and nurture the landmark legislative decision of 1972.

**Sharon Taylor:** *The point at which I began to feel a threat to my position (and my reputation) came in 2004, just after Craig Willis retired as president. President Willis never said anything to me, but I later learned from associates that he felt a sense of concern for me after he retired. He told Peter Campbell, assistant A.D., "there are people that want to get Sharon out of here."*

*As head of the USA Field Hockey Association, I was in Athens for the 2004 Olympic games. As I often did, I brought back small souvenir gifts from the Games to give to colleagues and staff. While I was away, new LHU President Keith Miller took over the reins. I brought his gift to my first meeting. He was a nice man, very cordial. But at this very first meeting, he told me a story about a woman from his previous institution that worked at the college for 30 years. Although she had done a lot of good things, she began to slow down.*

*After I left, I began to walk back to my office thinking about his comments. I went into Peter Campbell's office and related the story to him. I told Peter, "I think he is talking about me." That was the beginning of it.*

*Starting that year, there were some issues. The wrestling people were unhappy. President Miller called a wrestling meeting and brought in a bunch of people, including John Moore, the former president of Indiana State University in Terre Haute. New college and university presidents frequently work with a mentor to get them oriented to the job. John Moore was Miller's mentor.*

*The decision was made to commission an audit of the entire athletics department. I mildly protested the use of the word audit. I suggested he call it a review instead. He agreed. John Moore nominated Andrea Myers, the director of athletics at Indiana State, to conduct the review.*

*Although I never felt Keith Miller attempted to undermine me, he did seem to be overly receptive to external influences, especially certain alumni and trustees. I knew there were several people that just thought*

*I never should have been the athletics director. They thought the athletics director should be 6'4" tall, blue-eyed, blonde-haired former football or wrestling coach.*

*I think Miller felt pressure right from the start to get me to retire. The search committee included three trustees, Guy Graham, Chris Dwyer, and Don Faulkner. All three later proved to be highly motivated to get me out. As the Andrea Myers report later showed, their interview topics (for Keith Miller) included a suggestion to "reassign me."*

*Another trustee later told me that if this type of thing (external pressure) would have taken place while Craig Willis was president he would have just called them up personally and told them to stop it and stay away from his staff. I used to say that Craig might beat us up over something, but he would never let anyone else do it.*

*So, yes, from my first conversation with Keith Miller, I did begin to have a heightened sense that things had changed.*

### The Andrea Myers Review

Sharon's detractors claimed that a decline in men's sports programs, particularly wrestling and football, resulted from a bias toward the women's teams. A female athletics director who had coached women's teams had to be the source of this bias.

In 2005, at John Moore's urging, Indiana State University athletics director Andrea Myers set out to evaluate the status of Lock Haven's athletics department. Her stated purpose: "A program review for the intercollegiate athletics department at Lock Haven University."

Before traveling to the campus to conduct interviews, she reviewed the university's strategic plan, student athlete handbook, athletics department operating manual, position descriptions, performance reviews and the coaches' labor agreements.

To insure a wide range of perspectives, all interested parties had an opportunity to participate. From her report: "A number of groups were invited to provide input for this review. Those groups included: University Trustees, Community Representatives, Athletics Administration, Senior University Administration, Student Athletes, Head Coaches and University Administrative Personnel."

Representatives from all the above groups were asked to describe the positive elements of the university's sports programs, as well as suggestions for improvements.

The anti-Sharon Taylor movement, just beginning to coalesce, would have their voices heard. Community representatives, alumni and trustees could testify to the failures of Sharon Taylor and press hard for her removal. If this loose affiliation of critics expected to damage the athletics director with their testimony, they were greatly disappointed. Not only did Sharon Taylor emerge unscathed, she received high praise and support from the vast majority of internal participants such as coaches, students, athletics department staff and non-athletics administrators.

The first point in the Observations portion of the report: "Based upon the information gathered during the review it appears that the athletics program is very sound and well balanced. The fact that Lock Haven has won the PSAC All-Sports Award on numerous occasions would seem to support this observation. Numerous individuals throughout the campus visit spoke about the commitment and integrity of the athletics director."

At the time, the PSAC All-Sports Award, named the F. Eugene Dixon Trophy, was awarded to the Pennsylvania State System of Higher Education member with the best accumulative record in twelve sports, six men's and six women's. Each competing institution can choose from 23 different sports teams.

The trophy was first awarded following the 1995-1996 academic year. At the time of the Myers review, Lock Haven, the third smallest of the 14 PSAC institutions, had won the trophy in 2000 and 2001. In 2007, Lock Haven, still under Sharon Taylor, claimed the Dixon Trophy for a third time. A school with a gender bias, toward men or women, could not have beaten out 13 other schools. At least six successful men's programs would be needed to seriously compete for this trophy.

Myers continued: "The coaching staff and athletics administrators seem very dedicated and committed to excellence. This commitment is reflected in the overall success of LHU athletics program. Most of the coaches feel that A.D. Taylor does not micromanage; in fact the comment was that 'she lets them do their job.'"

Support from outside the university and community also arrived: "As the campus session with the head coaches was ending, I was provided several letters of support for Ms. Taylor that had been sent from athletics directors in the PSAC. None of the letters indicated or any way suggested that Ms. Taylor had solicited them. Without exception the letters spoke to Ms. Taylor's concerns for student athletes, her honesty, professionalism, knowledge and the respect she has among her peers within the conference."

After reporting almost complete internal support for Sharon Taylor, Ms. Myers added this observation: "It seems as though Ms. Taylor does not have the support of the trustees; perhaps she could meet with them independently and seek their input on issues of concern. An educational session for the trustees may help to answer many of the questions about the athletics director's leadership ability."

If the review disappointed the community, alumni, and trustees up to this juncture, it was about to get worse.

Recommendation number one: Athletics 101 presentation for the trustees. "I recommend the A.D. be a participant and deeply involved in preparation and presentation of these materials. Indications are that she is extremely knowledgeable. It may also be helpful to involve Associate A.D. Campbell and/or vice presidents to assist in the presentation involving their areas of administrative oversight." The report also listed suggested topics such as Title IX education and NCAA requirements.

As for the community unrest, Myers reported a "serious deep-rooted problem in community and alumni against Ms. Taylor." External voices believed that Taylor should be "removed." They very graciously suggested that she not be "blatantly fired."

Part of the problem, concluded Myers, was a "great misunderstanding" about Title IX among both the community and the trustees. Additionally, she pointed out a lack of understanding "about the internal operations of an athletics department."

Although the Lock Haven's athletics department received a good report card over-all, the Myers Review pointed out several institutional problems and provided recommendations for improvement.

LHU needed to include athletics in its strategic planning, and the coaches should be permitted play an important role in formulating that plan. More and better communication had to be engendered between and among the administration, the financial aid director and everyone in the sports programs.

To put out the fires developing among community members and alumni, Myers suggested a public relations initiative.

The report was submitted to LHU president Keith Miller in April 2005. Miller adopted virtually none of the recommendations, despite the fact that he had initiated the process (at the urging of his mentor, John Moore).

[Author's note: The complete Andres Myers Report can be found in Appendix C]

**Sharon Taylor:** *The Andrea Myers report showed that the criticisms of my performance came mostly from external sources. One or two people were from downtown. I pretty much know who those folks were. One of them was our district attorney who had been a member of one of our foundation boards. The other two were trustees. That scenario became a constant theme throughout (the ensuing years).*

*Not only did Myers feel that the trustees lacked a working knowledge of an athletics department and Title IX specifically, she felt deeply offended when some of them insulted her integrity by intimating that she could not be objective in her findings due to a close relationship with me. Interestingly, Andrea and I hardly knew each other, but I guess it was assumed that the small group of women athletics directors must all be good friends.*

*When Myers interviewed the coaches, there were one or two who were disgruntled, but they were the same people who didn't want to raise money. One of them was a swim coach who later filed a lawsuit after we let him go. We received great support from the inside. The coaches were very satisfied. The issues came from the outside. "Too much emphasis on gender equity" was one of the recorded comments." I guess there was too much emphasis on obeying the law!*

*The chief problem: outside forces had too much influence. Keith (President Miller) was a nice man. He wanted to be nice to everybody.*

*He didn't want anyone to be unhappy and it paralyzed him. Anybody would tell you that he wanted to do no harm. He couldn't be strong with that group like (former president) Craig Willis was. Plus, he was an African-American trying to fit into this small town environment in rural Central Pennsylvania.*

*I said to him once, "Keith, if you think they are any happier with you sitting where you are, than me sitting where I am..."*

*He said, "I know it, I know it."*

*He ultimately had anonymous threats to his family and to himself. I never learned the details but I know it was reported to law enforcement. He was in a very difficult spot. He followed a very long, long-time president who firmly handled this kind of outside interference. So Keith came into a situation where he felt he had to be very careful in his dealings with the community.*

*In a way, he felt he worked for the trustees, two of whom were my biggest critics. Consequently, he could not handle them in a strong manner. Guy Graham was the chair of the council of trustees; he still is. The other was Chris Dwyer. They were on the search committee that ultimately hired Keith. They pressured him at the time of the hiring to remove me if he became president.*

*At the time, I felt that the Myers Review was a threat to my position. I later came to understand that Keith launched the study as a means to support me. I think he felt that the Myers Review provided him with some ammunition to tacitly defend me.*

To borrow from the plot of an old Western movie, Sharon Taylor stood accused by the influential townspeople of a serious crime, reverse sexism. They wanted "frontier justice," a virtual lynching.

The sheriff, who owed his position to the town's leaders, was expected to deliver the accused to the angry mob. Keith Miller, in the role of sheriff, believed that Sharon Taylor deserved a fair trial. The Myers Review would serve as her day in court. When the one-woman jury (Andrea Myers) delivered a not guilty verdict, the film had a short-lived happy ending. Unfortunately, a sequel would bring new challenges.

Andrea Myers suggested in her list of recommendations several ideas to ease the tension from outside the university. She suggested a Title IX seminar for the entire Council of Trustees. In addition to educating the trustees on the intricacies of Title IX, a series of meetings could provide the trustees with a clearer picture of how well the LHU athletics department functioned in this vital area. Perhaps a groundswell of support for Sharon may have developed to counter the animus of her two main critics.

Keith Miller never arranged for those sessions to be held.

Myers also recommended a public relations campaign to educate the community on the positive work being done in the athletics department, as well as the steps being taken to improve the two men's sports that had fallen on hard times. The student athletes, as a whole, reported their satisfaction with Lock Haven sports. The community needed to hear from the athletes themselves to get a more balanced perspective.

Keith Miller never acted on that recommendation, either.

## The Council of Trustees

As early as 2002, a faction of the Council of Trustees wanted Sharon Taylor out of the athletics department. Lock Haven alumnus Jim Swistock joined the board that year. A successful businessman from State College, he attended his first meeting and was surprised by the unabashed comments of two or three trustees. "At the first meeting I thought I would be getting some orientation. A couple of trustees came to me and said they wanted to get rid of Sharon Taylor. I replied, 'Who is Sharon Taylor?' I knew who she was, but that was my response. I didn't have an axe to grind with Sharon. From what I could tell at that point, she did a pretty good job, actually, a very good job as athletics director over the years. That's the only thing I saw. A lot of people voiced their opinion that they wanted her to retire."

Craig Dean Willis still occupied the president's office in 2002 causing the anti-Taylor forces to lay low and bide their time.

When Keith Miller replaced Willis in 2004, the uprising began to take shape. Part of Miller's agenda was to reshape the image of the university to show that it could change with the times. The trustees felt that Miller would do their bidding and remove Sharon Taylor.

Following the results of the Andrea Myers audit, Sharon Taylor was still firmly entrenched in her position. If the new president could not, or would not, remove Sharon Taylor, a new force began to emerge that was ready and eager to do the dirty work. A grass roots organization gained momentum based on the desire to recapture the past glory of Lock Haven wrestling. The mission of this group was to eliminate what they deemed the cause of the problem, Sharon Taylor. The small faction of trustees looking to oust Taylor was making little headway, but they would soon have a mercenary army assembling to take over the job.

Virginia "Ginny" Roth slipped in the back door in 2007. Trustee Ron Jury had recently passed away leaving his seat vacant. Eight weeks later Roth received a call from a friend working in Senator John Wozniak's office. Roth was informed that her resume was needed ASAP. The Pennsylvania governor's office was prepared to name her to complete Jury's term on the council. Jury had garnered much favor working with the past two gubernatorial administrations. Ron Jury had suggested and strongly recommended Ginny Roth, a close friend of his, and a 1981 Lock Haven graduate.

Roth's reply, "There aren't any women on the Council, why would I want to go up there?" With the assurance that more women would be named later that year, she made up her mind to accept the appointment. She was already a member of the LHU Foundation, the fundraising arm of the university. She thought her skills in marketing and communications would be helpful during the tough financial times gripping the nation.

Left up to the machinations of the other trustees, Roth would never have been invited to join the boys' club. That would hold doubly true for a woman of her ilk, strong and outspoken.

Roth's first reaction was a slight tinge of intimidation. LHU had not featured a female trustee in over a decade. She contacted the chairman, Guy Graham, and suggested a lunch meeting to display her respect and try to survey the lay of the land. She wanted to know from Graham what he thought went into becoming a good trustee. Roth opened the meeting with a request. "I said, Mr. Chairman, tell me the major issues facing this university." I had done a lot of marketing for our firm (PPO&S) so I actually understood the business of education. I thought he was going to talk about the shift in enrollments, the economics of affordability, or the competition of this new thing called online education. He said to me in a hushed tone, 'We got a real issue. We're going to be eaten alive by Title IX.' I didn't know how to respond, but I knew before lunch was over, exactly where things stood, and what I was getting into."

Graham's name surfaces frequently whenever the discussion turns to the Council of Trustees, but he was not alone in his resistance to Title IX. Roth has also singled out Chris Dwyer and George Durrwachter as part of the cabal that became the power behind the council.

The decline in football and wrestling was especially bothersome to the trustees and alums, but loss of pride was not the only consequence. Roth explains, "There were people who were high-end donors of a certain age demographic that were prime fundraising targets. What they cared about was football, and especially wrestling. For them to see that these programs were no longer Division I, and not performing at levels deemed successful from the perspective of the 1960s, they couldn't translate that." The donations from this group began to shrink.

Something had to be done. The problem, as plaintively explained to Ginny Roth by Graham, had an obvious source and an equally obvious solution. The ascent of women's sports at LHU was the cause. The architect of this affront to the pride of the institution was Sharon Taylor. The key to restoring LHU to respectability would be her removal. Pulling Keith Miller's strings didn't work out the way they had planned. Another tack was needed.

## The P.L.O.W. Years

Following the Myers Report, the external forces working against Sharon Taylor did not fold their tents and slink away in defeat. They formed an organization named PLOW, an acronym that spelled out the group's mission, to Preserve the Legacy of Wrestling. The goal seemed harmless enough. Lock Haven University, indeed, could claim a proud history of wrestling champions.

Beginning in the early 1960s, Lock Haven ascended to become a national wrestling power in the NAIA, the National Association of Intercollegiate Athletics. The NAIA officially began in 1952 as an organization designed to bring together teams from small colleges and universities to compete for national championships, as the NCAA had been doing for larger institutions since the early days of the 20th century.

In 1958, the NAIA added wrestling to its menu of post-season tournaments. Mankato State College in Minnesota claimed the NAIA wrestling crown the first two years. Beginning in 1960, Lock Haven State College and neighboring Bloomsburg State College dominated the national wrestling scene, grabbing a combined seven titles over an eight-year period. Only Moorhead State from Minnesota interrupted the stranglehold that these two Pennsylvania schools held over the small college landscape. When not claiming the top prize, the two schools frequently finished as runner-up.

Adams State in Colorado finally broke through in 1968 to begin a run of six championships in the next nine years.

While Lock Haven participated in championship tournaments with other NAIA level schools, they attained a high level of competition that enabled them to challenge, and frequently defeat, much larger universities, including Indiana State, Iowa State, Michigan, Oklahoma State, Penn State and Pittsburgh.

During the 1970s, Lock Haven and other Pennsylvania state colleges left the NAIA to participate in NCAA tournaments. A review of NCAA championship archives from 1970 through 1980 shows that Lock Haven wrestling had been eclipsed by sister schools such as Clarion and Slippery Rock. During that entire decade, Lock Haven only placed two wrestlers among the top six NCAA tournament finishers, a fourth place in 1971 and a fifth place in 1978. Tiny Division III school Franklin and Marshall (PA) matched that record during 1978-1979.

In contrast, Slippery Rock had seven wrestlers in the top six in their respective weight classes, while Clarion claimed six. The only PSAC school to finish among the top ten teams was Slippery Rock in 1971.

By 1981, individual athletes from Lock Haven and other small programs appeared less and less frequently among the top competitors, finding it difficult to survive the first round of matches.

Current wrestling juggernaut Penn State did not come into prominence until the 21st century, as they and other Division I schools finally began to take collegiate wrestling seriously. The entry of larger, richer programs into wrestling further pushed the smaller schools to the periphery of national competition.

How well did the LHU wrestling program succeed against sister schools in the PSAC championships? From 1970 until 1987, Lock Haven won the championship tournament just twice, 1971 and 1977. By the year 1987, when Sharon Taylor became interim director of athletics, four other PSAC teams had eclipsed LHU wrestling.

The halcyon days of wrestling in the 1960s, as remembered by Lock Haven alumni, were well in the past. The luster of Lock Haven wrestling had begun to tarnish years before Taylor moved into an administrator position. She, in fact, was busy turning the women's field hockey team into a national powerhouse as Lock Haven's second head coach.

Turning the coin over to the other side, the two most successful years LHU had in the NCAA Division I tournament were 1996 and 1997 when they ranked 11th and 5th, respectively, and out scored all other PSAC entries. Let's see...who served as athletics director during that time? Well, it was Sharon Taylor, the one person said to be responsible for the demise of wrestling at Lock Haven.

On the surface, PLOW had an honorable goal, to restore Lock Haven wrestling to its previous status. The removal of Sharon Taylor as director of athletics had to be the starting point, and perhaps was actually the end game for this group. In their eyes, she had taken gender equality too far, and deliberately set out to emasculate men's sports, particularly wrestling and football.

The emotional pitch of PLOW's members would rise to almost torch and pitchfork levels. More than just accusing Taylor of preferential treatment of women's sports, they alleged such practices as shredding incriminating documents, burying NCAA violations, discriminating against African-American coaches, using crude epithets to describe male athletics staff members, and even parking illegally.

LHU alumnus and former varsity wrestler Austin Shanfelter brought a whole new element to PLOW. A wealthy and successful businessman from South Florida, he infused the group with money, influence and credibility. As a valued donor to Lock Haven University, he held a very important trump card. The threat of losing his contributions made the trustees stand up and take notice. The scant trustee support of Taylor decreased even more when the cost of backing her rose appreciably.

After the NCAA cleared Taylor and LHU of alleged violations in the wrestling program, PLOW took its case public. On October 28, 2009, the Lock Haven newspaper, the Express, printed an unusually lengthy article penned by Austin Shanfelter and Jerry Swope. The 800-word opinion piece served as a manifesto for the PLOW organization. The article opens with a short review of the glory days of Lock Haven wrestling.

Paragraph two launches into a lament for the lost glory and bemoans the lack of action taken by university officials to address the concerns of alumni and the local citizenry.

In a classic example of "hurt and rescue" tactics, Shanfelter and Swope unveil the plan to save the day. "To form a more unified voice, more than 500 men and women have joined a new, permanent organization known simply as Preserve the Legacy of Wrestling, or PLOW.
[2]

The article proceeded with its case against Sharon Taylor by:

- o detailing the problems in the wrestling program including Sharon Taylor's plan to demote wrestling to Division II status

- o implying that the NCAA violations were whitewashed by an internal investigation

- o mentioning the "shameful" cancelation of the baseball program

- o reporting on the recent winless football season

- o subtly warning that the ongoing audit of the athletics department by Judith Sweet and Ronald Strattan may be compromised by a relationship between Sharon Taylor and one of the consultants

- o assuring readers that the PLOW group has "studied" the athletics department and consolidated their findings in a "white paper" provided to LHU and Pennsylvania State System of Higher Education

o    calling for the appointment of a new athletics director

The op-ed piece concludes with this informal mission statement: "PLOW ...will serve as a voice for university athletics alumni and friends for years to come. We have supported Lock Haven University in many ways in the past and desire to do so in the future. This is why PLOW is more than a handful of people expressing a one-time concern. It's an ever-growing group of people with a vested interest in Lock Haven University who have lost all confidence in the present leadership of athletics." [3]

If PLOW had been the plaintiff in a civil court trial, the above arguments would have ably served as opening statements by their lawyer. The defense attorney would have followed with opening statements in support of Sharon Taylor. Subsequently, PLOW would have to put witnesses on the stand to support under oath the allegations against Taylor. Again, the defense attorney would have the opportunity to cross-examine those witnesses and present oppositional testimony. The jury would have listened to the entire court proceedings.

Such was not the case in the hypothetical PLOW v. Sharon Taylor case in the court of public opinion. President Keith Miller had instructed Taylor in writing that she would refrain from speaking on behalf of the university without permission. That permission never came. Nor did any official response ever emanate from LHU. In fact, no one responded in defense of Lock Haven's athletics department. Had the entire academic community been put under a blanket gag order? That was not likely, but it became a de facto silence if not de jure.

The most glaring falsehood was the claim that Taylor wanted to downgrade wrestling to a Division II sport at LHU. If the PLOW organizers had done any homework at all on Title IX, they would have known that a complementary downgrade to a women's program would have to follow. If wrestling took a hit, then so would field hockey. No one would suggest that Taylor would propose any strategy that would hurt the very team she had nurtured for decades and delivered to national prominence.

That scare tactic and all of the other allegations went unchallenged. Accusations against the athletics department were a combination of unsubstantiated claims and actual facts interpreted inaccurately. An alumni organization boasting 500 members implied a certain amount of credibility. While it was probably true that PLOW was "more than a handful of people," the number 500 most likely came from a mailing list of former LHU graduates, not necessarily those actively involved in PLOW.

Late in 2009, with the PLOW imbroglio consuming the Lock Haven campus, President Keith Miller once again looked outside the academic walls to seek a peaceful solution. Despite the mounting pressure from certain trustees and the PLOW group to fire Sharon Taylor, Miller did not seem to have the heart to do it. In 2005 he was under the same kind of duress to make a change in the athletics department. His decision to bring in Andrea Myers to audit the athletics department gave him room to breathe and ultimately the ammunition to retain Taylor in the A.D. position.

There is every indication that Miller knew, or hoped, that he would soon be leaving Lock Haven to become president of Virginia State University. Another credible audit would show the world that he was taking the situation seriously, as well as to allow himself the time to "leave town" before he had to deal with a very messy personnel problem. This time he found two very professional and highly regarded experts who would explore all aspects of Lock Haven's athletics programs and the university's commitment to governing them fairly and competently.

Judith Sweet and Ronald Strattan were chosen to perform the audit. Sweet had logged 24 years as Director of Athletics at the University of California at San Diego before serving as NCAA Senior Vice President for Championships and Education. During her six-year tenure with the NCAA, she was the primary contact for Title IX and other gender equity issues. Strattan, a former head football coach at Portland State University, also served in the NCAA's education services department.

Sweet and Strattan hit the LHU campus in January of 2010 like a tornado, conducting over 30 individual meetings in three days. They even interviewed PLOW members. They reviewed numerous documents including strategic plans, policies, manuals and previous audits, such as the Myers Report. When the dust had cleared, they issued a ten-page report that included Weaknesses, Strengths, Other Observations and Recommendations.

The first impression one receives in reading the report is how very similar the findings were to those issued by Andrea Myers five years earlier. Among the list of weaknesses are these:

- The report submitted in 2005 by consultant Andrea Myers, which included many relevant recommendations, was provided to President Miller and the Council of Trustees, but there was no follow up. Several of those recommendations addressed issues that appear to have continued to be problematic since the report was submitted and correspond to issues that we have also identified. It is unclear to us why there was no follow–up to this 2005 report.

- The lack of follow up to the 2005 Myers report has led to questioning the administration's commitment to both intercollegiate athletics and to the Director of Athletics.

- Relationships among the university, athletics administration and some alumni and members of the community are fractured.

- There is an unhealthy divisiveness within the athletics department that appears to be delineated by sport and gender of teams and may be influenced by pressures from outside the university.

Among the listed strengths were these:

- Coaches and athletics administrators are dedicated to excellence at LHUP, and for the most part, they have been successful beyond what might be expected given the limited resources available.

- A review of the Equity in Athletics Disclosure Act (EADA) submitted by LHUP in 2009 shows that there is equitable financial support for men's and women's athletics. Ongoing evaluation of participation opportunities consistent with Title IX requirements should continue.

- In the past several years, as Title IX requirements were more consistently met, the LHUP women's teams have enjoyed increasing success. While most people have applauded this success, it has also been viewed incorrectly by individuals not knowledgeable about Title IX as the reason for some men's teams not being successful in recent years.

The recommendations from Sweet and Strattan mirror what Andrea Myers suggested: better strategic planning for athletics, clarified accountability for fundraising, establishment of an athletics advisory committee, better communication between athletics and administration, community outreach programs, Title IX education programs, and a campaign to end negative attitudes pitting men's sports against women's sports.

While the general tone of the report was supportive of Taylor, her coaches and her staff, the lack of any intent on Miller's part to follow-up on the recommendations did not change a thing at LHU. PLOW intimated that the fix was in because Judith Sweet must have been a close friend of Sharon Taylor. After all, they are both women. What more evidence does one need?

[Author's note: The complete Judith Sweet Report can be found in Appendix D]

PLOW's assault on Sharon Taylor in the local newspaper continued unabated. As an avalanche of lawsuits began to hit LHU, the public had a one-sided perspective on where to cast the blame. Every legal action found its way back to Sharon Taylor, according to PLOW. The following chapter will break down the origins and results of those lawsuits.

# Chapter Three – A Flurry of Litigation

Following the release of the Andrea Myers Review in April of 2005, Lock Haven president Keith Miller allowed the athletics department to drift further into dangerous waters. The observations and recommendations enumerated by Myers remained unrealized. The administration constructed no plans to educate the trustees, assemble a public relations campaign, or schedule more meetings to increase communication between and within departments. Ongoing and future incidents and problems that might have been avoided or mitigated flared out of control and into the courts.

**Garlick**

The swim team requested a meeting with Taylor and associate athletics director Peter Campbell. During the meeting, three of the women stated that they were quitting the team if coach George "Bart" Garlick remained as coach. The swimmers made numerous accusations about Garlick, several of which were later corroborated.

LHU opted not to renew Garlick's contract in June of 2005.

In 2007, Garlick filed a lawsuit naming Lock Haven University and Sharon Taylor as co-defendants. The ex-coach claimed that the university's decision not to renew his contact was because Sharon Taylor wanted the head swimming coach to be a woman. [1]

Garlick alleges that Taylor met with the women and asked them if they preferred a female coach. He felt that Taylor sabotaged his ability to function as a head coach. [2]

LHU actually replaced Garlick with another male coach, Andy Waeger. The already flimsy case lost one of its principal claims. The court sided with Lock Haven and dismissed the sexual discrimination case.

**Sharon Taylor:** *Peter Campbell worked very closely with Bart. He really tried to help him. There was no reaction from the trustees or alumni. He no longer had any support around the campus. Craig Willis had championed his hiring because of his relationship with Garlick's stepfather, Bill Piper of the Piper Aircraft Corporation. The Pipers* *were wealthy contributors to LHU. With Willis gone, Garlick had no one in his corner.*

*The case he brought to court was without any merit whatsoever. He wasn't fired; his contract was simply not renewed after President Miller came into office. Had President Willis still been in charge, it might have been different.*

George "Bart" Garlick III died on May 16, 2012 from injuries sustained while driving a truck for his employer, QC Energy Resources. [3]

## Guerriero

A lawsuit filed in 2003 by an assistant professor in the Department of Academic Development and Counseling named Joseph Patrick Guerriero alleged that LHU and Sharon Taylor removed him from his position as assistant athletics director because of his opposition to the "sexually hostile" atmosphere of the University. His case was settled in 2006.

**Sharon Taylor:** *Guerriero had been the Director of the Clearfield Campus, which at the time consisted of one building. He was brought into LHU to fill in when Assistant A.D. Bob Weller went on sabbatical leave. Patrick had the ambition to be an athletics director and President Willis gave him a chance to work in the department. When Weller returned from his leave, Guerriero returned to duties in his own department, which involved student services.*

*When Bob Weller decided to retire in 1998, Craig Willis once again selected Patrick to fill the position of assistant A.D., where he served for a couple of years. Things did not go well and, in January 2001, President Willis and Provost Roy Stewart made the decision to return him to his duties in student services. He sued.*

University personnel at the time indicated that the judge handling the Guerriero case pressured LHU to work out a settlement. According to a USA Today article by Erik Brady in July, 2010, Guerriero's grievances included such "sexually hostile" actions toward men in athletics as: men not permitted to have their dogs on the grass fields, while women could; and, umbrellas were not permitted in the stadium for football games, but spectators could have them at field hockey contests (with no regard for the difference in numbers at the events). Such was his idea of "gender bias."

By the time any settlement was agreed upon in the Guerriero case, President Willis had retired and a new president, Keith T. Miller held the reins at LHU. The University appeared to have a strong case; surely such claims of "gender bias" would be ridiculed in court. But, the judge's encouragement of a settlement was noted, and one was reached which resulted in an award of $47,000 to Guerriero, as well as an assignment in the University Foundation. While the assignment called for the sale of advertising for athletic teams, the position was totally unrelated to the Athletics Department and Sharon Taylor.

The settlement of the Guerriero lawsuit appeared to open the floodgates. If Guerriero could extract that kind of money from LHU with such charges, others felt they could correct every perceived injustice with a legal action of their own.

## Rudy

In addition to the normal duties, responsibilities and stresses of running a university athletics department, Taylor now had the added burden of dealing with concurrent lawsuits, even those not involving her, specifically.

If Taylor thought life would get any simpler in 2008, she soon found out otherwise. A class action suit filed in June of 2007 hit the fan. Lock Haven's field hockey coach (and Taylor's successor), Patricia Rudy, filed suit against the Pennsylvania State System of Higher Education (PASSHE) and the 14 schools therein, including her own employer Lock Haven University. [4]

Rudy claimed job discrimination in that male coaches in PASSHE schools were paid substantially more than female counterparts. On the one hand, Taylor, as administrator, had to defend her department and her employer. On the other hand, as a former head coach, and strong supporter of Pat Rudy, she naturally had to feel some empathy for her field hockey coach and former student-athlete.

In 2008, Rudy dropped PASSHE from her suit leaving LHU as the lone defendant. The university settled with Rudy to the tune of $200,000, another costly hit to the athletics department. [5]

To Taylor's critics, this put one more black mark next to her name. To the public it added to the growing perception that something was not right in Lock Haven.

**Sharon Taylor:** *Rudy was dead right. The women that were coaching hockey throughout the conference had salaries so much lower than any of the men's coaches in almost any sport. Rudy and her attorneys determined that it would be too cumbersome to bring a class action suit. The Lock Haven situation was unique; women's field hockey had to be compared with men's wrestling because both were Division I sports. Rudy made the decision to go on her own and sue Lock Haven individually. It was simply a pay-equity issue, a Title VII fair pay action.*

*When Rudy came to LHU in 1996, she had 15 years of very successful coaching experience at Cortland State (NY). She had won three consecutive championships in Division III, and I had been concerned that she would not consider leaving Cortland. But, she did and she was the logical successor to the LHU field hockey program.*

*Rudy arrived at LHU needing only to complete her dissertation to earn her doctorate. Nine years into her tenure at Lock Haven she was making around $20,000 less than Rocky Bonomo, the wrestling coach.*

*After the court settlement, a reporter from the Harrisburg Patriot-News called me and told me the case had been settled. I knew nothing about it until he called me for comment. The reporter knew more than I did about the case. I told him I thought she was very courageous for doing what she did. Keith Miller became upset with me for speaking without permission of the University and instructed me not to do so again. That de facto "gag order" would have consequences a year or so later.*

*Prior to the Rudy lawsuit, I had presented President Miller with three different plans to improve most of the women's, and three of the men's coaches' salaries. I submitted the first plan in June of 2006, the second in August, and the final version in February of 2007. I told him that the plans were not perfect, but they would keep us out of trouble. I thought he was going to act on this, but he never did.*

59

## Guerriero, the Sequels

The Guerriero name resurfaced again in 2008. Guerriero filed a new suit claiming that LHU reneged on the settlement agreement. His position as Director of Sports Marketing was to run for two years. LHU relieved him of those duties less than a year after the court settlement. His supervisor in the Development area claimed that his job performance was unsatisfactory.

Guerriero maintained that his marketing goal of $20,000 was not realistic because of the difficulty in selling advertising outside of the Lock Haven area. He further alleged that "a supervisor" told him that LHU did not intend for him to succeed. The latter situation provided proof to him that he was marked for retaliation for his 2003 lawsuit.

This time he filed a suit against LHU in federal court. The near future for Taylor now called for more testimony on behalf of the athletics department and more legal fees for LHU.

When Guerriero was reassigned following the settlement of the first lawsuit, he was given duties in the Development area. Even though his function was sports marketing, he had no direct involvement with the Athletics Department, and hence, no connection to Sharon Taylor. A jury verdict awarded him another $60,000 for LHU's failure to uphold the terms of the 2006 settlement. The university quickly appealed the jury's decision.

Despite the fact that Taylor and the athletics department were not involved in the legal action, a Williamsport radio station aligning itself with ESPN headlined: "Taylor and LHU Lose Another Court Battle."

Guerriero remains at Lock Haven as a tenured faculty member.

## Wright

In January of 2008, another incident took place that soon boiled over into a monstrous controversy, eventually leading to more litigation. A highly touted wrestler from the town of Wingate near Lock Haven injured his shoulder during a match. Landis Wright, attending LHU on a wrestling scholarship, could not practice for the upcoming meet in early February against archrival Bloomsburg. His shoulder pain sent him to Mount Nittany Medical Center in State College. According to the later lawsuit, the emergency room doctor diagnosed the injury as a separated shoulder and advised him not to wrestle until completion of four to six weeks of rehabilitation.

Wright claimed that the wrestling coach, Rocky Bonomo, pressured him to practice and that the trainer allegedly suggested injections to ameliorate the pain.

This new controversy contained two very toxic elements, an alleged mishandling of an injured student athlete, and a victim from the Lock Haven area. The athletics department was accused of actions meant to punish the wrestling team, and the community had one more reason to rail against Sharon Taylor. The PLOW movement grew out of LHU's perceived mismanagement of the wrestling program. In the absence of any action by President Miller, PLOW continued to smolder. The Landis Wright affair tossed a gallon of gasoline on the fire. The involvement of a local kid fanned the flames.

Landis Wright filed a lawsuit on October 30, 2009, naming Sharon Taylor, Rocky Bonomo and Keith Miller as defendants. His father, Paul Wright, secured the legal services of Buchanan, Ingersoll and Rooney, a high-powered law firm headquartered in Pittsburgh with a branch in Harrisburg.

According to an article written by "staff" on LockHaven.com, the online version of The Express newspaper (Lock Haven), Landis Wright learned that he must wrestle injured or lose his scholarship. The staff writers failed to note who exactly threatened to void Wright's scholarship. [6]

The article stated further that Landis and his father, Paul Wright, met with Taylor and five other unnamed "people from the university, causing Landis and Paul to feel pressured by Lock Haven and its coaching staff." At this meeting, the Wrights alleged numerous NCAA violations occurring within the wrestling program. [7]

The LockHaven.com article goes on to quote from the lawsuit, "During the meeting, Ms. Taylor told Landis he could keep his scholarship at Lock Haven if Landis would sit in the bleachers and keep quiet." [8]

President Miller informed the Wrights by letter on April 16, 2008 that he would hold an investigation into their complaints.

The lawsuit also alleged "Taylor conducted the 'so-called investigation' even though she was part of the meeting on February 12" (where the NCAA violations were revealed). [9]

During the investigation of NCAA violations, other wrestling team members testified that the coaches did not prescribe or condone any of the practices outlined by the Wrights. The lawsuit explained this away by concluding that the wrestlers could not be candid because they had been interviewed in small groups, thereby inhibiting testimony that may have been gained by interviewing them separately.

The Express news article continued, "The suit states Taylor and (head coach) Bonomo removed Landis' scholarship. Dr. Miller then allegedly caused his tuition bills to be paid, but did not restore his athletics scholarship, according to court papers." [10]

The Wrights contended that Landis could not join the team the following fall semester because he had failed to turn in his paperwork on time.

For PLOW, the lawsuits were grist for their mill. Sharon Taylor now resided in the center of an ever-widening storm.

The LockHaven.com article contained information gleaned from the plaintiff and the lawsuit, but presented little in the way of rebuttal. The last sentence in the article reported that Lock Haven Director of Marketing and Communications Mary White declined comment on a current litigation. No one on the "staff" that shared the byline of the story could uncover any involved parties to corroborate or deny various aspects of the complaints.

Any local citizen reading this article could easily deduce that Landis Wright had been mistreated and the University attempted to cover-up NCAA violations.

Anyone not previously belonging to the PLOW organization now had solid proof that Sharon Taylor needed to be removed. By 2010, PLOW boasted "more than 500" members. [11]

**Sharon Taylor:** *Landis Wright claimed that a University trainer with Bonomo's knowledge and encouragement simply applied ice and said that it would be examined two days later. That is just a flat out lie. Jack*

*Bailey, our team physician, was at the match. He examined Landis carefully at mat side. Jack looked at him before he left and told him that it was not a shoulder separation, but a shoulder strain. He said further that he would see him again the following Tuesday when he came to campus. So, a physician did examine him the night of the match. And, yes, a trainer did put ice on it.*

*His father decided to take him to the hospital that night. All that stuff about the surgeon telling him that he could risk permanent injury and could never wrestle again was just not true. As a matter of fact, the young man turned up with what was pretty clearly an incomplete prescription form where someone had written, "not permitted to wrestle, could do permanent injury." It was not signed by a physician.*

*Landis said further that Bonomo pressured him to wrestle. Bonomo simply said that he had been cleared by the physician, by the orthopedic doctor and by the trainer. Landis did not want to wrestle against Bloomsburg, for whatever reason.*

*Before the Bloomsburg match, the suit claimed that the trainer offered an injection to numb Wright's shoulder. Again, this was a flat out lie. Dr. Jack Bailey offered to give him a shot of cortisone to assist or speed up the recovery. He didn't offer Novocain or anything to numb the pain. This wasn't the night of the match, it was the prior week. By the day of the Bloomsburg dual meet, everyone knew that Landis was not going to wrestle because he had flatly refused.*

*They did meet with me on February 12th. There was a blizzard raging outside. All of the local schools had been closed. Paul Wright called me and said that he wanted to come over. I told him that I would be there if he really had to make it that day. I would have to round up the coaches and the trainer because I didn't know a thing about it. I told him I would not meet with him without them. He said okay. I also invited my assistant Peter Campbell. Peter is the only one that Paul Wright did not expect to see there.*

*During the meeting Paul Wright claims that he brought up the subject of NCAA violations. Anybody who knows me can tell you that if anyone mentioned the "v" word, everything would come to a screeching halt. There absolutely would have been no discussion of his shoulder, his scholarship or anything, had he mentioned violations. We would have started an investigation of any violations immediately. I swear to God, they never mentioned any violations as they later claimed. Peter can attest to that. They never brought up violations until they met with the University provost, Roger Johnson, some weeks later. Almost as an afterthought at that meeting, they mentioned the rubber suits, the saunas, etc.*

*At the meeting with Johnson, they claimed that I said Landis could have his scholarship if he sat in the bleachers and kept his mouth shut. What I actually said was...well, a little background first. Paul Wright and coach Rocky Bonomo were arguing back and forth like two kids. Each threatened to punch the other. Landis actually behaved himself. After a whole lot of back and forth, Rocky said he would free Landis to go anywhere he wanted, but if he wanted to stay at Lock Haven he could keep his scholarship.*

*Mr. Wright listened to that and looked at me. And I said, "Well, to tell you the truth, it's worth $10,000 to me not to have this kind of meeting in my office." I probably shouldn't have said it that way, but at that point, that's how I was feeling.*

*Mr. Landis turned to his son and said, "What do you think of that?"*

*Landis said, "No, I want to wrestle." He still wanted to be on the team. So it was his father who wanted to take the money and run.*

*Later, the quote became me telling him to sit in the bleachers and keep quiet. Believe me, I wouldn't sit in a room with five other University employees and make that kind of dumb statement.*

*The Wrights eventually went to the provost and filed an official complaint. By then, the wrestling season had ended with Landis still injured.*

*Rocky then decided that he didn't want Landis on the team any longer. So we fought a battle for a few months over the issue of whether a coach had the right to determine which students would be on his team. Because Rocky was adamant that he did not want Landis back, we went step-by-step through the NCAA process. We went through the financial aid office. They notified the athlete that his scholarship would not be renewed for the following year. We planned to do it in April, well in advance of the NCAA-dictated July deadline, so Landis would have plenty of time to speak to recruiters from other schools.*

*Then the president became involved. He said that he was "going to fix it" despite how he had been treated by the student's father. Truly, many of these problems occurred because Keith (Miller) wanted everybody to like him. People would be shocked if they saw some of the awful and rude things Paul Wright said (in writing) about Miller. And Wright even sent it to the president.*

*Keith scheduled a meeting and asked Rocky and me, along with LHU's attorney, to sit down with the Wrights and a local lawyer they had hired who had no previous knowledge of the case. We met in the president's conference room because he wanted to take control and get everything worked out.*

*Because the attorneys were going back and forth, the doggone July 1 NCAA deadline passed and Landis never had his hearing with Financial Aid. The parties never came to any agreement. So the new school year arrived with nothing settled.*

*Landis decided he wanted to wrestle again but he did not turn in the necessary paperwork. This went on for quite awhile. I even called his father to remind him of the deadline. After the final date passed, Rocky informed Landis he was not on the team.*

*The Wrights then contested the $10,000 tuition. Keith Miller forgave the unpaid tuition and just wrote it off as a bad debt. He didn't consider it as a scholarship, and certainly not as a mea culpa payment. That is what occurred with the $10,000 mentioned in the lawsuit. The tuition was not waived, Landis still owed it, but Miller just told Financial Aid to write it off. The 2008-2009 wrestling season went on without Landis Wright.*

*With regard to the "violations," President Miller actually required a two-step process. He brought Human Resources in to investigate the alleged NCAA violations instead of the athletics department. They asked me how to proceed; I suggested that they bring all of the wrestlers together in a classroom. The wrestlers were informed that some allegations had been made and they would be asked some questions. Three people from HR took them into separate athletics department offices, one at a time, to be interviewed. I was not present at all for the questioning.*

*All students were asked the same questions. When each session ended, the student had to leave and could not reenter the room where the others waited. The kids waiting to interview were not permitted to talk or to use their cell phones. The lawsuit claimed they were interviewed with other wrestlers present, thus inhibiting their testimony. This was another big lie. We would never interview students two at a time.*

*I was then asked by Keith Miller to run an additional investigation and compare it to the results obtained by Human Resources. I met with each wrestler still in the program and questioned them again, individually. Assistant A.D. Danielle Barney sat in on the interviews and took copious notes. I forwarded the results to the administration and the NCAA.*

*The wrestlers reported that some of them would occasionally show up for practice with a plastic bag or rubber garment under their clothes. In every case, the coaches would send them away to remove the illegal items.*

*I called Bruce Baumgartner, Olympic wrestling champion and athletics director at Edinboro University (PA). He said, "That happens all the time, Sharon. As long as the coaches try to stop it, that's all you can do. You can't follow them around 24 hours a day."*

*So that was the whole story of these violations. No rules had been broken. When Austin Shanfelter, the power behind PLOW, received the results of the investigation, he accused us of a cover-up.*

The Council of Trustees was so invested in the NCAA investigation that one member went totally off the rails when he learned that no sanctions would be forthcoming against the University. The normal reaction from a school official would be relief and joy. Former trustee Ginny Roth describes the incident. "A Lock Haven town colleague had what can only be described as a profound emotional rampage during a private Council of Trustees work session. His fury was over the lack of substantive findings in the Wright case. After a heated display of words, he stormed out of the meeting. There was sufficient disarray and chaos that the university police were summoned to be present at the public sessions scheduled for later in the day. We later found out that he spent the rest of the day at a local bar. He is no longer a trustee. One of our colleagues on the board had given him the nickname 'the village idiot'."

This individual wanted Sharon Taylor gone so badly that he would have welcomed sanctions against his institution as a trade off. The very program that PLOW wanted to revive would take a step backward, but that would have been fine with him. Such was the attitude in Lock Haven at the time.

Former LHU Vice President Linda Koch commented on why Keith Miller involved Human Resources in a possible NCAA investigation: "One might speculate that on the advice of legal counsel, President Miller brought in the Human Resources Office because they were used to conducting investigations of employee complaints. This might be considered a normal and customary practice. However, human resource personnel are not educated in NCAA violations and not trained to conduct such investigations. Note also that PASSHE legal counsel are likewise not trained (in this area)."

Six months before Landis Wright filed his suit, Taylor found herself tiptoeing carefully through a minefield even more dangerous than the NCAA violation threat. Lock Haven had decided not to renew the contract of men's basketball coach John Wilson, Jr.

### John Wilson, Jr. - Dead Man Walking

John Wilson, Jr. began his tenure as Lock Haven's men's basketball coach in 1999. By the year 2002, Wilson, an African-American, received the first in a series of poor performance evaluations. In April of 2009, Wilson learned that he would be the coach only until his contract expired in 2011.

According to court records, Wilson failed to effectively engage in fundraising, the life-blood of scholarship money at LHU. His players consistently earned low grades, and worst of all, he committed the biggest crime in college sports: he guided his teams to very poor won-loss records. Moreover, the NCAA suspended him twice for allowing students to play while clearly ineligible under conference rules. [12]

Instead of using the two years' notice to find another position, Wilson fought back. Calling himself "dead man walking," he filed a complaint with the Pennsylvania Human Relations Commission in December of 2009, just two months following the filing of Landis Wright's legal action. The PHRC took no action, but issued Wilson a "right to sue" letter and a suit hit the court docket in 2010. [13]

Wilson cited discrimination on the basis of race and a hostile work environment. In an effort to explain the NCAA suspensions, he stated that LHU failed to adequately defend and support him, again because of his race. [14]

Within a year, Magistrate Judge William Prince recommended dismissal of the case against LHU and Sharon Taylor. The U.S. Middle District Court accepted the recommendation and found in favor of the defendants. Prince held that Wilson could not prove any of his allegations. Taylor had no authority over Wilson's salary except where poor performance evaluations precluded pay increases. Furthermore, all of the reasons for the unsatisfactory ratings had been substantiated. [15]

U.S. Middle Court Judge John E. Jones III concluded, "In this case, plaintiff has offered little more than his own suppositions in support of his allegations that race factored into the behavior of the defendants upon which he bases his claims." [16] But the documents presented by both sides in the discovery process exposed a basketball program with serious issues.

**Sharon Taylor:** *Coach Wilson's case was a short one. There were so many issues: poor performance, lack of fundraising, a couple of NCAA violations, and some significant issues of personal conduct by several players over a number of years. The team's overall record was 57 wins and 266 losses, but some of the other issues were far more troubling. One young man had been caught on video stealing items from a locker room; I also discovered that he had been banned from the residence halls for stalking female students. I instructed John to suspend him. That story led to a tragic ending.*

Domenique Thomas Wilson, of Philadelphia, no relation to the head coach, was accused of entering the apartment of three female Lock Haven students in February of 2009. Police said he attacked the three women, raping two of them several times at knifepoint. Wilson terrorized the women for four hours and later used stolen ATM cards to extract cash from their accounts.

Domenique Wilson claimed that a man named Jonathan planted the semen in the women to frame him. [17]

He was convicted in March of 2010 of 37 counts. The judge set the sentencing for June. The Clinton County D.A. predicted that Domenique Wilson would be put away for the rest of his life. [18]

In June, the 6'7" former West Philadelphia High basketball star received 76 to 196 years in prison. District Attorney Salisbury successfully argued for a penalty in the "aggravated" range. The standard range would have netted Wilson 57-74 years. [19]

DNA taken from the Lock Haven case later showed Wilson to be the perpetrator of several other rapes that took place in Philadelphia prior to his enrollment at Lock Haven. He was charged and convicted of raping a Philadelphia woman in October of 2008 and a University of Pennsylvania student two months later. He was sentenced to 230 years and declared a violent sexual predator. Counting the Lock Haven sentence he faces a total of 154 to 426 years in prison. [20]

The poor judgment of John Wilson, Jr. in fighting to keep Domenique Wilson on the Lock Haven basketball team did not help his fight to retain his coaching position. The coach claimed that he wanted to give the kid a second chance. He undoubtedly wanted to keep a 6' 7" high school all-star on his roster to try to reverse the poor won-loss record of recent years.

One particular NCAA violation clearly illustrated Coach Wilson's lack of judgment. The player identified by the NCAA as ineligible happened to be the head coach's son, hereafter referred to as JW. JW had received some very bad advice from his academic advisor. That advisor was his father. Because coaches are part of the staff at LHU, this arrangement was legitimate, if not particularly wise.

NCAA eligibility rules are complex. Not only are there minimum credit hour standards, but the aptly named 75% rule states that 75% of all yearly credits must be earned within the two main semesters (or three in a trimester schedule). Passing grades also factor into the equation. JW's academic history led to serious sanctions against LHU.

**Sharon Taylor:** *From the moment I became Director of Athletics, I insisted that all evaluation of initial or continuing eligibility would be handled in the Registrar's Office, not in the Athletics Department. I wanted there to be no question of objectivity in evaluations. Presidents Willis and Miller supported that position from the start.*

*A change of grade was submitted in one of JW's courses and the Registrar's staffer suspected a problem with the NCAA's "repeated course" rule. She sent the transcript to me for review. The instant I looked at it, I realized we had a big problem, not just with the repeated course, but also with several years of the 75% rule.*

A review of the transcript indicated that the student would take 12-14 credits each semester, fail several courses, and repeat them in summer school. The result was that 75% of his course work was not completed in the two academic year semesters. Looking back over the past year that JW played, he was actually not eligible. As luck would have it, that year was the most successful of John Wilson's coaching tenure. With the help of a very talented assistant coach, the team won 12 games that season.

**Sharon Taylor:** *I composed a very compelling appeal to the NCAA trying to explain the unexplainable. The NCAA turned us down flat, declaring JW ineligible for the past season. They forced us to forfeit all of those wins during our "best" season. Further, they fined us $500 per game in which an ineligible player appeared. Coach Wilson received a slap on the wrist for his coaching and his advising failures, but nothing more serious.*

Most students would not have fallen prey to this rule, because of the prohibitive cost of repeating courses. JW, however, paid no tuition due to his father's position as a staff member of the Pennsylvania State System of Higher Education. He continued to repeat courses and take others that did not lead to any particular degree.

Normally, a department suffering fines due to a coach's lack of vigilance had to pay them out of their budget. In this case, because there was virtually no money in the men's basketball account, President Miller stepped in and arranged for LHU to pay the men's basketball fines. Wilson never accepted responsibility for this misadventure.

Interestingly, when Keith Miller left LHU to become president of Virginia State University, he took John Wilson with him to become an assistant director of athletics.

As to the fate of John Wilson's son, he became academically ineligible going forward given the number of credits he needed for reinstatement, and the very few semesters he had left. He is not known to have played college level basketball again.

In November of 2007, Pennsylvania Attorney General Tom Corbett announced the arrest of four Lock Haven students for dealing in large quantities of marijuana. Operation Fouled-Out was named for the fact that three of the four men arrested were current or former Lock Haven University basketball players under coach John Wilson. Bruce Kennedy of Ambler (PA) and Rodney D. Armstrong of Harrisburg (PA) were on the team when arrested. Michael J. Dye of Fleetwood (PA) formerly played for Wilson. The fourth, Matthew Eshelman, was a student at LHU at the time, but had not been a member of the basketball team.

Corbett reported that the group allegedly bought marijuana in Philadelphia for around $2,000 per pound and sold to Lock Haven students and town residents grossing as much as $6,000 per pound.

The combination of NCAA violations and poor judgment in recruiting and retaining players proved to be ample and justifiable reason for the court to uphold LHU's decision to not renew the contract of John Wilson, Jr.

**Sharon Taylor:** *John and I were having a conversation in my office after he had filed the lawsuit. I asked him if all of this had happened somewhere else, would he still be employed. He said, "No, but I was smart enough here to wait until I was protected." How was he protected? He was protected by the relationship between his wife and the wife of the president, Keith Miller. The wives were the best of friends. There was a marked difference in John Wilson when Keith came to the University. He had made an effort up until 2004.*

*During a meeting about Wilson, I said to Keith, in front of Provost Roger Johnson, "I know this is hard for you to do, just based on the relationship between the two wives." He replied that the relationship had nothing to do with it. He became very testy and defensive.*

*What John meant was that he had a president in his corner, not based upon race, necessarily. And I don't think John and Keith were friends, but the closeness of the relationship through the wives was a factor. This also explains why Keith took John with him to Virginia State*

71

*University as an assistant athletics director. I guess you could explain it as a close relationship between two families.*

The chair of the Council of Trustees, Guy Graham, was aware of the eligibility issue of Wilson's son. Former trustee Ginny Roth reports that it was a source of major disagreement between her and Graham. "I went to Graham and said, 'Don't you think we ought to be looking into the issue of our basketball coach playing his son while academically ineligible?' Guy said, 'Ginny, Ginny, Ginny. Now come on, dear. I've been a coach. Don't you think I would know if my son was academically eligible?' I told him he was probably right, but it was my job to ask questions. He came back later and said, 'Well there was a misunderstanding.' I said, Bullshit, you're covering up.' I told him that Wilson needed to go."

Lock Haven Legal Scorecard

Garlick: Win - Case dismissed for lack of evidence

Guerriero I: Loss. Plaintiff received $47,500 cash settlement and reassigned another position

Guerriero II: Loss. Jury verdict for plaintiff resulting in a $60,000 cash and another job reassignment

Rudy: Loss. Plaintiff received cash settlement of $200,000 and retains coaching position

Wright: Loss. Plaintiff received cash settlement of $200,000

Wilson: Win: Case dismissed for lack of evidence

## Chapter Four – Taylor Fights Back

Preserve (the) Legacy Of Wrestling, a group that had formed for the purpose of returning Lock Haven wrestling to its former glory, had expanded to an all-out effort to pin the blame for all athletics problems, real and imagined, on Sharon Taylor. More importantly, according to Taylor, they did so using false and defamatory accusations.

With each new lawsuit filed against Lock Haven University and Sharon Taylor, the PLOW group grew more daring with their accusations and ploys to get Taylor dismissed as A.D. Whenever a legal action went against Lock Haven, Taylor was excoriated, whether or not she played any part in the underlying incidents.

After the supposed NCAA violations in the wrestling program were shown to be unfounded, PLOW cried "cover-up." When the court findings went in LHU's favor, as in the John Wilson, Jr. race discrimination case, PLOW members continued to believe and state publicly, that she was guilty of all sorts of evil deeds.

On or about July 12, 2009, PLOW released a document entitled *Lock Haven University Athletics in a Crossroads*. This pamphlet was distributed to PLOW members and posted on the PLOW website. *Crossroads* enumerated the problems that they had determined to be the reasons for the decline of Lock Haven athletics.

On July 14, Taylor secured the services of Goodall and Yurchak, Attorneys At Law, located in State College, PA.

Three months later, PLOW released a publication entitled *PLOW Emergency Update*, a bulletin created and distributed by a Harrisburg (PA) public relations firm owned by David La Torre. This publication outlined new outrages committed by Sharon Taylor that would lead to further decline in LHU athletics.

Taylor tolerated the early criticisms and false allegations, such as parking illegally and calling a male staff member her "bitch." By late 2009, however, PLOW resorted to an all-out blitzkrieg, designed to destroy her hard-earned reputation and secure her dismissal. Funded in part by wealthy alumnus Austin Shanfelter, PLOW turned to the professional public relations firm, La Torre Communications, later chosen by Penn State University to help rebuild their reputation in the wake of the Jerry Sandusky scandal. PLOW also had the ear of an ESPN radio affiliate managed by Todd Bartley. Many of the PLOW pronouncements aired unfiltered through ESPN Radio Williamsport.

To make matters much worse, LHU put Taylor and her staff under a de facto gag rule. As the "evidence" against her accumulated, she had no clear channel to correct publicly issued falsehoods and inaccuracies. In short, she could not defend herself. Nor did the University release official responses to the criticisms.

The siege mentality of PLOW began to take its toll on Taylor. Like a boxer pinned against the ropes, unable to punch back, she had to look off campus for relief. She faced the difficult decision of whether or not to file her own lawsuit.

On December 16, 2009, her attorney filed a lawsuit against PLOW and naming the individuals she felt were most responsible for the group's more egregious accusations.

The suit specifically named Austin Shanfelter, Ronald Bowes, Neil Turner, Thane Turner, Jerry Swope, Todd Bartley, and ESPN, Inc. as defendants. Thane Turner and ESPN were ultimately dropped from the suit. [1]

### Defendant Austin Shanfelter

Shanfelter, understood to be the unofficial leader of PLOW, resides in the Fort Meyers, FL area. He is a graduate of Lock Haven University and a former wrestler. His wealth and status enabled PLOW to grow into a formidable foe of LHU's Athletics Director.

Bloomberg Businessweek profiles Shanfelter as a Director and Chairman of the Compensation Committee of Orion Marine Group, Inc. earning $124,500. Further background information reveals that he held the position of CEO and President of MasTec Inc. from 2001 through 2007. He has been chairman of Global HR Research, LLC. since 2008. He additionally serves on a number of boards including Sabre Industries.

His board memberships and directorships most likely have provided a nice living beyond the Orion Marine Group paycheck.

Compared to the financial clout that Shanfelter brought to PLOW, Sharon Taylor had to fight an uphill battle to influence the perceptions of the public and the LHU community with regard to her fitness for the job. Additionally, President Miller had a virtual gag order working against her with regard to the lawsuits and accusations against her integrity.

Shanfelter attempted to use his past largesse to LHU as a stick to spur President Miller and the Council of Trustees into removing Taylor. For Miller to do otherwise meant risking the loss of a large annual donation to the school. Forbes.com's profile of Shanfelter reports that he held 326,678 shares of MasTec in 2008. MasTec's website describes the company thusly:

"Engineering and construction for electrical transmission, oil and natural gas pipelines, renewable energy and wireless networks"

Shanfelter is no stranger to the legal system. In 2004, while serving as CEO of MasTec, Inc., he and CFO Donald Weinstein were named as defendants in a securities fraud class action lawsuit. The defendants were alleged to have made "material misstatements with respect to a company's financial results." More specifically, they were alleged to have inflated financial results, prematurely claimed revenue on contracts, and overstated inventory, all violations of GAAP, Generally Accepted Accounting Principles.

When MasTec's true financial picture appeared, the stock price took a nosedive, costing investors considerable losses.

While there was no organization formed calling itself Preserve the Legacy of MasTec (PLOM) there was a group called the S.E.C. that investigated the alleged fraud. One of the more interesting documents gathered by the SEC investigation was Shanfelter's employment contract with MasTec. On top of his base salary of $600,000, he received stock options and performance bonuses. His base salary alone equaled his alma mater's entire annual budget for the athletics department.

Several more class action suits were filed. Company founder Jorge Mas, Jr. was added as a defendant. Judge Federico A. Moreno of the United Sates District Court, Southern District of Florida, joined the cases together. In April of 2006, a settlement of $10 million in cash was agreed upon. Following a settlement fairness hearing in November, the court approved the settlement.

**Sharon Taylor:** *As a wrestling booster, Shanfelter remained tight with the wrestling community. He has always been one of those boosters who wants to have a say in how the program is run. Joe Paterno used to say to the Penn State football boosters, "I want your money but I don't want your two cents."*

*Shanfelter wanted to be rid of Rocky Bonomo (as wrestling coach). He saw me as an impediment to that. He offered Keith Miller a half million dollars (donation) to fire me.*

### Defendant Jerry Swope

Swope wrestled for Lock Haven, capturing individual PSAC crowns from 1963-1965 in the 177-pound weight class. LHU failed to claim the team championship in any of those three campaigns. [2] He graduated from LHU in 1966 and later earned a Masters Degree in Education leading to a career as a teacher at Warrior Run High School and Millersville University. Swope has been named to the Lock Haven University Wrestling Hall of Fame, the Clinton County Sports Hall of Fame, the Pennsylvania Wrestling Hall of Fame and the West Branch Wrestling Hall of Fame. On November 15, 2012, he joined the LHU Council of Trustees. [3]

### Defendant Ronald Bowes

Bowes, also a 1966 graduate of Lock Haven, never claimed an individual PSAC championship, but performed well enough to earn entry into the Lock Haven University Wrestling Hall of Fame in 1994. More recently, he joined the Maryland Wrestling Hall of Fame for his efforts in establishing wrestling programs at Thomas S. Wooton High School in Rockville and Quince Orchard High School in Gaithersburg. He guided the two programs to a combined 135-32-4 record during his tenure. [4] Bowes serves on the Lock Haven University Foundation's Board of Directors and chairs the Athletics Committee. [5]

## Defendant Neil Turner

Turner coached the LHU wrestling team from 1979 to 1990, earning coach of the year awards in 1985 and 1988. Turner wrestled for Penn State, graduating in 1961. [6]

**Sharon Taylor:** *During the 1989-90 season, LHU President Craig Willis received information that several NCAA violations had occurred in the wrestling program. He asked me to begin an investigation. Coach Turner had allowed students ineligible for intercollegiate athletic competition under Proposition 48 (academic eligibility rules) to participate in practice sessions. Coach Turner was also accused of using boosters to go on the road and recruit prospective wrestling candidates, another NCAA violation.*

*When I called Turner into my office to discuss the alleged violations, he became very defensive and offered his resignation. I told him that I was not seeking his resignation, just information. He returned to my office a short time later and handed me a written resignation that stated that I forced him to resign. Because that was not true, I refused to accept the letter. He had the department secretary revise the letter and resubmitted it.*

*One day later, Turner came to my office again to tell me that he had had a change of heart. He had reconsidered and did not want to give up his coaching position. I was ready to agree with his new decision and proceed with the inquiry into the NCAA violations. At that point, he informed me of a list of conditions recommended by his lawyer. When the word "lawyer" entered the conversation, I concluded the meeting and made an appointment to see President Willis. Willis made the decision to accept the resignation and find another position for him within the University.*

*Tom Justice accepted the position of interim wrestling coach to complete the season.*

*Neil had always done a fine job running the summer wrestling camps, earning a lot of money for his program. So, he wasn't fired, just "reassigned" to the position of Director of Camps and Conferences. Several months later, President Willis learned that Turner planned to run his own camps in direct competition with the Lock Haven camps that he was organizing.*

*Willis informed Neil that he could not operate his own camp programs; it was a conflict of interest as outlined in his employment contract. Turner refused to acquiesce and Willis fired him.*

*You might think that this episode motivated Turner to join PLOW and attempt to drive me from my position. Actually, Neil was never happy about me running the athletics department. He voiced his opposition to my promotion from the very beginning.*

*During that period, we launched an internal investigation into the alleged violations. Except in very serious and widespread cases, the NCAA actually expects the schools to perform their own investigations. A committee of three non-athletics department employees investigated the allegations. Two highly respected faculty members and an associate dean confirmed that the violations had, in fact, occurred. LHU suffered some minor sanctions, including forfeiture of some wrestling victories.*

*Neil's son, Thane Turner, was eventually dropped from the lawsuit. We learned that Thane was much more passively involved that we first realized. He was just there to help Neil where he could. He never took an active or vindictive approach like the other guys did.*

Over the three previous years Taylor had spent considerable time and energy defending her employer and herself against relentless criticism and a seemingly endless chain of lawsuits; this in addition to handling the complex and time-consuming leadership of LHU's athletics department.

Kathleen Yurchak, Taylor's attorney, speaking about Taylor's state of mind, said "I don't know that it's accurate to say she was affected by the lawsuits that she was a defendant in, because in my mind she felt she was right in all of those. It was the PLOW organization attacking her even though she was doing her best to defend the institution. If she felt that the administration was supporting her in the lawsuits, or PLOW wasn't attacking her [it might have been different]…well, I think that is where things broke down."

Paragraph 89 of the legal complaint declared, "As a direct and proximate result of the conduct of Defendants, Plaintiff suffered anguish, humiliation, and embarrassment, as well as damage to her career and reputation, all directly causing her to endure severe emotional distress." [7]

Kathleen Yurchak believes that Taylor was deeply hurt over the constant allegations that she did not support the men's teams at LHU. The fact that Lock Haven won the Dixon Trophy three times for the best total athletics department, men and women, made no difference to her critics. Though she had always advocated for gender equality in sports, her tenure as A.D. was dedicated to maximizing the potential of men's and women's teams alike. Coaches of the men's teams readily acknowledged her support.

The crux of the legal action can be reduced to two paragraphs from the Background portion of the complaint: "Specifically, PLOW and the Individual Defendants have published and distributed literature containing numerous defamatory falsities and inaccuracies in order to portray Plaintiff in a negative light and to accomplish the organization's ultimate goal of forcing Plaintiff out of her position as athletics director."

"PLOW and the Individual Defendants have also used various media outlets, including ESPN Radio and The Express, the newspaper in the Lock Haven region, as a means for publishing and disseminating their defamatory statements about Plaintiff." [8]

The complaint cited five examples of inaccurate or false statements from the "Crossroads" publication, including the implication that a $20,000 shortfall in football funds had been misappropriated. Another item stated that the men's swimming team coach sued LHU for wrongful termination following the elimination of the men's swimming team. The complaint contests each of the inaccurate items. The complaint further states that each of the named defendants "had knowledge that the statements were false" or served in a capacity "which would have made them privy to the process surrounding the athletics department..."

The complaint also spelled out additional falsehoods and inaccuracies that appeared in an article in The Express authored by defendants Shanfelter and Swope. The article, entitled "Time for a change in LHU athletics department is at hand," incorrectly stated that NCAA violations had been improperly investigated under Taylor's watch.

Taylor was not the only target of PLOW. They also aimed their guns at head wrestling coach Rocky Bonomo. Rocky made two mistakes that placed him in the gun sights of PLOW. Firstly, he supported and believed in Sharon Taylor. Secondly, he embraced Neil Turner as a confidant to the wrestling team. Said Bonomo, "I brought Neil Turner back into the fold - (he was) a former coach who was very jaded about Sharon and LHU. Sharon warned me about bringing him back. That turned out to be a huge mistake for me. He turned on me very quickly, Neil did. Then Shanfelter turned very shortly after. Austin is a very successful businessman. He was my friend and a tremendous ally. Shanfelter wrestled for Neil. He really connected with Neil. He (Shanfelter) was just a spot starter, so I don't think he had much of a wrestling career at Lock Haven. But he really appreciated Neil Turner."

Bonomo's allegiance to his boss cost him his job. His contract was not renewed. Bonomo continued, "They wanted me to turn against Sharon. If I would have turned against her I would probably still be working there. I still had two years left on my contract. They manipulated the president into not renewing my contract. I left with two years left on it because they started to attack my team. I couldn't protect my team so the best thing for everybody was for me to get out of there. I got a pathetic settlement."

Anthony "Rocky" Bonomo became collateral damage in PLOW's quest to dethrone Sharon Taylor. Today he operates a gym and wrestling club called Rock Solid near Wilkes-Barre in Northeastern Pennsylvania.


### Defendant Todd Bartley

The lawsuit also went after Todd Bartley of ESPN radio in Williamsport: "Defendant Bartley is the general manager of ESPN Radio, Williamsport. Upon information and belief Bartley is a 'member' of PLOW and/or has been actively involved in the PLOW organization from its inception. Defendant Bartley, in his capacity as general manager for ESPN radio, has used the ESPN station as an outlet to disseminate the false information provided by PLOW." [9]

Bartley requested and received various records and emails pertaining to "matters concerning plaintiff." With this information in hand, Bartley proceeded to publicly air accusations against Taylor that contradicted the information released by the University.

Bartley falsely and inaccurately included Taylor in a lawsuit in which Taylor played no part. The headline of an Internet article on the radio's website carried the title "Taylor and LHU lose another court battle."

Taylor's lawsuit asserted that Bartley and ESPN ventured beyond the normal scope of media reporting into dangerous waters. They actively took one side in a quest to damage a reputation and deprive someone of their job.

The legal action consisted of five counts of "libel per se," one count of "intentional infliction of emotional distress," and one count of "conspiracy." The defendants faced a 30-day deadline to file their pleadings or risk a summary judgment against them.

After the court documents had been filed, and preparations began for the deposition process, attorney Yurchak observed a pronounced silence coming from the PLOW organization. This temporary ceasefire suggested that legal action should have been initiated sooner.

In March of 2011, a motion for summary judgment for the defendant Todd Bartley was filed by his attorney Michael J. Zicolello of Williamsport, PA. In his motion Zicolello asserted he following:

- Sharon Taylor is a public figure.

- Bartley was never a member of PLOW

- He did not author any of the allegedly defamatory statements contained in PLOW documents.

- The lawsuit referred to in the Internet headline, "Taylor and LHU lose another court battle" did originally not mention Sharon Taylor.

- Plaintiff suffered no physical harm, injury or illness.

- The claim of conspiracy fails because no unlawful act was committed in agreement with any other party.

- As a member of the sports press, Bartley did not act with malice in reporting about Sharon Taylor.

The motion called for a summary judgment because the case contained insufficient evidence and failed to prove that allegedly defamatory statements were made with actual malice. [10]

In April of 2011, attorney Timothy J. Nieman of Rhoads and Sinon in Harrisburg filed a motion for summary judgment on behalf of PLOW, Austin Shanfelter, Neil Turner and Thane Turner.

This motion hinged on two claims by Sharon Taylor. The first being a denial that she is a public figure because "her access to the media was limited by LHU and she did not have adequate opportunity to counteract the false statements made." [11] The defendants maintain that LHU allowed Taylor the option of speaking out as long as she did not speak "on behalf of the University."

The second disputed argument was that the defendants acted with malice. The motion states simply that Taylor is unable to prove malice by "clear and convincing evidence."

Plaintiff Shanfelter supplied President Keith Miller of LHU with a draft of the "Crossroads" publication before it was released. After 30 days with no response by LHU, Shanfelter published Crossroads under the belief that Miller would have investigated and commented on any inaccuracies. [12]

Kathleen Yurchak quickly filed briefs on behalf of Sharon Taylor in opposition to the Bartley and PLOW motions for judgment in their favor. The Bartley response included transcripts of radio programs entitled *The Locker Room Show*, a program Bartley himself describes as "monologue driven." "This show aired four times each week on ESPN Radio Williamsport, with Bartley anchoring two of the four shows.

Transcript excerpts display Bartley's flair for self-promotion as well as his zeal in seeking Sharon Taylor's resignation or dismissal.

Quoting Todd Bartley from the Brief:

*"Trust me, I've picked on plenty of people, and let me get this out there. I called for John Cooper's head when he was head coach of the (Ohio State) Buckeyes, okay? When I am (sic) in Eastern North Carolina, do you remember the bowl game, the GMAC Bowl is what it was down in Mobile, AL? Marshall's playing East Carolina. East Carolina is*

*thumping Marshall at the half like 70-5. All right, that wasn't the score but you get the idea. Marshall comes back and beats East Carolina. Why? Because Tim Rose's defense brought a three-man line instead of four and Byron (Leftwich) just picked apart the defense all night. The next day we're on the radio...Tim Rose gotta go, Tim Rose gotta go, Tim Rose gotta go...Well, 48 hours later, guess what happened? Publish Report, Hammer has a meeting with Logan and Logan says guess what? I have a lot of money left on my deal? If you want me to fire Rose I'm going to. They were both gone within 48 hours. That's how it works, Sharon, in the real world." [13]*

How does one interpret the above rant? Todd Bartley wants the audience to understand that he is not afraid to take on the big dogs, such as Ohio State Coach John Cooper. Further, Bartley claimed that he had played a role in getting head coach Steve Logan and defensive co-coordinator Tim Rose fired from East Carolina University. He ended by warning Sharon Taylor that she may be next.

Seven days later on his show Bartley let the other shoe drop:

*"So I will offer you this, will offer you this, Sharon, I have a seat, which I swept the floor over the weekend by the way, so I do that too, sweep the floor, take out the garbage and everything. I will offer you this seat. Mic position number 4, to come on the show and do the student athletes of Lock Haven a favor by tendering your resignation the next time we have the show and I am in town. I will make that offer to you right now, it's a standing offer whenever you're ready. You are more than welcome to resign, because that, Sharon, will save taxpayers of this state and those student athletes a lot of heartache and make it easy that Keith Miller does not have to make a decision on firing you.* [14]

During his deposition Bartley testified that it is against journalistic standards as an investigative reporter and against his own general policy to broadcast unconfirmed reports.

Despite Bartley's self-proclaimed high journalistic standards, he made this pronouncement on his show: "We also have an unconfirmed report, and again I want to state that it's an unconfirmed report, that since our last show Ms. Taylor has again dropped the ax on the football program and two coaches have been dismissed. That is unconfirmed. We are trying to track down and confirm that as we speak."

Two weeks later, this investigative reporter, unable to track down the truth, repeated the unconfirmed story, this time citing no source, confirmed or otherwise. Actually, the football program remained and no football coaches had been fired.

Bartley denied under oath belonging to the PLOW organization. He did not attend Lock Haven University. His Facebook home page states that he studied at the University of Mount Union in Alliance, Ohio. His radio station operated out of Williamsport, 27 miles from LHU. What connection put Sharon Taylor in his crosshairs? Sharon thinks she has the clue to unlock this mystery.

**Sharon Taylor:** *Up until April of 2009, Bartley broadcast various LHU sporting events including football on his radio station. He had worked these deals out with Troy Miller, the Director of Athletics Development. LHU would soon participate in the NCAA Softball National Championship. Troy simply did not wish to deal with Bartley any longer. Bartley approached Miller and learned that his requests now had to go through me. I agreed to let his station cover the tournament, but explained that we required a broadcast fee of $350 per game. The money would go into the softball program. Bartley declined.*

*Two weeks later, he sent me an email saying, "It is my understanding that since softball just won a second national championship, you had shared with certain folks (that) you were considering retiring as Athletics Director, I wanted to confirm with you if this was true or not?"*

*After learning that his understanding was not correct, he began his campaign of publicly calling for my resignation. In the meantime, he continued working behind my back to secure the play-by-play rights to Lock Haven sporting events.*

*On June 15, 2009, he sent an email to the Lock Haven Foundation complaining about the licensing fees for radio sports coverage. In the same email he stated, "In short, we have taken on the task to uncover the truth in regard to some allegations that have been made in regard to the Athletics Department and Ms. Taylor, to date." He failed to reveal the nature of the "serious allegations."*

On July 30, William Hanelly, Vice President for Finance Administration and Technology, in a letter to Bartley, formally declined to accept his unsolicited proposal. The University officially stood behind Sharon Taylor. Nevertheless, Bartley blamed Taylor for his failure to secure important programming for ESPN Radio Williamsport.

Bartley had no stake in returning Lock Haven wrestling to its glory days. He had no connection to Lock Haven football or baseball. What he did have was the need to create or exploit controversy to attract listeners to his radio programs. Thousands of sports journalists attempt to accomplish that everyday. That, by itself, could not account for the zeal with which he zeroed in on Sharon Taylor. The inability to acquire the programming rights to Lock Haven's participation in the NCAA softball championship at no cost must have put him in a delicate position, especially if he had prematurely informed station ownership that it was a done deal.

Bartley claimed in court documents that he was never a member of PLOW. His claim may have been true in a literal sense. By adopting the well-known proverb, "the enemy of my enemy is my friend," he became an important ally of PLOW, if not technically a member. When emails were addressed to "PLOW members" and Bartley was among the recipients, it could be assumed that he was considered to be a member. Bartley was the only media person consistently listed as such.

On April 21, PLOW member Ronald Bowes emailed fellow members Austin Shanfelter, Jerry Swope, and Thane Turner informing them that, "Todd Bartley of Williamsport's ESPN Radio wants to be included in the PLOW loop. He is working to get the Taylor agenda exposed. His email is tbarkley@xxxx.com." [15]

As proof that PLOW had sunk its roots into the Lock Haven Foundation as well as the Council of Trustees, Taylor's legal team unearthed an email from Foundation member Don Houser who conveyed encouragement to Bartley: "Keep them coming (sic), its working." Bartley, in turn, forwarded the email and his letter to the LHU Foundation members to David La Torre, the publicist for PLOW. The subject line was "ESPN Radio Williamsport – Food for Thought." [16]

Sharon Taylor's case against Todd Bartley seemed to be strong, but her legal team needed to present it before a jury. Bartley's motion for a summary judgment would short-circuit that goal. "There is ample evidence for the issue of conspiracy to be submitted to a jury. Conspiracies are by their very nature carried out covertly so allegations of conspiracy are based on circumstantial evidence and logical deductions."

"In the case before this Court, the Defendants crossed the line. The jury is entitled to make the determination of whether the defendants, including Bartley, knowingly used the pretext of legitimate business transactions to lead the public to a conclusion about Taylor based on false and misleading information to further their own agendas." [17]

## Defendant ESPN

At the time of the court filing, ESPN Radio Williamsport was owned by Daniel Klingerman, Larry Allison, Jr. and the Colonial Radio Group headquartered in Olean, New York. ESPN had no ownership interest in the station, but permitted the use of the ESPN brand due to an affiliate agreement. Consequently, ESPN was removed as a defendant in the case.

Colonial sold its shares to Klingerman and Allison in 2010, just months after the lawsuit was filed. The new ownership group became known as Colonial Radio Group Williamsport. The Olean based group changed its name to Colonial Media and Entertainment and currently operates four simulcast radio stations in southwestern New York State.

## USA Today Article

While the PLOW attacks slowed down during the discovery phase of Taylor's lawsuit, a national publication became aware of the Lock Haven imbroglio and elected to run a feature article on it. On July 22, 2010, USA Today aired Lock Haven's dirty laundry for the whole country to see. The article was written by Erik Brady and actually gave both sides a decent chance to state their case. The headline, in fact, caught the essence of the conflict: *School locked in gender war. Men allege bias, women assert fairness, both file lawsuits.*

Brady reported that Taylor's "critics say she favors women over men and that's why women's teams fare better than men's at the Division II school." The article stated further that women's teams had won 70% of their contests since 2007. The men's teams had won 37%.

Pat Guerriero, he of the multiple lawsuits against LHU, held nothing back in his quote. "Oh, it's worse than that. Sharon hates men."

John Wilson, whose court case had not yet been decided, accused Taylor of wishing for failure on the part of his basketball team.

Neil Turner, former wrestling coach, talked cautiously about Taylor because he was a plaintiff in Taylor's lawsuit. Still, somebody had spoken anonymously on PLOW's behalf, and that person could have been Turner.

Brady did his best to provide a balanced report. He had quotes from Pat Rudy, the long-time head coach of the field hockey team as well as Donna Lopiano, a nationally known expert witness in gender equity cases. Rudy and Lopiano held similar views: when women seem to have equity in athletics, that equality is somehow viewed as unfair in the eyes of the male-dominated establishment.

Former president Craig Dean Willis stated simply that he saw no bias during his tenure.

One fact that Brady could have presented in support of Taylor was this: Lock Haven won the Dixon Award three times for the best overall season in athletics among the 14 state universities in Pennsylvania. This award required excellence in both men's and women's sports.

The online version of the story followed the basic outline of the print story, but the headline implied something more: *Lock Haven AD Taylor lightning rod for controversy, litigation.* This unfortunate headline cast a shadow over Taylor to anyone reading this on the Internet. While she played a part in some of the events leading up to certain litigation, she had little or no role in other cases.

Keith Miller had moved on to Virginia State University shortly before the USA Today article hit the newsstands. This might have been the best timing he displayed in several years. Interim president Barbara Dixon had a perfect alibi: she had just completed her third week on the job and could offer no opinion as to whether the bias toward women was fact or perception.

Thanks to USA Today, Lock Haven had become synonymous with the battle over gender equality.

**Sharon Taylor:** *Actually, I was very satisfied with the USA Today article. I think it uncovered some of the crazy things that these guys had leveled against me and held them up to ridicule. They were furious, especially Guerriero, who had contacted Brady in the first place.*

## The Court's Decision

The defendants in Taylor's lawsuit filed motions for summary judgment for dismissal based on the principle that Sharon Taylor is a public figure. As such, freedom of speech issues come into play. Lawyers for the defendants stated in the motion, "Therefore, the United States Supreme Court has found that to be successful, a public figure must prove that any defamatory statement was made with actual malice." Quoting Curtis Publishing Co. v. Butts 1975, they continued, "Evidence of ill will or a defendant's desire to harm a plaintiff's reputation, although prohibitive of the defendant's state of mind, without more, does not establish actual malice for defamation purposes." [18]

In several similar lawsuits, the defendants demonstrated that a Georgia University athletics director, a Temple University basketball coach, and a high school football coach from Ohio all were deemed public figures by the respective courts. [19]

In other words, even if Taylor could show that PLOW did act to intentionally harm her reputation, more evidence would be needed to prove "actual malice" if the plaintiff is determined by the court to be a public figure. The higher standard of proof requires the plaintiff to show clearly that the defendant knew the defamatory statements to be false, yet proceeded with a careless disregard for the truth.

With regard to the malice issue, Taylor's legal team felt that they had met the standard for proving that PLOW had ample opportunities to learn, and to know, that many of their criticisms of Taylor were false. PLOW was tightly tied into key members of the Council of Trustees who met regularly with the president. Copies of emails bore this out. According to the plaintiff, PLOW continued to publicly issue the alleged defamatory accusations, thus displaying a reckless disregard for the truth.

The matter of whether Sharon Taylor could be categorized as a public figure was more subjective.

On May 3, 2011, Judge Craig P. Miller of the Court of Common Pleas of Clinton County, Pennsylvania rendered this opinion: "Defendant Todd Bartley's motion for summary judgment is granted and judgment is entered in favor of defendant."

> •    "Defendant Ronald Bowes' motion for summary judgment is granted and judgment is entered in favor of defendant."

> •    "Defendant Jerry Swope's motion for summary judgment is granted and judgment is entered in favor of defendant."

> •    "Defendant Preserve the Legacy of Wrestling (PLOW), Austin Shanfelter and Neil Turner's motion for summary judgment is granted and judgment is entered in favor of defendants."

> •    "All remaining counts and therefore all actions against all defendants are dismissed."

> •    "The jury selection and subsequent trial are cancelled." [20]

In addition to ruling on the charges, Judge Miller admonished both parties: "This action has consumed a great deal of time for this Court, and this Court would assume that the litigants have expended significant time, money and energy in bringing this action and in defending this action. This Court believes that better use of this time, money and energy can be made by these litigants who are all successful intelligent individuals. All appear to have a love for Lock Haven University and its athletic teams. This Court would suggest that the parties move forward in an appropriate forum to resolve their differences in a civilized manner that will not result in further litigation, but in the betterment of Lock Haven University and its athletic teams." [21]

# Chapter Five - The Day of Reckoning

Taylor's lawsuit against PLOW members and Todd Bartley seemed to douse the flames of the vigilante action aimed at her removal. The pre-trial depositions had a sobering effect on the defendants. Their claims now had to be substantiated under oath in the presence of lawyers and stenographers. The more reckless accusations now promised possible consequences in a court of law. Even though the court eventually dismissed the case, all of the defendants appeared to put down their torches and pitchforks and walk away.

With interim president Barbara Dixon in place, and PLOW subdued, Taylor could perform her duties with many fewer distractions. Yet, the PLOW cause still burned with a low flame in the person of several members of the Council of Trustees. Dr. Michael Fiorentino moved into the president's office July 1, 2011. The calm that had settled over Taylor's life was not destined to last very long.

On February 3, 2012, Sharon Taylor received an email asking her to report to the office of Michael Fiorentino, Lock Haven University's new president. Seven months earlier Fiorentino was chosen to relieve Barbara Dixon of her duties as interim president following Dr. Keith Miler's departure to take the reins at Virginia State University.

When asked the reason for the meeting, Fiorentino's administrative assistant, Gwen, would not reveal the true agenda. As Taylor walked from her office in the Thomas Fieldhouse to Sullivan Hall, she surmised that her earlier suggestions for restructuring the athletics department would be discussed.

As Taylor entered the lobby of the president's office, the presence of the human resource vice president Deana Hill raised no immediate red flags. Perhaps something important needed to be discussed relating to someone on staff.

**Sharon Taylor:** *He had someone in his office so I sat down in the lobby across the room from Deana Hill. After Deana and I exchanged pleasantries, I asked her if she knew what the meeting was about. She picked up her cell phone like she was looking for an answer. She asked me what was in the email, implying that she had no idea why we were* *there. I told her I thought it was about the structuring of the athletics department.*

*That's what really disappointed me. Up to that point, I thought that Deana was an honest broker. All she had to say was "I know, but you need to let the President tell you," or something like that. That would have been fine. At least she wouldn't have lied to me. That changed all my future interactions with her.*

Taylor had no inkling that her job was about to be taken away from her. Had she suspected that she was walking into an ambush, she most likely would not have been totally devastated. After all, the threat of losing her job had hung over her head for the past eight years. During her very first meeting with incoming president Keith Miller in 2004, the subject of her retirement entered the conversation in the form of a subtle anecdote whose meaning could only be interpreted as a suggestion for her to call it quits.

When the PLOW group emerged, supported by key members of the school's Council of Trustees, Taylor could not escape the possibility that the axe would fall one day. PLOW unabashedly set out to destroy her reputation and induce Miller to fire or demote her.

When Todd Bartley began to carry the PLOW banner on his radio show, a call for Taylor to resign blasted over the airwaves constantly. Every perceived negative event that occurred at Lock Haven was laid at her feet.

Keith Miller never enthusiastically supported Sharon Taylor, but he refused to render the decision that would remove her as head of the athletics department. Month after month, year after year, she lived with the reality that her job was in constant jeopardy.

During Barbara Dixon's one-year stint as interim president, Taylor, herself, created a plan that would allow LHU to replace her.

**Sharon Taylor:** *I proposed a settlement to retire while Barbara Dixon was there. She and I sat and worked it out. I offered a suggestion as to how the department should be structured. I had a sabbatical coming up. If LHU would give me the financial equivalent of the scheduled sabbatical, I would retire. I showed them how much money they would* *save. In our proposal Peter Campbell would be named A.D., Danielle Barney the associate A.D., and LHU would refill the event manger position that had been eliminated. My $100,000 salary goes out the door. They could surely hire someone as the event planner for around $30,000. They could have saved a lot of money and not had to deal with me any longer.*

*Dixon was all for it, but the State (PASSHE) rejected it because I wouldn't take my name off the lawsuit that the athletics directors around the system had filed. Looking back, I guess I should thank PASSHE*

*Athletics directors are considered faculty by contract. The average faculty member might be on campus 25-30 hours per week. Athletics administrators on average probably work 60-70 hours per week. I never got into my office before 9am but I never left before 6-6:30. I would always be there on weekends. The suit was filed around 2010 and is still pending today. I did ultimately remove myself from the list of plaintiffs, but I didn't want to abandon my colleagues without good reason.*

Fiorentino did not fire Taylor that day, nor did he offer her an inducement to retire. He "reassigned" her to a teaching position. Taylor's new assignment would be effective June 1, the end of the spring semester.

A brief press release was quickly disseminated: "In order to achieve greater efficiency and to meet the needs of a growing department, Lock Haven University will consolidate the athletics faculty and the Department of Sports Studies. This consolidation entails a shift of responsibilities. Effective at the end of the semester, Sharon Taylor will assume teaching duties while Peter Campbell and Danielle Barney's major responsibilities will continue to reside in directing the LHU athletics programs."

The release was not attributed to any specific administrator.

**Sharon Taylor:** *Here's what happened that morning when he told me about the reassignment. He was very matter of fact, not nervous at all. He announced that he was making a change in the structure of the athletics program, combining the two components, sports studies and athletics. He told me that I was being reassigned to the classroom. He* *told me that I knew more about athletics administration than anyone at LHU and the university really needed me in the newly established graduate program. That was his rationale, which was happy horse manure, of course, because I couldn't teach graduate classes due to the fact that I don't have an earned doctorate degree.*

*I sat and let him talk. I didn't interrupt or make a comment. He said Peter Campbell and Danielle Barney would carry on in athletics. He went through a lot of different aspects of the restructure.*

*Then apropos of absolutely nothing, he said, "I wasn't brought here (LHU) to do this." At that point I had to speak up. I replied, "Don't tell me that. I know exactly what you were told when you were brought here, because Keith Miller was told the same thing." He didn't deny it. He never said another thing about that.*

Linda Koch, Vice President of Student Affairs at that time, reacted to the suggestion that a quid pro quo agreement never actually existed between Fiorentino and the trustees. "He (Fiorentino) and I had a meeting the very day he met with Sharon to tell her she was being reassigned. He told me what he planned to do, reassign her to a teaching role. He then told me that if he had been put in a position before accepting the job (of president) to 'do this,' he would not have accepted the job. I must add that he volunteered this statement. I did not ask or suggest it."

Fiorentino's premise for the change was illogical: no one on campus could match her administrative skills, so he was removing her from an administrative position and placing her in the classroom, where she had not functioned in almost 25 years. Additionally, she did not have the academic credentials necessary to teach graduate courses.

**Sharon Taylor:** *I was due to go on a sabbatical during the fall semester coming up. After returning for the spring semester in 2013, I would take another sabbatical during the summer and fall terms. Fiorentino offered no settlement or compensation for the value of the two sabbaticals.*

*Surely, he couldn't have thought that I would accept the reassignment to the classroom. He must have also known that I was not going to simply walk away. I have no way of knowing what was going through his mind. Maybe he anticipated exactly what did eventually happen.*

Taylor left the president's office upset, but not crying. She felt that she deserved better, considering the successes she had brought to the university. The sabbatical alone carried a value of almost $100,000. She returned to her office and placed a call to her attorney, Kathleen Yurchak.

Yurchak and Taylor decided to bring in another law firm with experience in Title IX retaliation litigation. She consulted with Diane Milutinovich who recommended Baine Kerr of Hutchinson Black and Cook in Boulder, Colorado. Milutinovich experienced similar retaliatory abuse at Fresno State (See Chapter 9). Kerr had the reputation of a "rock star" in the Title IX arena.

On April 23, approximately six weeks after Taylor's reassignment meeting, Kerr sent a certified letter to Dr. Michael Fiorentino and University Legal Counsel Michael S. Ferguson notifying them that his firm, along with Kathleen Yurchak, would be representing Sharon Taylor in negotiations (and litigation, if needed) with Lock Haven University in the matter of her reassignment as director of athletics.

The letter clearly indicated that Taylor's "overarching" goal was reinstatement to her previous position. According to Hutchinson et. al., Taylor possessed a viable claim of Title IX retaliation action and he spelled out the legal precedent of Jackson vs. Birmingham Board of Education in 2005.

Roderick Jackson, a physical education teacher and girl's basketball coach in the Birmingham, Alabama, school system complained that girls' teams did not receive the same resources and facilities as the boys' teams, as required by Title IX. Jackson's complaints led to unsatisfactory evaluations and ultimately removal from his coaching position. [1]

He filed suit in the U.S. District Court and lost. The court held that Title IX does not provide any private relief for retaliation. In other words, he was not discriminated against under the law. The Court of Appeals likewise dismissed the case for the same reason. [2]

In 2004, the United States Supreme Court decided to hear the case. In March of 2005, the Court voted 5-4 in favor of Jackson. Justice Sandra

Day O'Connor delivered the opinion that Title IX does allow suits for retaliation against individuals who report sex discrimination. The "Yes" votes came from Stevens, O'Connor, Ginsberg, Souter and Breyer. The "No" votes belonged to Rehnquist, Scalia, Kennedy and Thomas. [3]

Taylor's legal team was prepared to detail the "factual and legal bases" for their client's claims. As long as Taylor's position remained open, a negotiated solution remained on the table.

The letter concluded with the assumption that Lock Haven University would be interested in receiving a settlement package.

Two weeks later, Taylor's legal team received a response from Michael Ferguson. The University would welcome a proposed package that would include "Ms. Taylor's retirement and a cash payout." In return, Taylor must withdraw all current litigation against LHU and PASSHE, and she must agree to refrain from any future legal action. No provision was mentioned for her reinstatement.

Taylor may have correctly assumed that LHU stood ready to get out the checkbook and pay the cost to bring about her retirement.

Baine Kerr and his associate Jonathan Boonin, working with Kathleen Yurchak, needed only one month to put together the settlement package. The cover letter to LHU legal counsel stated:

"Ms. Taylor is not looking to retire. Her objective remains to convince Lock Haven University ("LHU") to reverse the unwise and retaliatory "reassignment". She wants to retain her job as Athletics Director and continue the successful program she has worked for a quarter century to build, and that she deserves to keep. The alternative of litigation is the last thing Taylor and LHU want. So that you know where we are coming from, however, this letter will spell out the basis for Taylor's Title IX Claims, should it come to that."

What followed were sixteen pages laying out the basis for litigation and 43 more pages of exhibits.

The document highlighted a history of Sharon Taylor's efforts to bring about gender equity in athletics, as well as her steps to convey Title IX issues to both President Keith Miller and President Michael Fiorentino.

The Jackson vs. Birmingham Board of Education case was explained and named as a "roadmap" for Taylor's complaint.

To hammer home the likely consequences of going to court to fight the Taylor complaint, Kerr cited a "laundry list" of a dozen similar cases of Title IX retaliation that did not end well for the universities involved. One such case was Diane Milutinovich vs. California State University at Fresno. The case was settled for $3.5 million.

Ms. Milutinovich, Kerr added, had agreed to consult with Hutchinson Black and Cook in Taylor's case. Other Title IX experts signed on to consult were Donna Lopiano, Linda Carpenter and Nancy Hogshead-Makar.

Although Lopiano may not be a household name, former Tennessee University women's basketball coach Pat Summitt has called her "the most powerful woman in women's athletics." [4]

Linda Carpenter is the co-author (along with R. Vivian Acosta) of the book *Title IX*, the bible of gender equity law.

Nancy Hogshead-Makar, a three-time Olympic gold medalist in swimming, is currently a civil rights attorney. She served for several years as the Women's Sports Foundation's Senior Director of Advocacy.

Kerr wanted LHU to know that if they wanted a legal fight, his firm would bring the equivalent of the 1992 U.S. Olympic "Dream Team."

LHU most likely expected an entirely different sort of negotiation. Instead of a suggested monetary cash payout, they were given a choice of Sharon Taylor's reinstatement or "see you in court."

**The Surveillance Begins**

June 1 arrived with no resolution. Sharon Taylor was no longer the director of athletics. Officially, she would begin her sabbatical on July 1. Peter Campbell took over the position as interim director. Fiorentino put an exclamation point on Taylor's new role by forcing her out of her office. He offered her an office on the seventh floor of the Robinson Learning Center. She emphatically refused to move there.

**Sharon Taylor:** *When pigs fly I would go up there. I did clear out my office so they could do whatever they wanted to do with it. Peter offered me the use of an extra desk in his office. It was normally used as a student worker's desk. All I needed was a telephone and some space for my computer. I didn't need any storage because I wasn't doing anything in athletics.*

*The president then called Peter into a meeting with Deana Hill present. Fiorentino told Peter that he was not allowed to have me in his office. My presence gave people the impression that I was still running the department. That's when Peter just lost it and asked to be reassigned.*

Peter Campbell, born in Northern Ireland, played professional soccer in the Irish League and later the Canadian National Soccer League. He had earned a scholarship to Gannon University in Erie, Pennsylvania, graduating in 1992. After attending Cleveland Marshall College of Law he passed the bar and began to practice law in Cleveland. He coached soccer part-time at Baldwin-Wallace College. The coaching experience convinced him that a law career was not for him.

Taylor offered him the position of head coach of the women's soccer team in 1999. He led the Lady Eagles to their first-ever PSAC title and an NCAA Division II tournament berth his first season. His team repeated as champions the following year. He was named PSAC and Northeast Region Coach of the Year both seasons. He became the Associate Director of Athletics in 2002.

Taylor's former office had to remain unused and locked. According to colleagues, Fiorentino walked from Sullivan to the Thomas Fieldhouse three times to see if she was occupying any athletics department office space. Someone was obviously alerting him to any Taylor sightings in the Fieldhouse.

One day, Campbell and his staff worked on a project requiring research into files stored in Taylor's old office. Time after time, they had to unlock the door, access the file, and then relock the door. Eventually, they decided to keep the door cracked a fraction of an inch, but technically still locked. Within minutes Fiorentino began lurking just down the hallway, apparently trying to catch Taylor in the act of trespassing. His spy had observed the breach of security and both had jumped to the conclusion that Taylor was using the office.

When Campbell met with Fiorentino and Deana Hill in October, he was overwhelmed by the absurdity of the situation. He asked the president, "Why are you so scared of Sharon Taylor? If you don't trust me we should make a decision right now."

They did make a decision. Campbell was reassigned out of athletics administration. Former wrestling coach Carl Poff became the interim athletics director and Peter Campbell assumed the new role of professor of Sports Studies.

**Sharon Taylor:** *The man who runs the maintenance department had a small empty office in the Facilities Building on the south edge of the campus. He graciously allowed me to use it for several months. Someone in the spy network saw me going or coming and told him (Fiorentino). The next morning he sent someone into maintenance and took my computer away. That's how I got kicked out of there. Those folks in maintenance became some of my best friends!*

*When the fall semester started, wherever I went on campus, President Fiorentino seemed to appear within minutes. Unlike his predecessor, he did not have an "open door" policy. Faculty members had a particularly hard time securing an audience with him. People on campus joked that if you wanted to see the president, invite Sharon Taylor to your office.*

Attorney Blaine Kerr, in his November 5 settlement statement to the mediator, Judge Donald E. Zeigler, added this paragraph:

"There is one other matter we need to bring to your attention. We believe a serious Impediment to resolving this dispute is the attitude and conduct of Lock Haven's President Michael Fiorentino. As we will explain to you in mediation, Mr. Fiorentino has recently continued the retaliatory and harassing conduct towards Ms. Taylor by forcing her out of her office and by attempting to limit her communications with her colleagues who have been requesting her assistance. His conduct and attitude towards her are vindictive, bizarre and appear to border on real paranoia. If this matter is going to be resolved, it is essential that he get an attitude readjustment and be made to act reasonably."

On November 13, 2012, the settlement between Sharon Taylor and Lock Haven University garnered the approval of all parties. The most salient result was that Lock Haven would have a new athletics director. Taylor would retire. The remaining details were to remain confidential.

All of the legal paperwork was signed in early December. On January 1, 2013, Sharon Taylor became a former employee of LHU. The sabbatical dissolved into "full released time to assist with the transition."

In deference to her long experience managing the athletics department, Taylor would be available to guide the interim athletics staff until a permanent leader came on board. The settlement carried no restrictions or limits to her presence on campus. Even so, Dr. Fiorentino still persisted in his harassment.

**Sharon Taylor:** *On February 8, I stopped into Pat Rudy's office at the Fieldhouse to give her a check for $10,000. It was a personal donation from me to the women's field hockey team. As I neared the doorway to my former office, I heard someone speak my name and I turned around to find the president. He said, "Sharon, you shouldn't be on campus." I explained to him why I was there. I told him that I wouldn't be doing that again (donating).*

*Before leaving, I said, "Michael, if you don't want me on campus, you'd better tell security to keep me off. Otherwise, I will be here as an alum. I will be here as a retired faculty member. And I will be here as a donor."*

*He replied, "No, Sharon, I wouldn't do that."*

### Reaction

Two written examples serve to display the spectrum of response to the news that Sharon Taylor had been reassigned.

The first is an undated letter sent shotgun-style to "Dear Alumni and Friends" by Head Football Coach John Allen Jr. The letter began with an update on recruiting efforts then announced "a couple of things that are newsworthy."

The first bit of news involved scheduling information: a new opponent and a Thursday night game. Then the big news: "Secondly, and most important for many, Sharon Taylor – Athletics Director, has been reassigned to teaching... Many of you stated that you would not give (donate) until this day came. The day is here, and you control the dawn of a New Era in LHU Football."

Coach Allen's glee over the demotion of his former boss is palpable. Now the faithful alumni can begin to financially support the beleaguered football program. All of the recent problems would go away now that Taylor was gone.

Seven months after the "new dawn," with Sharon Taylor no longer at the helm, Lock Haven lost to Shippensburg University and established an all-time Division II record of 47 straight losses. The losing skein would continue to 52 games before the Bald Eagles stunned Cheyney University to end their long and painful losing streak.

One question that hangs in the air involves the alumni donations that were withheld to protest Sharon Taylor's continued tenure at LHU. Could the horrible slide into the football record books have been halted by more scholarships funded by alumni money? The losing record doubtless discouraged athletes from attending Lock Haven. A few more skilled players each year could have made a difference. Coach Allen should have been upset with the alums for leaving him and his players out in the cold.

The second example of reaction to Taylor's reassignment was an open letter to Lock Haven University published by the online version of the (Lock Haven) Express on April 24, 2012. The headline was "Reinstate Sharon Taylor" submitted by Julie Shumaker:

*I was in a state of shock after reading the Feb 4, 2012 article in the Lock Haven Express that Sharon Taylor has been "reassigned."*

*This is a slap in the face of a woman who has dedicated her entire life to the athletics department of Lock Haven State College and Lock Haven University. In fact, this is a slap in the face to all women in the home, work place and athletics.*

*During my four years at Lock Haven, I witnessed Sharon attending all sporting events even before she was promoted to the athletics director position. She always encouraged all students and athletes to attend events and show support for the college. I was witness to her attention to detail as she could address by name almost every student/athlete.*

*After graduation, Sharon became a mentor/model for me as I navigated the world of teaching/coaching at the high school and college levels, and other employment. Her guidance has been invaluable to me and to many who have had the chance to know her. She is a well-respected representative of the university on the local, national, and international levels with her involvement in AIAW, NCAA, USFHA, USOC Board of Directors and other initiatives.*

*Elizabeth Stanton Cady, Billie Jean King, Babe Zaharias, Betty Friedan, Cathy Rush, Carol Eckman, Martina Navratilova, Pat Summitt, and Sharon Taylor are a few of the pioneers of women's rights that have given their lives for the betterment of all. Demoting Sharon is a step backwards for the equality of all. With all due respect, let's end the "old boy network era" of treating women as less than equal.*

*I am recommending that you reinstate Sharon Taylor to her position of AD and let her retire on her own terms and recognize her for a job well done. My continued advocacy of the university depends on this.*

Gayatri Devi has served as a professor of World Literature and Women's Studies at Lock Haven since 2005. She states her relationship to Sharon Taylor as a colleague. As the campus coordinator of Women's and Gender Studies, she has witnessed first hand Taylor's commitment to all facets of women's issues, not just in athletics.

Devi offers an example of Taylor's commitment to all women at LHU. "We have an annual event on campus called Take Back the Night. Sharon's speech in 2012 about the urgency to protect the bodies and minds of young women from sexual and other kinds of assaults was so enlightening and inspiring to all of us in the audience. She cares very deeply about social justice for women."

"Take Back the Night" started as a demonstration in Philadelphia in 1975 to protest the murder of a young professional woman. Susan Alexander Speeth was stabbed to death a block from her home. Since then, the movement has gone international, and is now marked by events at thousands of universities, women's centers, and rape crisis centers all over the world. [5]

Devi says of Taylor, "She embodies the best aspects of the Title IX mandate. She made sure there was equality for women and men in athletics. Her coaching, her teaching, and her professional decisions have been to wholeheartedly put into practice the federal mandate."

Devi's reaction to the reassignment: "Frankly, I was absolutely shocked. No one who followed the growth of LHU athletics under Sharon could see this as anything but a demotion. To many of us, it was surprising and shocking. I never thought it would be done, and done so privately. I felt that within the justice of the "system" that it would not actually be done in that way. I could understand the community's behavior toward her, but I thought the University would be different. Perhaps that was naïve of me."

Devi continues, "I believe she has paid a price for her advocacy. It used to be very painful to read the criticism of her in the local newspapers. Such a humble and honest person should not have been publicly pilloried. The comments of some of her disgruntled male colleagues were physically and emotionally painful to me. Almost all of it (the criticism) was defamatory and false."

To Devi, the PLOW assaults were ideological in nature. The critics could simply not understand, or they refused to try to understand, Taylor's efforts to provide the best experiences possible for both men and women students at LHU.

LHU's head field hockey coach, Pat Rudy, was traveling to Lebanon (PA) to visit her mother on February 3, 2012, when her cell phone rang. The caller was Sharon Taylor. She advised Rudy that she might want to pull over. Rudy tells the story. "While I sat in my car outside of a restaurant, Taylor told me what had just happened. I was in shock, really upset. I told her it was ridiculous and she had to fight it. I was adamant with her. I could tell Sharon was very upset. After the call, I just sat there in that restaurant parking lot. Everyone was shocked. She was a tenured faculty member who had been there for a long time. She was a very respected administrator and very successful in her job."

"The trouble started back when Keith Miller became president and PLOW started up. PLOW was very destructive and derogatory toward Sharon. They launched a very personal attack on Sharon. They needed someone to blame (for the failure of the wrestling program). She was an easy target. Instead of looking where the money (funding) came from and how it was allocated, they just blamed her and the women's programs. They didn't agree with gender equity and Title IX. She was very threatening to them. Even today, anyone speaking about Title IX is perceived as a threat to them."

After witnessing years of vicious personal attacks against Taylor, the reassignment still shocked Rudy. She explains, "After Keith Miller couldn't fire her, and (interim president) Barbara Dixon wouldn't fire her, I thought she was safe."

Former LHU president Craig Dean Willis was in the minority. He was not particularly surprised about the reassignment. Said Willis, "I knew from what Sharon told me that Keith Miller kept asking her when she was going to retire. He openly told her he needed to get rid of her. I guess I had developed a persona that I think the trustees were really afraid to talk to me about it." The forces that were trying to depose Taylor for the better part of a decade finally found a willing ally in the new president.

Taylor's friends and associates from around the country may not have been totally aware of her recent struggles at Lock Haven. Most of them could not fathom the decision to demote someone who had brought so much goodwill and positive attention to the university.

Most local Lock Haven people, however, knew about the contentious relationship between Taylor and the factions determined to oust her. But even they were shocked, or at least surprised, by the timing of the reassignment. There had been no obvious flare-ups or warning signs. But things were happening under the surface. Some of the precipitating events took place more than two years before President Fiorentino's decision to make a change.

The next chapter will deal with those incidents that ultimately dictated the timing of Sharon Taylor's dismissal from her position as director of athletics.

# Chapter Six - The Brock Parker Saga

One of the mysteries surrounding the reassignment of Sharon Taylor on February 3, 2012, has been the timing. The fact that Taylor did not have the credentials to move from her position in athletics to the Graduate faculty, suggests that President Fiorentino acted hastily, not allowing the university enough lead-time to fully understand the academic realities of her reassignment. The lack of an earned doctorate left her unqualified for the graduate-level position that the president indicated had inspired his decision.

Why would Fiorentino make such a move shortly after the start of the spring semester? While it is true that he had pressure from some of the trustees and many of the alumni that made up the group known as PLOW, or Preserve the Legacy of Wrestling, he knew that Taylor had two sabbatical leaves planned in the next year. Considering her age, and the difficult times she had withstood over the past seven years, Taylor may have been amenable to a retirement arrangement. Lock Haven could have recognized her many achievements and accolades. They could have approved her for emerita status. This could have clearly been a "win-win" situation, Taylor leaving to much fanfare, and Fiorentino fulfilling his pledge to the anti-Taylor contingency. Instead, he shocked the LHU community, as well as Taylor's many friends and colleagues around the nation.

To unravel this mystery, we must go back to 2009 and examine an act of violence that took place in Thomas Fieldhouse. That event ultimately led to an email that Sharon Taylor sent to Fiorentino and HR Director Deana Hill more than two years later. Eleven days after that, Taylor lost her job as athletics director.

### The Alleged Assault

As the 2009 wrestling season began, LHU had a new head coach. Robbie Waller, a former national champ from Oklahoma University, took over following Rocky Bonomo's departure. At age 30, he now coached a Division I wrestling team.

Bonomo, the year before, had recruited a promising athlete from Canton High School in northern Pennsylvania, not far from the New York border. Brock Parker completed his high school career with just one loss out of 25 matches. Coach Bonomo red-shirted Parker during his freshman year so he could work on improving his grades and his wrestling skills. He practiced with the team but did not compete in any of Lock Haven's dual meets.

As the 2009 season got underway, Brock Parker was eager to begin his collegiate wrestling career. Parker and Robbie Waller discussed a strategy of moving Parker down to the 141-pound class to compete in the Binghamton Open in early November. The wrestler would have to lose 14 pounds. With several weeks of lead-time, both agreed it was doable. Parker worked out, dieted and monitored his weight daily.

Coach Waller called Parker on a Sunday evening to inquire about his progress. The wrestler reported that his weight was down to 149.5 pounds: right on target with two weeks to go.

The next day Parker entered the wrestling room and jumped on the scale for his official Monday weigh-in. The scale reported 151, up from the previous evening but still in a good range.

Parker began warming up with a small group of his teammates when the coach entered the mat room. The wrestler describes what happened next: "Waller came in the room and said, 'Come here.' He didn't seem mad. He said it in a normal voice. So I jogged over to him not thinking anything was up. My weight was fine and I had been performing and wrestling hard. I had prepared for the tournament the right way. "

"As soon as I got close to him, he grabbed the back of my neck and grabbed my left arm and just smashed my head off the wall. Then he said, 'Get the fuck out,' and threw me."

"I was like, 'Whoa!' I didn't say anything else, just 'Whoa,' in shock. Then he grabbed me again and said, 'Get the fuck out.' He threw me again."

The walls in the mat room were padded, but Parker bounced off a steel partition separating the two sides of a double door, one side of which appeared to be permanently closed.

Waller was not finished. "And then he threw me out into the hallway and kept pushing me until I left. He just kept swearing at me and telling me to leave. It was lose-lose for me either way so I just left as fast as I could."

Parker emphasizes the fact that he was never confrontational with his coach. A combination of fear, intimidation and respect for authority trumped a wrestler's instinct to fight back.

Badly stunned, he retreated to the locker room. He stood in front of a mirror watching his nose spurt blackish blood while he tried to staunch the flow. He feared the nose might be broken. He noticed also that his lip was split and bleeding. Finally, not wanting further contact with Waller, or his teammates for that matter, he plugged the nose, got dressed, and left the building as unobtrusively as possible.

Parker returned to his room and tried to process what had just occurred. He couldn't fathom any justification for the coach's eruption, or the violent nature of the act itself. Around 7:30 that evening, the team captain, Dan Craig, phoned to relay a message from the coach. Waller had been trying unsuccessfully to call Parker and now he was really pissed. If Parker did not take his phone call, he would be kicked off the team. Craig had not been in the mat room when the outburst occurred and could not fully appreciate the terroristic intent of Waller's threat.

Wrestler and coach spoke that evening. Waller did not apologize, blaming Parker for lying to him about the weight loss. Parker tried to explain that the Monday workout would drop his weight another two or three pounds. He told his coach he would return to the team the next day, but he would not continue to pursue the weight loss necessary to compete at 141 pounds. He would wrestle at 149 instead. "I knew I just couldn't cut weight with him (Waller). If he got that aggravated two weeks out, I didn't want to deal with that all year round."

Brock Parker did not seek medical treatment for his injuries. More regrettably, he never told anyone about the incident, not even his parents. The incident went viral throughout the wrestling team and local wrestling supporters. No one informed Athletics Director Sharon Taylor, or any other university administrator.

To the best of Brock's recollection, there were just a handful of people who witnessed the confrontation. Two of them had just begun to work out with Brock: Harry Turner, Brock's roommate, and Brad Marquart, who left the team a short time later. Parker believes the departure had to do with Robbie Waller.

## The Witness

Parker described one other witness as "an older man." That man was Tom Justice, the women's volleyball coach at the time. Justice had served as a very valuable assistant wrestling coach from 1985 through 1990 under head coach Neil Turner. Why was Justice in the wrestling room? He explains, "We had a new wrestling coach. When Robbie came, he came in all alone. He had no assistant coach. I offered to volunteer, just help out, so the kids would have some additional help. It's hard to coach 35-40 kids as one person. You just can't do it in wrestling. Robbie was glad to have me."

Justice stood close enough to Parker and Waller to hear the brief discussion about the wrestler's weigh-in results. Justice recalls clearly what happened next, "What I saw, after the exchange about the weight, Robbie went ballistic. He reached out and grabbed Brock and he bounced him up against the wall. He shoved him out the wrestling room doors. He went out the doors after him. At that point, both of them were out in Thomas Fieldhouse."

Justice emphasizes that he did not see Parker's face after he had been forced into the hallway. He did not witness the bloody nose or split lip. Justice laughed at the suggestion that Parker may have talked back to his coach. "I'm sorry. Excuse me for laughing. If you look at the human dynamics, when someone like Robbie Waller is bigger than you, and much stronger, and much more aggressive than you, people don't talk back."

When Waller returned to the wrestling room, the practice continued with no discussion about the Parker incident.

Without being asked, Justice explained why he did not report the incident. He felt that it was a one-time outburst on Waller's part. He did not personally witness any further aggressive acts toward the athletes. Additionally, he recalled other incidents of uncontrolled anger by former head wrestling coach Neil Turner, implying that in the course of managing a wrestling team, these things happen.

Justice did not report the incident to anyone. Nor did any wrestlers come forward. The victim, Brock Parker, elected to remain silent but he made two very important decisions. He would continue wrestling until the PSAC tournament, and then he would transfer out of Lock Haven University.

## The Admission

Professor Bridget Roun taught courses in Sports Administration. One of her favorite students was Brock Parker. His demeanor and personality took a quick turn for the worse midway into the fall semester of 2009. "He just changed," said Roun. "He wasn't doing the work and he wasn't attending class." She was also concerned about the red marks on his face. She worried that the reason for one problem might also explain the other. She had heard a rumor circulating around campus that a coach had physically abused a student.

One day before class, professor and student met in the hallway. Parker remembers the conversation quite vividly. "She said, 'I have to ask you a question.' I was like, sure, yeah. She caught me off-guard. I could tell something was wrong. She asked me, 'Did this happen to you?' I just said, 'Yeah.' She started crying. She apologized to me for it."

Roun was very uncomfortable when Parker asked her not to do anything with the information. She was unaware that Parker had not told anyone else on or off campus about the Waller incident. Someone must have reported it by then. Parker's words still haunt her. He said that Waller "jacked him up against the wall."

She begged him to go talk to Director of Athletics Sharon Taylor and report the incident. Taylor definitely needed to know about the alleged assault. Parker made it clear to Roun that he didn't want to be identified as the student who had been manhandled and beat up by his coach. He was embarrassed. He didn't want to be viewed as a complainer. He had already made the decision to leave Lock Haven, so why bother?

## The Transfer

On November 11, 2009, Parker did make an appointment to speak with Athletics Director Sharon Taylor. He sat down in her office and announced that he wanted information on how to transfer. He steadfastly refused to state his reason. He told her he loved being at Lock Haven. Based on that comment, Taylor suspected he might be having problems at home, so she didn't probe further.

On December 3, he visited Taylor again to inform her that he intended to leave at the end of the semester and enroll at East Stroudsburg University. He wanted to make sure that he did nothing to get either school in trouble. He learned that East Stroudsburg competed at the Division II level. Taylor assured Parker that Lock Haven would release him from his scholarship and sign off on the transfer so that he could be immediately eligible to compete at East Stroudsburg

In January of 2010, Brock Parker officially became a former student of Lock Haven University. He remained on campus during the semester break.

Had Parker filed charges against Robbie Waller outside of the university's campus security system, the police would have investigated. According to a Pennsylvania law enforcement officer, police most likely would have charged the coach with simple assault and possibly disorderly conduct, if satisfied that the complaint had merit. Simple assault carries a punishment of up to seven years in prison. What if Waller could credibly claim that he pushed the student in anger and the injury was accidental? "Simple assault would still be the charge," the officer replied.

But no charges were filed. Waller went about his mission to return Lock Haven's wrestling team into a national power. Parker moved on to East Stroudsburg, 130 miles east on Interstate 80. On the surface, it looked like a case of "no harm, no foul," but serious harm had occurred to Brock Parker. It was the kind of damage that couldn't immediately be observed or measured.

The negotiations between colleges went smoothly. Brock Parker received a scholarship from East Stroudsburg. The transfer from a Division I program to Division II enabled him to step right into the 2010 wrestling schedule. "I'll be honest. I wasn't really holding up my end of the deal there," Parker admits. "Part of me didn't want to wrestle anymore. I had lost the love for something. Wrestling was all I ever wanted to do, every day of my whole life. I never missed practice. I never missed school because I didn't want to miss practice."

Parker could not stop obsessing on what he had lost. A wrestler he had defeated while competing for LHU had been named an All-American. That could have been him. He felt sorry for himself. He still hadn't told anybody (other than Bridget Roun) about what happened.

Finally, Brock Parker had to pull into the breakdown lane. He knew he was lost, "stuck in limbo." He left East Stroudsburg after one semester. He gave up his scholarship. He gave up his dream of becoming a nationally recognized wrestler.

Joey Rivera, the wrestling coach at East Stroudsburg University, felt he had scored a windfall. A top-ranked wrestler dropped into his lap. But the Brock Parker that joined his team was not what he expected. Rivera and Parker never had a sit-down meeting to discuss the discrepancy between expectation and actual results. Consequently, Rivera was unable to discover the details of Parker's decision to leave Lock Haven. He felt it was just a falling out between the wrestler and coaching staff.

Rivera said regretfully, "The only thing I can do is try to help them with every facet of their life. I can only do that if they are forthright with me and let me know what's going on. He had some medical issues that he was going through that we were trying to figure out. Rivera concluded, "He never got back to where he once was with the love of the sport."

At the end of Parker's first semester at ESU, Rivera received a copy of Parker's failing grades. He reached out to Parker, but he had already left the campus -- gone for good.

Rivera would not learn the details of Brock Parker's alleged assault for another two years.

Parker moved back home to Troy, PA. His mother, Lori Baker, still did not know what had happened at Lock Haven. She knew something had changed her son, but she had no clue what it might have been. She says, "He was looking for me to give him answers, but he wouldn't tell me the problem." She would not hear all of the details of the incident until 2013.

She still refers to Robbie Waller as "that terrible person." She does not want to say his name aloud. During the transition period between universities, Waller called her several times and engaged her in very heated discussions. Waller wanted to prevent one of his best wrestlers from leaving his program. Baker, a school nurse at nearby Athens School District, didn't know why her son needed to get away from Lock Haven, but she likewise looked forward to having no further contact with Waller.

Wrestling was the constant in Parker's life that kept him moving in the right direction. Now he was just adrift. He went to work as a guard at the Bradford County Correctional Facility. After working at the jail for a year, he resumed his educational studies at Mansfield University. Mansfield does not have a wrestling program, nor do they have a major in Sports Administration. Parker had lost almost an entire year's worth of credits because of this. He wonders why schools in the same state system do not accept credits from their sister schools. He has begun to formulate some plans for the future. He would like to return to Lock Haven University at some point.

## The Terry Fike Affair

As the year 2010 expired and the calendar flipped to 2011, life went on at LHU. Waller was still the head wrestling coach. His team went 6-20 in dual meets in his first two years at the helm. Brock Parker was in everyone's rear-view mirror.

A gradual change began to manifest itself by the fall semester of 2011. More and more women were now appearing in the wrestling room; not to compete against the men, but to build the women's wrestling club into a legitimate varsity team. Former Lock Haven wrestler and men's wrestling strength and conditioning coach Terry Fike had the assignment to recruit female wrestling candidates and to find schools with which he could schedule competitions. There were probably less than two dozen colleges with a full-blown women's program. Very few of them were near Lock Haven.

On November 9th, a misunderstanding would lead to a confrontation that would bring Brock Parker's name back to the forefront at Lock Haven University. Fike's team had the wrestling room scheduled from 6:30 to 8:30 pm. Fike had a woman on the team that weighed over 160 pounds. Wrestling her lighter teammates would not contribute much to her ability to compete against women in her weight class. Consequently, Fike was working with her that evening and was not wearing his glasses.

A small group of male wrestlers entered the mat room and began to work out on weights. Fike did not recognize graduate assistant Brad Pataki with the group. Had he seen Brad, he might have let things slide. But he didn't want unsupervised men in the room. He asked them to step outside for the remaining 30 minutes of his practice. They all quietly and quickly exited the room.

A short time later, head coach Robbie Waller burst into the room. Hearing what had happened, the coach raced from his home back to the fieldhouse. Fike describes what happened next: "He made no introductory remarks when he walked through the door. He started shouting. He was profane, dropping f-bombs, to use the expression. Extremely unreasonable. I could tell he was sort of out of control so I saw there was no use trying to deal with him or discuss it any further. I just said you're interrupting my practice can you step out until we're done."

Waller then stepped over the line, according to Fike. Still shouting, he informed Fike that he wasn't a real coach. He was just a "nanny." The implication was that the women weren't real wrestlers, they weren't a real team, and Fike was not a real coach. Waller turned and left the room.

On the way out of the fieldhouse after practice, Fike stopped at the equipment room to talk to a male wrestler who sometimes helped with the women's team. The student had heard the ruckus from one floor above the wrestling room. Fike made a facetious comment and both of them laughed. The wrestler then retorted, "That was nothing. Did you hear what he did to Brock Parker?"

Fike had not heard the story. He was now getting it from one of the athletes who had been in the room when Waller physically put hands on Parker. Much like Brock Parker's version, he related how Waller pushed the athlete into the metal partition between the doors and bloodied his nose.

The younger man informed Fike that he wanted to remain anonymous. He said he was a physical education major who wanted to become a coach. He would need a good reference and the blessings of the Lock Haven athletics department. Apparently a number of other wrestlers viewed the situation in the same manner.

The following day, Fike went to A.D. Sharon Taylor's office and reported the Waller incident from the night before, as well as the alleged assault on an unnamed wrestler. True to his word, he did not reveal the name of the individual describing the physical attack, or the name of the victim.

That afternoon, Taylor called Fike, Waller, and Pataki into her office. An athletics department staff member attended as a witness to the proceedings. After gathering facts on the recent confrontation between Fike and Waller, Taylor addressed the rumored physical abuse incident. The allegations were presented to Waller. She had no details with which to pin him down to a specific incident. Taylor asked him about any excessive physical hands-on incidents. He denied any such episodes, and he did it in front of Terry Fike.

On November 12, 2011, Taylor reported the incident to Deana Hill, Director of Human Resources.

On November 22, Taylor reported the incident verbally to Michael Fiorentino during her regular meeting with the president.

On January 19, 2012, she sent President Fiorentino an email outlining three different issues with Coach Waller.

The next morning, Sharon Taylor experienced an epiphany, a head slapping, light-bulb moment. The student athlete who had been slammed into the wall, or door, or both, may have been Brock Parker. She called Terry Fike on the phone and demanded to know if it was Brock Parker who had been slammed against the wall. Fike admitted that it was Parker. Taylor then dialed Parker's cell phone number and left a message, asking him to call her.

Later that afternoon, Parker returned the phone call. Taylor asked him if he had been involved in a physical confrontation with his coach. He admitted that he had.

Taylor then asked, "Did this have anything to do with you leaving Lock Haven University?"

Brock said, "It had everything to do with me leaving."

On January 22, 2012, Sharon Taylor put everything she had into a memo to Deana Hill with a c.c. to President Fiorentino. She hand-signed the documents.

Twelve days later, Michael Fiorentino called Sharon Taylor into his office with Deana Hall present, and "reassigned" her to teaching in the Sports Studies Department. She was no longer the athletics director and held no official authority to shepherd the Parker investigation to a conclusion.

## The Stalking

Following Sharon Taylor's removal from the athletics director position, President Fiorentino began a mission to prevent her from physically appearing in the athletics department, almost to the point that he seemed to be stalking her. Taylor and others soon noticed that wherever she went on campus, Fiorentino seemed to appear within minutes.

Apart from the Brock Parker incident, his actions seem to be inexplicable. Why would the president of a university care if a long-time, well-regarded athletics director hung around her old office and that of her interim successor, Peter Campbell? If for no other reason than a smooth transition, Taylor should have been invited to assist Campbell in any way she could.

As reported in the previous chapter, Taylor's attorney Baine Kerr wrote to the mediator in her case against Lock Haven University: "Mr. Fiorentino has recently continued the retaliatory and harassing conduct towards Ms. Taylor by forcing her out of her office and by attempting to limit her communications with her colleagues who have been requesting her assistance. His conduct and attitude towards her are vindictive, bizarre and appear to border on real paranoia."

Were his actions bizarre and vindictive? Possibly, yes. Did they border on paranoia? Perhaps not. Had Taylor understood the nature of the investigation that was taking place, she would have acted to see that the truth was discovered. His fear was quite rational. The trustees and alumni that made up the PLOW group would not be happy if the head wrestling coach had to leave because of an assault on a student. They would not be happy if Sharon Taylor found a way to "hurt" Lock Haven wrestling even though she had been officially removed from the athletics department.

## The Investigation That Wasn't

Associate Athletics Director Peter Campbell was named interim athletics director. Taylor cleaned out her office in May of 2012 and passed along all of her files on the Brock Parker incident. Shortly after taking the reins, Campbell asked Deana Hill about an investigation. "I was told that there was nothing to it," said Campbell. "I accepted it. I trusted the people that looked into it."

Campbell brought it up again later that summer and was told that nobody saw anything. By the fall of 2012, he learned that the two witnesses whose names were provided, Tom Justice and Bridget Roun, had never been interviewed. The most amazing thing of all? The alleged victim, Brock Parker was never contacted.

The first time Campbell met with the new president in his office, the main topic of conversation was keeping Sharon Taylor out of Thomas Fieldhouse and away from the athletics department. During the period from June to October of 2012, President Fiorentino went out of his way to show up anywhere on campus that Sharon Taylor was sighted.

On October 14, 2012, Campbell was asked to come to Fiorentino's office. Deana Hill was present. They wanted to discuss Sharon Taylor. Campbell had had enough. "I asked him why he was so scared of Sharon Taylor." Campbell continued, "Coaches assault students; we have issues with Title IX compliance, and you're calling me in here because I am sharing my office with Sharon Taylor while she is on sabbatical?"

Three issues coalesced in Campbell's mind that day. "The first was salary," explained Campbell. "They basically asked me to assume a lot of extra duties and responsibilities without any additional compensation, even though the president originally stated he would give me additional compensation. Then he reneged on that."

The second issue was the way they treated Sharon Taylor. He figured that they could do the same to him.

The third, and ultimately the last straw, was Brock Parker. "It wasn't a proper investigation that was done, obviously. I was told that it was looked into and there was nothing there. But then they didn't talk to any of the witnesses and they didn't talk to the victim himself. They never even went to Paul Altieri (Director of Law Enforcement and Public Safety). I just felt that something was being hidden."

Campbell asked to be reassigned out of the athletics department. Effective in January of 2013, he would join Bridget Roun as a professor in the Sports Studies Department.

With Sharon Taylor and Peter Campbell gone from the athletics department, the alleged assault of Brock Parker now had a good chance of dying a quiet death. The human resource department, under Deana Hill's direction, had not advanced the investigation of a possible crime against a student. Robbie Waller's denial was apparently sufficient to warrant no further interviews. The decision not to contact campus police most likely came from someone higher in the organization than Deana Hill. Was Michael Fiorentino orchestrating a cover up to protect his wrestling coach, as well as the reputation of his university?

About two weeks after Campbell's meeting with Fiorentino and Hill, the president of Penn State, Graham Spanier, was charged with trying to "hush up" the child sexual abuse allegations against Jerry Sandusky. Pennsylvania's Attorney General, Linda Kelly said, "This was a conspiracy of silence by top officials to actively conceal the truth."

The accusations against Waller certainly pale in comparison to the horrific acts ascribed to Sandusky, but the concept of protecting the image of Lock Haven and the wrestling program specifically, at the expense of the health and safety of the students would be indefensible.

The administration is obligated to investigate the incident, if not for the benefit of a former student, then for parents of current and future students to assure them that their children are being, and will be, protected against such brutish behaviors.

### The Fateful Phone Call

Fast forward to March 18, 2013. The first day of spring break, ironically, finds the campus shut down due to a crippling snowstorm. Professor Peter Campbell does not go into work.

A phone call to his office phone is switched to his voice mail. That call would soon raise the Brock Parker incident back from the grave.

Tuesday, March 19th, Campbell entered his office and checked his phone messages. A woman's voice addressed him as Mr. Campbell, and continued:

*This is a friend of Lock Haven wrestling. We understand that rumor has it you're investigating coach Waller about the abuse of Brock Park (Pause) Brock Parker. But we know, I know, first hand, of other*

116

*physical and verbal abuses that have gone on with other wrestlers. Why do you think so many kids have quit the team in the past three years? Maybe you should look into this. Thank you.*

Peter Campbell had officially left the athletics department two months earlier. The caller, whose voice he did not recognize, obviously thought he was still the interim athletics director. He immediately sought advice. "I called the campus police chief after I got the message. I basically asked him how I should handle this. I asked him if he was aware of the situation. At the time he told me he had never been aware of that situation."

Campbell dispatched an email to the president, to Deana Hill in human resources, and to Paul Altieri at the campus police. He recommended to them that, "We should probably take this seriously and investigate it properly because my concern is it's already out there in the community." He phrased it with a hint of criticism because of the fact that he brought it up three times in the past year and was told three times that there was nothing there. "That's why I copied Paul Altieri on the email."

Campbell sought assistance from someone in the IT department who transferred the voice mail to a computer file format that would enable it to be duplicated, stored, or emailed.

On, or shortly after March 19th, Terry Fike paid a visit to Peter Campbell's office. There he learned that Campbell had reported the phone call to Paul Altieri, who claimed not to be aware of the Parker incident. Fike decided to go to Altieri to report what he knew about it and make sure an investigation would be initiated. Campus police told him that they could not investigate because they did not have a witness. Fike's response: "I said, wait right here, I will produce an eyewitness for you."

Fike immediately thought of Tom Justice. It had become widely known that Justice was in the mat room when the physical abuse took place. "Coach Justice and I were good friends. I was a student assistant when he was assistant wrestling coach. He had been a good influence on me."

Tom Justice received a call from Terry Fike, who sounded very upset about something. Justice recalled the conversation, "When I got the call from Terry, he was clearly troubled. He wanted to talk. I said come right over. We sat down and talked about the whole (Brock Parker) thing."

Fike returned to the campus police with Justice in tow.

## Another Investigation Launched

Tom Justice gave his statement to a campus investigator whose name he cannot recall. Paul Altieri was present at that time. Justice filled out a written report. Finally, it appeared that a proper investigation would be performed.

Brock Parker traveled to Lock Haven and gave his statement in front of campus police and human resources. That interview took place fourteen months after Sharon Taylor reported the Parker/Waller affair to Deana Hill and Michael Fiorentino.

Tom Justice, Terry Fike and Bridget Roun were likewise interviewed.

Linda Koch was not part of the investigation, even though she supervised the campus police. Still, she did her best to stay informed of the progress. Sometime between March 20 and April 2, 2013, Deana Hill spoke to Koch on another matter involving a faculty member and a student who were having an inappropriate relationship. Koch took the opportunity to inquire about the investigation. Hill said that she spoke with the people "who were there" and they didn't see anything.

Within that same time period, Bridget Roun attended a benefit to raise money for the Virginia Martin Scholarship. She saw Deana Hill there and inquired about the Brock Parker investigation. Hill said that the president killed it, or words to that effect.

On April 2, 2013, Rutgers men's basketball coach Mike Rice was shown on ESPN's Between the Lines physically and verbally abusing his players during practice. The next day he was fired.

## Waller "Released"

On May 9, 2013, Robbie Waller sent a broadcast email to virtually everyone on campus. It was subsequently published in the Lock Haven Express newspaper. The email began, "It is with great sadness that I am emailing you to inform you personally that I have been notified today by LHU President Michael Fiorentino that from this point forward I will no longer be serving in the position of wrestling coach at Lock Haven University. He has stated that he has chosen to 'take the wrestling program in a different direction' with no further explanation."

Fiorentino issued no official statement. The university web site had no announcement. They just removed Waller's name from the current season's web screens.

A further anomaly had Waller revealing his own severance package. Perhaps the generous nature of the buyout would make the dismissal seem less like a termination for just cause. An important and surprising part of the severance package was to be a positive recommendation from Fiorentino to assist Waller in securing future coaching opportunities.

On June 30, 2013, VP for Student Affairs Linda Koch retired after 26 years of service to Lock Haven University. One of her responsibilities had been oversight of the campus police force. Initially, the search for her replacement was announced. A short time later, perhaps as soon as July, President Fiorentino decided to abolish the position. Control of campus police would transfer to the president's office. The Vice President for Academic Affairs would pick up all other duties pertaining to student affairs. Koch was unaware of any earlier discussions about the need for this change.

There are fourteen universities in the Pennsylvania State System of Higher Education. According to Koch, exactly none of them place the campus security under the aegis of the president. Approximately half of the schools assign the responsibility to the vice presidents for finance and the other half to the vice presidents for student affairs. Koch knows this because she had served as liaison with all of the campus law enforcement directors.

About the change at Lock Haven, Koch made this observation: "I think you could reach the conclusion very easily that he (Fiorentino) was concerned about what was going on. That is one way to make sure that information is not shared with others on his staff." In other words, Fiorentino would be in total control of the investigation and its results.

Why would Fiorentino be worried about the Brock Parker investigation after he made the decision to remove Robbie Waller as head wrestling coach? Koch speculates, "The president was taken aback when Peter (Campbell) reported that phone call to law enforcement. Understand,

Peter is an attorney. Peter would understand the law and say this could be a criminal matter."

To Koch, the law she is referring to is pretty clear. "It is a criminal matter and should be reported to law enforcement. As a university official, Peter did what should have been done."

What Koch left unsaid is this: when Sharon Taylor first reported the Brock Parker incident in January of 2012, someone in the upper hierarchy of the administration made a decision not to notify law enforcement. If the allegations made in the anonymous phone message left for Peter Campbell were true, more student athletes were abused after Brock Parker. A swift, thorough, and conscientious investigation in 2012 may have prevented additional physical and emotional damage to other Lock Haven wrestlers.

**Another Victim Comes Forward**

On December 22, 2013, the other shoe fell and reverberated loudly throughout the Lock Haven wrestling community. The Williamsport Sun Gazette printed an article under the byline of Mitch Rupert. The article detailed the Brock Parker story but also added a new element, a second wrestler alleging physical abuse by Robbie Waller.

Aaron Fry was a red-shirt freshman during the 2011-2012 season. Sometime between the middle of November and early December of 2011, Fry was practicing wrestling from the bottom position when his head coach, Robbie Waller, told him to stop wrestling. He was instructed to get up and go to the other end of the wrestling room and ride the stationary bikes. Fry figured that Waller must have observed something that displeased him. Fry describes what happened next, "I got up and I started walking. I don't know if I wasn't walking fast enough or what. But he pushed me one time, kind of just shoved me. I kind of just looked at him and kept on walking and he pushed me again. By that time I was pretty much on top of the stationary bikes; not on top of them but standing right beside them. And the third time, was the final push where he grabbed me and shoved me into the bikes. I fell into the bikes and knocked one of them over."

If banishment to the exercise bikes was meant to be a teaching moment, the lesson became lost in the violent act that shocked Fry and his teammates. They stopped wrestling and quietly stared at Fry as he picked himself up from the floor.

The coach did not go to Fry and ask him if he was okay. Nor did he explain why he pulled Fry from the mats, or why he grabbed him and pushed him into the bikes. Waller just turned around and walked away.

Fry did not wait to be thrown out of the room like Parker had been. He regained his composure and walked out of the practice. Fry explains his reaction: "I wasn't injured. I guess I was kind of pissed. I was more in shock than anything. Did this really just happen?"

Unlike Brock Parker, Fry contacted his parents immediately. His parents quickly placed a call to Director of Athletics Sharon Taylor's office, but found no one was there to answer the call. In the meantime, Waller called Fry and asked him to come to his office. Waller apologized to Fry and assured him that nothing like that would happen again.

Fry thought the incident was over, but it remained with him as other events occurred involving both him and other wrestlers, behaviors that Fry characterizes as both physical and verbal abuse.

During Fry's true freshman year, his red-shirt status barred him from traveling with the team to any events. Since he wanted to participate in the Binghamton Open, he signed up for the tournament. He personally paid his entry fee, gas money, and hotel room.

Fry explains what happened in Binghamton: "I was cutting a lot of weight and didn't make the weight class that I wanted to be in and ended up wrestling at a weight up. And then, because I didn't wrestle the weight he (Waller) wanted me to, I ended up losing scholarship money. I think I lost $400 from my scholarship for that semester."

According to Sharon Taylor, withholding scholarship money is a rare occurrence, and normally happens when a student gets in trouble with alcohol or minor scuffles with the law. When it does happen, the funds are pulled from the following semester.

After two years under Robbie Waller, Fry had had enough. "That last year was the final straw," says Fry. "Just the way he treated people; the way he treated me. I don't want to say I hated wrestling, but it left a bitter taste in my mouth…I didn't want to do it anymore because it wasn't fun anymore."

Fry also related an incident that took place at a summer wrestling camp. Waller took an athlete outside and allegedly punched him in the chest. According to Fry, the force of the blow was so great as to injure Waller's finger. The student's name is being withheld at this time because he is still involved in Lock Haven wrestling.

Speaking with Robbin Fry, Aaron's mother, one hears a story almost identical to that of Lori Baker, Brock Parker's mom. A kid who has loved wrestling since elementary school loses all interest within the hostile environment created by Robbie Waller. While Baker is very angry at Lock Haven for not investigating the assault of her son and thus enabling Waller to negatively influence more LHU wrestlers, Fry is furious that Michael Fiorentino sent Waller away with a positive recommendation that may someday expose other college athletes to the same experiences.

The Fry incident may not seem important due to the absence of any injuries, but it does demonstrate that the Parker assault was not an isolated event. When asked to list other wrestlers who quit the team possibly due to Robbie Waller, he named five former teammates: Colton Dalberth, Aaron Ernst, Kris Gratalo, Jake Bachman and Troy Dolan.

Dolan is an interesting case. He was a three-time Pennsylvania state champion at Derry Area High School near Latrobe, Pennsylvania. He matriculated at the University of Missouri but later transferred to Lock Haven. Dolan left the LHU program after just one semester. Fry explains, "I know he hated Waller because Waller was a jerk to him."

The anonymous call to Peter Campbell had made reference to the large number of students who quit the wrestling team. In additional to the names provided by Aaron Fry, the following individuals left the wrestling program in a two-year period:

2011-2012
- Greg Barnish
- Korey Gillen
- Eric Kimble
- Matthew Martoccio

2012-2013
- Vinnie Pellechia

- Jacob Powers
- Zach Heffner

Additionally, Tory Bennett and Cody Copeland sought transfers out of Lock Haven.

Some of these students may have left because of grades, curriculum changes, failure to make the team, financial stress, or personal reasons, but the sheer number of team desertions should have sent up a red flag, as suggested by the anonymous caller.

## A Cover Up?

Two big questions remain. Was there a cover up of the Brock Parker incident and why would a cover up be necessary?

The first question was directed to the principals in this story. Peter Campbell answered, "Absolutely. That's why I didn't feel comfortable (remaining in the athletics department) and had to get out. When I found out that none of the witnesses had even been interviewed, that sent up some red flags."

Tom Justice draws the same conclusion, "All the evidence points to it. Without a doubt."

Terry Fike also believes that a cover up took place that went all the way up to the president's office.

Bridget Roun believes that Sharon Taylor's dismissal as athletics director is circumstantial evidence that a cover up took place. She also cites Deana Hill's comment about the president killing the investigation.

Sharon Taylor would not comment on whether or not a cover up occurred, but she noted that, "Based on 25 years as an A.D., an internal investigation of this nature need not take more than three or four weeks to complete."

The fact that the inquiry spanned 15 months and never resulted in a public finding hints strongly that the LHU administration wanted to conceal the truth.

Taylor would not comment on a thought shared by others: that her removal as athletics director was related to her reporting the physical abuse of Brock Parker and was designed to remove her from a position where she could push for a thorough investigation; that she was hastily assigned to a faculty position from which she had no authority over athletic matters.

Further, does Fiorentino's mysterious surveillance of Sharon Taylor whenever she came near the athletics department now have a possible explanation? Maybe he didn't want Taylor around to keep the Brock Parker case bubbling on the surface. Peter Campbell's question to Fiorentino about why he was scared of Sharon Taylor can now be answered.

When did the alleged cover up begin? The November 2011 email from Sharon Taylor about an incident involving Robbie Waller did not have a student name attached to it. Waller denied that any physical hands-on abuse took place. It is understandable why an investigation would not take place at this point. The fact that the incident had buzzed around the wrestling community for two years might have warranted a deeper look. Such an inquiry would certainly upset the wrestling community.

Two months later, the story became clearer. Brock Parker was identified as the alleged victim; Robbie Waller the alleged abuser. Witnesses were named. In a similar fashion to the Penn State scandal, lip service would be paid to finding the truth. Beginning in January of 2012, the investigation that should have begun in earnest, was either botched or whitewashed.

Why a cover up? Terry Fike has a theory about the initial reluctance to delve into the allegations. Michael Fiorentino came into the Lock Haven presidency with the strong backing of the pro-wrestling alumni and trustees. Fike believes that Fiorentino felt obliged to appease this contingency.

Jerry Swope was one such trustee, and Ron Bowes, a wealthy alumnus. Each wielded power and influence. Robbie Waller was seen by many to be "their boy." Prior to a wrestling trip to the Midwest, Bowes asked to accompany the team on the bus. According to emails at the time, Taylor recommended against it to President Fiorentino, who overruled her. He claimed that he spoke with an NCAA official who cleared Bowes to make the trip. It turned out that he contacted Steve Murray, PSAC commissioner who does not generally handle NCAA rules interpretations. Taylor followed up with an individual who was an NCAA rules interpreter. That individual was aghast that a conference office would support such a request involving an athletics booster.

Another Bowes episode caused Lock Haven to self-report a violation to the PSAC. The parents of a wrestler attended a party hosted by Bowes. Bowes replied that he had not invited the parents but did not turn them away either. Taylor reported the violation and took other actions within the department to avoid similar issues with boosters.

By the time the anonymous phone call arrived in Peter Campbell's office, the motivation for a cover up became more urgent and important. A few miles away at Penn State, Graham Spanier, Tim Curley and Gary Schultz were being severely criticized for not reporting the Jerry Sandusky shower room incident to law enforcement. How many more victims had been abused after that event that could have been spared life-altering sexual abuse? The same argument could have been made at Lock Haven, though the level and scope of abuse did not compare. The legal responsibility to report physical abuse had been abdicated by the president and the director of human resources.

Spanier, Curley and Schultz were later charged for lying to a grand jury.

When Terry Fike and Tom Justice went to the campus police, a proper investigation had to be initiated. The administration had to be "all in" at that point. Damage control would be the new strategy. The dismissal of Robbie Waller served that purpose. Waller was gone. He had a year and a half severance package that included health insurance and pension credits. Additionally, he would get a personal letter of recommendation from the president, perhaps enabling him to secure another coaching position.

The whole Waller file could then be buried under the cloak of personnel confidentiality. Only outside law enforcement, the courts, the justice department, or Right To Know laws may be able to retrieve it.

There is no one left at Lock Haven to challenge Fiorentino on the way this case was handled. Linda Koch, Peter Campbell, and Sharon Taylor are now gone from the University or from any position of power or authority.

Gadfly Terry Fike has been pushed out of his position as women's wrestling coach and Tom Justice has retired.

Robbie Waller and Brock Parker are gone, as well.

Albert Jones has also left LHU. Who is Albert Jones? He was Deana Hill's assistant in the human resource department who is now working for a private corporation. He was present during interviews and likely was a part of internal discussions about the Parker case. When contacted to seek a statement about the Brock Parker investigation, he replied, "I'm not in a position to answer any questions because of my involvement in the investigation (of Robbie Waller), in light of possible litigation in the future."

Mr. Jones must be expecting rain; he has his umbrella ready.

**What's Next?**

Perhaps someone has read Lock Haven University their Miranda rights. They certainly feel they have the right to remain silent. Five requests sent to Lock Haven University under Pennsylvania's Right to Know Law each resulted in a denial.

The first request, submitted to LHU in March of 2014, asked for a copy of the email Director of Athletics Sharon Taylor sent to Deana Hill and Michael Fiorentino dated January 22, 2012; the subject of which was allegations of abuse (Robbie Waller against Brock Parker). This request was denied to protect the privacy of the student.

The second request asked for the results of the investigation by Deana Hill into allegations of abuse outlined in the Sharon Taylor email noted in request number one. This request was likewise denied to protect the privacy of the student.

The third request asked for a copy of the email sent by Peter Campbell to Michael Fiorentino, Deana Hill and Paul Altieri on or about March 19, 2013; the subject of which was the anonymous phone message left on Campbell's phone alleging physical abuse by Wrestling Coach Robbie Waller. Because this request mentioned Paul Altieri, Director of Campus Security, it involved a criminal investigation and was exempt from disclosure. This denial is the most interesting. The results of the investigation are protected because of a criminal inquiry, yet no criminal activity must have been uncovered because of the "positive" recommendation given to Robbie Waller.

The fourth request asked for the results of the investigation launched by Lock Haven campus police in March of 2013 following the email mentioned in request number three. This request hit the exacta, denied because of student privacy and involvement of a criminal investigation.

The fifth and final request asked for a copy of the recommendation given to Robbie Waller as part of his severance package. This request was denied because it did not relate to a vacancy of an elected office or one requiring Senate confirmation.

If Lock Haven University paid as much attention to the physical and emotional welfare of their students as they do their rights of privacy, the university would have been a safer place for parents to send their children.

The time has arrived for an outside agency to pull back the curtains and find out what happened at Lock Haven University. If a cover up took place, the people involved need to face termination, resignation, possibly even criminal charges. The victims need to find some solace in knowing that the story will be made public.

The list of 16 wrestlers who left the wrestling program would suggest a pattern of physical and/or verbal abuse that needs to be investigated. Young men do not enroll in college to have their dreams dashed and their spirits crushed, participating in a sport they love.

Sending Waller out to possibly become a coach at another school could start the abuse again somewhere else. Waller is a man with undeniable skills and knowledge but clearly seems to be a candidate for anger management training, which may not occur under the present circumstances.

If an investigation does not reveal anything more sinister than incompetent handling of an alleged assault, a valuable lesson can still be gleaned from the events at Lock Haven University. Apparently, the Jerry Sandusky affair at nearby Penn State was not enough to convince Lock Haven officials of the value in a timely, honest and thorough investigation.

# Chapter Seven – A Slap in the Face

Author's note: The Merriam Webster dictionary defines emeritus as one retired from professional life but permitted to retain as an honorary title the rank of the last office held. Emeritus is masculine and emerita is feminine. The plural is emeriti.

On May 17, 2013, the Lock Haven University Council of Trustees convened at the Durrwachter Alumni Conference Center for a regularly scheduled meeting. According to the agenda, the committee meetings would take place at 1:00 pm followed by committee reports at 1:30. The executive session was scheduled for 2:30 to be followed by the general meeting at 4:00 pm, which was open to the public. After the previous meeting's minutes were approved and various people were officially recognized for meritorious deeds, the usual reports were presented. Toward the end of the session, it was time for "Matters for Decision."

The trustees made motions, seconded and approved them for purchases, fee schedules and retirements. Then item number four came up: "Resolution for Emeriti Status." The minutes of the meeting announced the following:

"Dr. Fiorentino recommended that the usual resolution be passed recognizing the retirement and emeriti status of Dr. Stephen Marvel with 16 ½ years of service as Professor in the Biology Department, Ms. Sharon Taylor with 40 ½ years of service as Assistant Professor in the Sports Studies Department, and Mr. Bruce Wooley with 29 ½ years of service as Associate Professor in the Business and Computer Science Department."

As the minutes continued, the motion for Marvel was made, seconded and approved with "all ayes."

The minutes however, failed to mention a very important communication between Council Trustee Guy Graham and President Michael Fiorentino. Following the reading of the resolution, Graham asked, "Shall we take these as a slate?" Taking them as a slate would have allowed the trustees to vote on all three candidates at once; all aye, or all nay.

Fiorentino said, "No, take them separately."

So they took them separately, first bestowing emeritus honors on Dr. Marvel. Then it was Sharon Taylor's turn; the same Sharon Taylor who remains the winningest coach in LHU history, bringing home seven national championships. She was athletics director from 1988 to early in 2012 and the architect of three Dixon Trophies awarded to LHU for overall sports achievement.

A silence fell over the entire council. No comment from Graham, no motions from any of the eight trustees officially listed as "Council Members Present," just total bloody silence.

The meeting minutes state simply: "No motion was made to address the recommendation for Ms. Sharon Taylor."

Graham gave the signal to move forward and a motion was made to approve the emeritus status for Mr. Wooley. It was seconded and approved. One must assume that Mr. Wooley received the honor; the minutes reported the recipient as Mr. (left blank).

The meeting proceeded to the next item on the agenda. The deans, vice presidents, directors, lawyers, and others in attendance must have been confused at first, then possibly stunned when they realized what had happened. Not only had the council snubbed Sharon Taylor, they did it in a manner unprecedented in the history of LHU, going back to the 1982 creation of the Pennsylvania State System of Higher Education. Emeriti candidates had always been voted in as a group, on a slate as Guy Graham would say.

Scott Johnson, who covered the meeting for the Lock Haven Express, recognized the deviation from the normal procedure. He began his article about the emeriti vote by reporting: "In a somewhat unusual move, the Lock Haven University Council of Trustees refused to give the university's former director of athletics an "emeriti" status. [1].

Mr. Johnson's choice of the words: "somewhat unusual" may be an understatement.

**Sharon Taylor:** *After all this occurred I went back under Right to Know and requested the minutes from the Council of Trustees meetings going back, well, I picked two or three years in each decade going back* *about thirty years or so. Looking through it, the language is almost basically the same. Typically what happened was a faculty member who served the university, who didn't get in trouble like getting arrested (although some got arrested after the fact), people who served honorably -- they were all given emeriti status.*

*The usual resolution was presented and Dr. Willis requested that the following be given... they did the same for Keith Miller and for Barbara Dixon when she was there (as interim president) and they did the same in Fiorentino's reign. In fact, in one case, Miller was already here for nine months and it had Dr. Willis' name (on the resolution) because they used the same stock language for the stem of the sentence and they forgot to change the name of the president. So, it was very pro forma.*

*As far as breaking up the slate of names, I am certain that Guy Graham has never asked a president that question before. This was in the public meeting. I will tell you as I sit here, in their private executive session they had this discussion and they worked out how this would happen. The names would be taken separately. They would present the nomination and no one would make the motion. They manipulated the whole thing.*

The following trustees were present at the general session of the May 17 meeting: Brent Barge, Mary Coploff, George Durrwachter, Daniel Elby, Guy Graham, Donald Houser Jr., Deb Suder and Jerry Swope. (The minutes neglected to mention the presence of Juliet Seidel, the student representative on the council), Krystjan Callahan, Christian Dwyer and Margery Krevsky (aka Margery Brown Dosey, as noted on the LHU web site) were listed as council members not in attendance.

Author's note: Christian Dwyer passed away on August 17, 2014.

Taylor's scenario in which the silent boycott of her recommendation was rehearsed seems quite believable. Though two of the trustees were critics of Sharon Taylor, at best, and adversaries at worst, another half dozen ranged from neutral to sympathetic to her. Upon hearing Dr. Fiorentino's recommendation, and accustomed to the formerly pro forma procedure, one of the trustees most likely would have made the motion to approve her. A seconding motion would not have been out of the question. Common courtesy would dictate that you don't leave your colleague "hanging in the wind".

The outcome of the resulting vote is highly debatable, but everyone voting against Taylor would then have had to do it in public, for all to see.

What possible argument could have been leveled against Taylor prior to the general session? A comment made to former president Dr. Craig Dean Willis by an unnamed trustee provides the motive: "If she wants to give back the $625,000 we'll grant it (emerita) to her in a minute. You know, she's costing the state and the university all this money and she doesn't deserve it." Taylor heard a very similar comment shortly after the May session.

The weekend following the May trustees meeting, Taylor attended the dedication of a building named for Dr. Willis. She had occasion to meet up with trustee Dan Elby.

**Sharon Taylor:** *I've known Dan since he was a student here. We made eye contact. I didn't mention a subject. I just said, "Dan, just tell me why." He said, "Well, Sharon, it was just the $700,000." Of course, he didn't have the right amount.*

Dr. Linda Koch, in her final month as V.P. for Student Affairs, was present at the event. "I was there that day, and here is what I think was so perverse about the whole emerita thing. Graham, Dwyer and a couple of other Trustees pushed four presidents ... three of whom just ignored them; but, they pushed these presidents to get rid of Sharon Taylor. And then, when they found a president who would do their bidding, and the action resulted in an allegedly large settlement, they punished her for it!

An associate dean, recently fired by President Fiorentino, asked another trustee why Taylor was not approved for emerita status. The trustee reportedly answered, "We had 650,000 reasons."

For his part, Dr. Willis does not agree that a connection exists between Taylor's legal settlement and eligibility for emeriti status. Said Dr. Willis, "I'm not pleased that they chose to connect them."

Lock Haven University agreed to settle with Sharon Taylor, because they recognized that a court trial would likely result in a verdict for the plaintiff in an amount over which they would have little or no control. A settlement is designed to make a person whole, to make up for a loss. The emeriti snub was a chance to get in one final shot against her. And, interestingly, each trustee seemed to have a different opinion of the settlement amount.

The reaction to the trustees' non-action came quickly and passionately. The first public response appeared in the Express Yourself column in the Lock Haven Express newspaper just five days after the council's meeting. The writer was Lock Haven professor Gayatri Devi. She titled her article "Sense of Shame." Professor Devi explained, "It fills me with shame that we do not value a colleague who has opened the eyes and ears and gave such lasting memories and victories to our daughters and sons." [2]

"Just last week...we read about the 2013 Presidential Award presented to Prof. Taylor by the National Association for Girls and Women in Sport (NAGWS). Prof. Taylor, a woman who has never blown her own horn under any circumstances, and is one of the most humble and dignified women that I have met in three different continents, is in the company of our Secretary of State Hillary Clinton and other similarly accomplished women, with this latest accolade I am filled with shame that we think nothing of erasing Prof. Taylor's legacy at our university by not honoring her with emeriti status." [3]

The next local reaction appeared in the Opinion-Editorial section of the Lock Haven Express newspaper, one week after the meeting. The writer was Dr. Betty Baird Schantz, former associate dean at LHU and emerita. Schantz wrote: "The refusal of the board to act on the rewarding of emeriti status to Sharon Taylor is unbelievable." Schantz continued by describing the contributions Taylor had made to LHU in her 40 years of service. [4]

Schantz speculated, "It would seem that there must be some other personal reasons and, if so, those members should excuse themselves from this process." [5]

She concluded, "This issue will be viewed by the university community – and certainly by those who support the rights of women – as a black eye to our beloved university and a backhand to professional women who serve universities everywhere." [6]

One day later, LHU alumnus Mark Temons had his say in the Express Yourself column. Temons' approach notched up the outrage a level or two. He took the trustees to task and added a vituperative theme to his article.

Temons reminded the council that they have been entrusted to do what is best for LHU, regardless of any personal biases. He asks, "Which one of you has ever contributed as Sharon Taylor has? Who among you has singlehandedly worked to place the name of LHU on the national map? Which one of you has touched the lives of so many young people and cared so little for personal glory? Are you so weak that you act simply out of jealousy?" [7]

Former president Craig Dean Willis concurs with the last allegation. Speaking about the trustees and alums determined to drag Taylor down, Dr. Willis opined, "Certainly, there were always those who were upset with Sharon. A lot of it, I think, was jealousy. Here is a person who could stand up in front of a thousand NCAA delegates and speak her piece in a literate way. With her national and international connections, I think there was jealousy over that." [8]

The trustees have maintained their silence on the matter.

The same day as Temons' article appeared, the shockwave over Taylor's snub went national. Ellen Staurowsky penned a very thoughtful five-page article in the online version of College Sports Business News. Dr. Staurowsky is among the very few women with a resume as comprehensive as Sharon Taylor's, particularly in the realm of women's athletics and sports education. She currently serves as Professor of Sports Management at Drexel University in Philadelphia.

Staurowsky brought up a potential legal issue not previously mentioned by other writers. "In the absence of an explanation or statement from the Council of Trustees regarding the Taylor case, questions remain. And the cloak of silence cannot obscure the uncomfortable possibility an actual violation of Title IX might have been committed if the motive for withholding emerita status was done in retaliation against an accomplished, strong woman who was simply doing her job."

Staurowsky generously granted the trustees the benefit of the doubt by postulating that they may be contemplating how best to honor Sharon Taylor. She concluded, "There are sons and daughters, and citizens of Lock Haven watching this unfold, watching how this is being handled, asking whether they too, if they devoted their lives to the place they have come to call The Haven, may be greeted with a similar stone wall of silence." [9]

By the middle of the summer, a petition had been drafted by the faculty union to present to the Lock Haven Council of Trustees prior to their scheduled September 12th meeting. The Association of Pennsylvania State College and University Faculties (APSCUF) posted their resolution on-line via change.org, a website created to facilitate and disseminate petitions. [10]

The petition summarized Taylor's career and accomplishments and outlined the events that had taken place at the trustees' May meeting. They petitioned the Council of Trustees to move and second President Fiorentino's recommendation to grant emeriti status to Sharon Taylor so that a debate may be held. They further petitioned the council to vote affirmatively on the recommendation.

Mark Cloud, Lock Haven's APSCUF chapter president, released this pronouncement:

"APSCUF strongly asserts that granting emeriti status to a faculty member is an academic decision and should be left to the best judgment of our academic leaders and peers." [11]

A Facebook page named "Rally Around Sharon" that was originally created a year earlier to protest the reassignment of Taylor, displayed an article about the emeriti situation and provided a link to the change.org site.

Moments after the September Council of Trustees meeting was gaveled to order, Chair Guy Graham asked for public comments. Five people indicated the desire to speak, Dr. Betty Schantz, Mr. Peter Campbell, Dr. Brooke Harlowe, Dr. Stan Berard, and Ms. Bridget Roun. Each in turn asked the trustees to reconsider its inaction on the granting of emeriti status to Sharon Taylor. The comments having been made, the meeting moved on.

Later in the meeting, Mark Cloud gave his scheduled union president report. According the minutes of the meeting:

"Dr. Cloud directed the trustees to a packet of information that was provided in their packets containing a resolution from the faculty, signed by 321 faculty, staff and community members, in support of granting Sharon Taylor emeriti status."

When the time came for "Matters for Decision," six items were discussed and voted. No discussion of any kind on Sharon Taylor and emeriti was forthcoming. Graham brought down the gavel and the meeting ended.

Dr. Cloud's comment about academic honors being left to academia brings up a very interesting point. Do trustees in the PASSHE have the authority to make decisions on emeriti recommendations? According to Act 188, the law that created the Pennsylvania State System of Higher Education in 1982, the councils of trustees in the fourteen universities do not have that authority. The Act enumerates thirteen duties, none of which involve the granting of academic honors. In fact, none of the thirteen items mentions faculty whatsoever.

If Sharon Taylor's life story were a Hallmark Movie Channel Original Movie, it would play out like this: The Lock Haven University Council of Trustees would hold their next quarterly meeting on February 6, 2014. All of the standard reports would be given and finally the meeting agenda would reach the Matters for Decision segment. After a handful of items are raised and dispatched, the council chair raises his gavel to end another meeting without a resolution to the Sharon Taylor emeriti issue.

Before the meeting can be terminated, a loud voice calls out, "Mr. Chairman! Mr. Chairman! Two meeting ago, a recommendation by Dr. Fiorentino to grant emerita status to Sharon Taylor was not acted upon, not voted down. I would now like to make a motion that the recommendation be approved. The trustee, Jane Doe, who missed the past two meetings, continues, "I believe the recommendation had been tabled by inaction."

An exited buzz fills the conference room. The trustees look around the table in confusion. The chairman is stunned by this sudden development. After collecting his wits, he makes a decision to allow the motion. He is convinced that no other trustee will break from the herd and second the motion. Indeed, no one speaks up.

One detail of the Roberts Rules of Order that he is sure of states that a chairperson may continue with the meeting if no one seconds a motion. He announces, "If there is no second…"

Before he has a chance to finish his sentence and drop the gavel, a male voice rings out, "I second the motion."

Most of the twelve non-trustees in the room begin to cheer.

Receiving no signal from the president or university legal counsel, the chairman nervously clears his throat. Several months earlier, the entire council spoke as one, or failed to speak at all, in this matter. He would have to take a chance that a vote would be in favor of rejecting the recommendation, so he calls for discussion.

Jane Doe asked for, and is granted the floor. She begins, "We are discussing an academic honor. First of all, I don't believe that anyone on this council is qualified to judge Professor Taylor. Secondly, we received a petition signed by almost every faculty member demanding that we revisit this matter in light of Sharon Taylor's 40-plus years of outstanding service to this institution. In the event that anyone in this room is unfamiliar with Ms. Taylor's career, I am distributing a summary of her accomplishments."

After passing around Taylor's resume, she continues, "I was not here two meetings ago, when this shameful travesty occurred. I would like to think that I would have had the courage to speak up and make that motion. But, if I'm being honest, maybe I would not have broken ranks, either. Maybe I would have acted the coward and remained silent like all of you. I know some of you on this council dislike Sharon Taylor, and some of you are influential enough to try to bully the rest of us. I hope everyone will vote their conscience and approve the recommendation."

Another hand shoots up and is quickly recognized. He almost spits out the words, "This is not personal, at all. Sharon Taylor cost this university around three-quarters of a million dollars. She doesn't deserve to be honored."

No one else volunteers to join the discussion, so the chairman announces, "A motion was made and seconded to approve President Fiorentino's recommendation to grant Professor Sharon Taylor emerita status. How do you vote?"

President Fiorentino betrays no emotion as the longest tenured trustee casts the first of nine votes.

"Nay"

The vote proceeds clockwise around the table.

"Nay"

"Aye"

"Aye"

"Nay"

"Aye"

It is a foregone conclusion that the chairman, voting last, would vote against the recommendation. So one more negative vote and the game would be over.

The conference room would fall completely silent.

"Aye"

The eighth vote would be critical. A vote for Taylor would make the count five to three in favor. With a quorum present, Sharon Taylor would receive the honor.

Intentionally, or not, the eighth trustee would pause for an eternity before shaking his head back and forth, and finally proclaiming, "Aye."

His vote now unimportant, the chairman reluctantly abstains, declares the resolution passed, and slams the gavel down, neglecting to ask for any further business.

The local newspaper reporter would quickly run into the hall while retrieving her cell phone from the bottom of her purse.

Several witnesses would fish their phones out of pockets and purses trying to be the first person to reach Sharon Taylor with the very unexpected news.

Sadly, the February council meeting did not play out in the above manner. In reality, no one resurrected the Sharon Taylor recommendation. In fact, two other recommendations were put forth to the council. President Fiorentino called for the approval of emeriti status for Dr. Zakir Hossain, Sociology Professor and Interim Dean of Arts and Science, for 22 years of service.

A motion was made by Trustee Durrwachter and seconded by Trustee Suder. The motion carried unanimously.

In a separate recommendation, Fiorentino also recommended granting emeriti status to Dr. Linda Koch, Vice President of Student Affairs, for 26 years of service.

A motion was made by Trustee Callahan and seconded by Trustee Suder. The motion carried unanimously.

While both of the new emeriti were highly deserving of the honor, neither served Lock Haven for 40 years.

Also noteworthy is the fact that President Fiorentino made the two recommendations separately. Chairman Graham did not have to ask Fiorentino if the council should vote them as a slate. Why is this noteworthy? In the matter of Sharon Taylor, Fiorentino appears completely uninvolved in the machinations that denied her the honor of emerita. The minutes of the meeting simply state that he passed along her name as a recommendation. His hands are clean. Those who attended the meeting witnessed his instructions to Guy Graham to vote the three names separately.

Without that "off the record" interchange, the three names would have been voted on "as a slate" and Sharon Taylor would have been granted the honor she deserved. The council would not have discredited the other two retirees by voting them down. As much as some of them wanted to "smack down" Taylor, the two deserving professors would have been too much collateral damage. The anti-Taylor cabal found another way to get the dirty deed done.

The February 6 meeting allowed Dr. Fiorentino to make separate voting a standard procedure going forward. This solidifies the actions of May 17, 2013, which broke a thirty-plus-year tradition of voting in all emeriti candidates at one time.

The following is Sharon Taylor's November 14th response to the actions of the LHU Council of Trustees as submitted to, and published by, The Lock Haven Express newspaper on November 8, 2014.

To The Editor, Lock Haven Express:

For 18 months, I have been something of a bystander observing the action/non-action of the Lock Haven University Council of Trustees (COT) in the matter of their recognizing LHU's awarding of Emerita status to me upon my retirement from Lock Haven University. I am more appreciative than I can express to my LHU Faculty colleagues for their support and efforts, not only on my behalf, but also for Faculty retirees into the future. And, I have responded to a multitude of question and comments related to the reaction of professional colleagues, friends, and LHU alumni both here in Lock Haven and around the country. Earlier this year, the "Our View" editorial, and a separate news article, in this newspaper made reference to the same absence of COT action upon which so many others have commented.

Since that time, I have been assured that the President of LHU has done all he can do in this matter. According to the official minutes of the May 2013, COT meeting, President Fiorentino formally "recommended" that I be given emerita status. This formal recommendation was subsequently confirmed to me, this year, by President Fiorentino's representative. So, the President of LHU, acting on behalf of Lock Haven University, made the recommendation but the COT then purportedly failed to act on his recommendation.

In 1982, Act 188 was passed by the Pennsylvania Legislature, creating the PA State System of Higher Education. The System is comprised of Lock Haven University and the other 13 Commonwealth-owned universities. One result of the System's creation was that most of the significant decisions for the universities would be made in Harrisburg by the System's Board of Governors; local COTs were given specific and limited powers and duties, none of which pertained to Faculty and their academic or employment processes. Indeed, the only place in Act 188 where the term "Emeriti Status" is mentioned is under the responsibilities of the Board of Governors, should they decide to confer such an honor.

When asked why LHU's COT "approves" the President's decisions on Emeriti status, one local administrator answered, "They wanted to be involved". Since the creation of the State System, perhaps local COTs are seeking relevance.

Quite simply, the decision to award Emeriti status to retirees of a college or university must rest with the academic leadership of the institution ... not with its trustees. Emeriti status reflects the final step in individuals' professional careers; it clearly falls within the purview of the institution that the individuals served. Any action by trustees in the matter of Emeriti status is no more appropriate than their action would be in a Faculty member's hiring, in the awarding of tenure to him or her, or in the multistep promotion process that the institution embraces.

Having Emeriti status conferred by politically appointed COTs is more akin to political patronage than it is to a process of higher education. In this matter, as in many other matters involving Faculty and academic integrity, COTs are, appropriately, irrelevant; the process must ensure that petty politics and the possibility of personal vendettas are minimized. Recognition of these facts is the reason that a vastly overwhelming majority of colleges and universities in the U.S. follow the recommendations of the respected American Association of University Professors (AAUP) and the American Council on Education (ACE) and hold these designations unto themselves.

At the September 2013, COT meeting's public session, a Faculty member spoke eloquently of "process", and the fact that it was absent in this situation. [NOTE: The LHU administration announced a formal "process" this fall that will apply to future retirees, but there was none in May, 2013, or in the 30 years prior.] If, in the May 2013, meeting, the LHU Trustees had truly believed that my contributions to LHU in the 40.5 years of service to my Alma Mater did not warrant Emerita status, fair enough! Perhaps they had some reason to believe that I was the ONLY Faculty member in the last 30 years [limit of the research] to have been recommended by any of four (4) University presidents who did NOT deserve to be so recognized. If that was their conviction, then they should have put the matter to a vote and (to borrow a term from former Secretary of State, Madeleine Albright) had "the cojones" to vote it down! Instead they hid behind a parliamentary maneuver of taking each name separately [again, a "first" in 30 years] and remained silent on the President's recommendation.

As I mentioned at the outset, time and again over these many months I have been asked by so many people: "what's going on?" and the answer is… nothing. And so, in the absence of an enumerated power in May, 2013, for the local COT to approve the awarding of Emeriti status, and with the conviction that all things of an academic nature related to Faculty rest with the academy, I accept, with appreciation, the aforementioned Emerita recognition awarded by Lock Haven University as stated in a letter, filled with laudatory comments, dated May 17, 2013, and signed by the University President, Michael Fiorentino.

Sincerely yours
Sharon E. Taylor
Director of Athletics/Assistant Professor Emerita
Lock Haven University

# Chapter Eight - A Tale of Four Presidents

The past four individuals who served as President of Lock Haven University each played a role in the denouement of Sharon Taylor's career as Director of Athletics. The first promoted her to the position, then supported and mentored her through the better times. She rewarded him with championship teams as well as accolades and national recognition. Her role with the USOC and the U.S. Olympic field hockey team directed an international spotlight onto a small state university buried in the mountains of Central Pennsylvania.

The second in this foursome failed to throw the bolt when the wolves were at the door. His inaction in defending Taylor emboldened the critics and allowed their efforts to snowball. Although he tacitly supported her in some ways, his penchant for avoiding decisions prevented the athletics department from correcting problems that may have silenced many of the critics. The de facto gag order placed on her department severely crippled her efforts to defend herself. His failure to fight the early round of lawsuits only led to a free-for-all in which employees felt confident in suing Lock Haven University when things didn't go their way. His decisions, and non-decisions, also brought the national spotlight down on Lock Haven and Sharon Taylor when USA Today published a feature article calling Taylor a "lightning rod for controversy, litigation."

The third president served for a little more than one year on an interim basis. She almost brokered a retirement package that would have allowed Taylor to leave Lock Haven with the dignity that she earned and deserved.

President number four came into power with an agenda that many believe included ridding the school of Ms. Taylor. When he accepted the job offer to lead Lock Haven University, Taylor's removal from the athletics department appears to be a quid-pro-quo. With no previous exposure to Taylor, he had no negative experiences that could have warranted the aggressive posture with which he began his tenure as President. Within a short period of time, Taylor was "reassigned" to faculty duties only. A lifetime of success and recognition meant nothing to him.

## Number One: President Craig Dean Willis

Dr. Craig Dean Willis joined Lock Haven State College in 1982. One year later the school became known as Lock Haven University. When he retired 22 years later, more than just the name of the school had changed. The 24 campus buildings had doubled to 48. Over 50 renovation projects now dot the campus map. The student enrollment also doubled as LHU added 20 new undergraduate programs and four new graduate degree programs. LHU became one of the first schools to offer a graduate degree in international studies. [1]

When pressed to choose his proudest achievement at Lock Haven, Dr. Willis pauses only slightly before naming the establishment of graduate programs, particularly the physician assistant program. His predecessor did not want them, but Willis observed that Lock Haven was constantly penalized for not offering master's degrees.

Said Dr. Willis, "There are others (achievements) too, but if you force me to name one, that is it. To be a university, you need graduate programs. Now there are five or six."

The Express newspaper described him as "a kind, hardworking and affable man who worked very hard to both protect and grow the interests of the university." [2]

What else can we say about Dr. Willis? First and foremost, he liked and respected Sharon Taylor. Before Willis ever sat down in his office chair on his first day at Lock Haven, Sharon Taylor had begun her tenth year as the school's field hockey coach.

In April of 2013, Sharon Taylor came to the Parson's Union Building, known on campus as the PUB, prepared to give a speech on the history and progress of Title IX at Lock Haven and education in general. She was unaware that 70 people had gathered to honor her for her many years of service to Lock Haven University. Two dozen people had requested an opportunity to take the floor and pay tribute to Sharon Taylor. One of those speakers was Craig Willis.

Willis spoke fondly of his former A.D., recalling how people warned him early on about Sharon Taylor. They informed Willis that Taylor was too pushy. They said she couldn't be trusted because she hated men and men's athletics. Said Willis, "Of course, I was here long enough to find out those things weren't true."

He did not have to regale the audience that evening with Taylor's accomplishments. Everyone present knew what Lock Haven athletes under her leadership had accomplished. Instead, he shared incidents that never made the local newspaper, incidents that show her character and dedication to her athletes and staff.

"I saw her handle a very delicate NCAA matter, save a whistleblower's job, unlike at Penn State where the whistleblower seems to be a pariah. I saw her handle a matter unrelated to athletics because she cared about the University and me, personally."

"I saw her stay calm and collected when the father of one of her athletes accused her of all sorts of ugly things in her personal life. She should have sued him. I understand that she kept her cool because of the student. The father forced his daughter to quit the athletic team. She eventually left school for the military just to get out from under the father's control."

Addressing Taylor he concluded, "I saw you as an A.D. where the number one priority was the athlete. You always looked at what was best for the kids."

Had President Willis remained at LHU for a few more years, he would not have let the wolves get past the door.

One of the trustees called Taylor to report that a couple of his associates were speaking against her. He told them that if Craig Willis was still there, he would have just called them into his office and told them to stop interfering with his staff. That would have been the end of it.

Before vacating the president's office, Willis told Dr. Linda Koch, Vice President for Student Affairs, "I'm really worried about Sharon. There are people here that really want to get her out of here."

### Number Two: President Keith T. Miller

Keith Miller paid his dues and moved steadily up the ladder of academia. Starting as a professor at Fairleigh Dickinson Teaneck Campus in 1987, he moved along to Quinnipiac College as associate dean and then became dean of the College of Business at Niagara University. In 2001, he took another step up by accepting the position of provost and vice chancellor of the University of Wisconsin, Oshkosh campus. In 2004, Lock Haven University offered him the opportunity to put "President" on his business card.

Miller most likely did not decide to accept the LHU position because of the school's history of excellence in collegiate wrestling. Yet wrestling's fall from grace would prove to be the catalyst that led to a very tumultuous tenure for Miller.

With Craig Willis retired, the PLOW group pressed its campaign to dethrone Sharon Taylor by accusing her of downgrading the once-proud wrestling program, as well as other male sports teams. A more potent threat also began to gain intensity. Several members of the Council of Trustees wanted Sharon Taylor gone. This small cabal of trustees and PLOW now had a common goal.

More than one person holds the opinion that Miller began his presidency with instructions from those trustees to get rid of Taylor. His right-hand man at that time was provost Zak Hossain, former professor and president of the faculty union. According to Hossain, there was no blatant public agenda to depose her. Instead, the mission was couched in the mantra, "If this institution wants to grow, there must be change." Even long-time president Craig Dean Willis needed to move on. Concerning the athletics department and Sharon Taylor, the plan was not personal. Times had changed, and new leadership would be needed. After twenty-plus years, the trustees wanted the athletics department to go in a different direction.

Hossain had no direct contact with the trustees, who deal directly with the president. Consequently, he had no evidence that a personal agenda was involved, but he "heard rumblings" to that effect.

Hossain and Miller agreed in principle that they needed to take LHU in a different direction, but there were far more important goals to chase than Sharon Taylor's position. For example, they planned to make LHU a laptop university, meaning that every student must have one. Hossain wanted to be the first school in the Pennsylvania system to achieve that status.

Whenever Miller reintroduced the subject of Sharon Taylor, Hossain reminded him of two issues. First of all, there was Sharon's place in the history of Lock Haven; as a coach and administrator, she led the school to national championships and garnered much positive publicity for the school. Any plan to remove her would be unpopular, and more importantly, distracting to their larger goals.

And the second reason was even more crucial. LHU could not fire her. Hossain explains, "Unlike me, Keith did not come from a union background. According to our collective bargaining agreement, coaches and athletics directors are faculty. Faculty cannot be fired."

If the director of athletics had been designated as an administrator, it would have been a very different story. "Administrators serve at the discretion of their superiors. I told Keith, that we could not do that. We would have to follow procedures. Keith agreed with me, but I pointed out that we needed some way to make a credible case that the athletics department is doing what it is supposed to do."

Miller wisely looked outside the campus and named Andrea L Myers to perform an audit of the athletics department. Miller and Hossain decided to give Myers "unfettered access" to anybody and everyone.

As noted earlier, the Myers Report found some areas needing improvement and outlined a program to "fix" the alleged flaws. Myers also found that Taylor's critics, especially the university trustees, were woefully ignorant of how an athletics department functioned in light of NCAA and Title IX regulations, as well as financial and scholarship facts of life. She recommended seminars to explain the mechanisms in place to deal with these factors.

The report was handed over to the Council of Trustees along with the conclusion that no action could be taken against Sharon Taylor, based on the results. Said Hossain, "The most we could have done is remove her from the A.D. position and she would go back to the classroom."

President Miller failed to act on most of the Myers' recommendations and consequently the calls for Taylor's ouster increased in frequency and volume. One of Andrea Myers recommendations called for better communication between the athletics department and the administration.

According to Hossain, Miller never brought up the Myers recommendation again after the initial meeting. Hossain feels that the Myers Report was Miller's way of keeping Taylor in her position.

The Guerriero lawsuit was filed in 2006. The decision to settle this lawsuit rather than defend it seemed to open the floodgates. By the time Miller resigned in 2010, half-dozen more legal actions had been filed against LHU.

The parade of lawsuits caught the attention of USA Today and suddenly Lock Haven's reputation had been stained in the national media.

Former trustee Virginia "Ginny" Roth sensed that Miller was under so much pressure that he had to be looking for a way out of Lock Haven. Eight of ten Lock Haven trustees voted to extend Miller's contract, but he had apparently found his escape route. He threw his name into the hat (mortarboard?) to replace the outgoing president of Virginia State University. The historically black land-grant school near Petersburg, Virginia chose Miller to begin his new position in 2011.

Had the road at LHU been less bumpy, or had he received a unanimous vote of confidence, Miller might have remained as president and Taylor might still be the A.D. Despite the fact that her litigation against PLOW failed, a lot of the steam escaped from the PLOW initiative after the cold reality of their leaders responding to the lawsuit and being deposed.

**Number Three: Interim President Barbara Dixon**

Keith Miller's somewhat unexpected departure from Lock Haven left the Pennsylvania State System of Higher Education, PASSHE, less than adequate time to mount a national search for a new president. The system wisely turned to the Registry for College and University Presidents. When the Registry learns that an institution is in need of temporary leadership, it broadcasts the opportunity to its members. Lock Haven sought a former president with experience in public education, accreditation, and athletics.

Dr. Barbara B. Dixon felt that her credentials were a good fit. PASSHE concurred. Dixon had recently retired from Truman State University in Kirksville, Missouri. She had served as president from 2003 to 2008. From 1997 to 2003 she was the Provost and Vice President for Student Affairs for SUNY Geneseo, satisfying the public education requirement.

147

Former music professor Dixon's resume did not feature any position in athletics, but her tenure at Truman State provided ample experience. She arrived at Truman shortly after a volleyball coach sued for discrimination based on Title IX violations. An out-of-court settlement provided the coach with $175,000 in reparations. Truman was also required to hire a gender equity officer with authority to overrule the athletics director if Title IX regulations were not followed. The process of cleaning up the Truman State mess gave Dixon a crash course in guiding an athletics department.

PASSHE offered Dixon the position and she became Interim President Dixon on July 1, 2010. She began the job with some knowledge of the problems with athletics. "I knew there were lawsuits. I knew there was controversy. I knew there was a group in town (Lock Haven) that was very interested, I would say, in getting her (Taylor) out of there."

Dixon quickly discovered that Lock Haven (administratively) "really didn't know how to handle athletics." The previous president had Taylor reporting to the VP for Finance and Administration, and then moved her under the Provost's authority, reporting to someone with "zero experience in athletics."

Dixon recalled, "One of things I determined pretty quickly was that I was never really going to find out what was going on, and help make any changes, or help settle any of those lawsuits if I didn't have athletics as a direct report. So, within a month or two, I pulled athletics into reporting to me, rather than to the provost. I did the same thing at Truman."

When asked to name the most challenging aspect of dealing with the athletics program, her surprising response was "football." The well-documented battle between Taylor and the PLOW group had cooled after Taylor's lawsuit was filed.

Lock Haven's football team was winless over the past two seasons, going 0- 21. Rumors swirled around the campus that football, as a varsity sport, would be dropped in favor of Sprint Football. The Collegiate Sprint Football League defines the sport on their web site:

Sprint Football is a full-contact, intercollegiate, varsity sport and has the same rules as regular college football, except that all players must weigh 172.0 pounds or less. The league has been in existence since prior to World War II.

LHU football could not compete in their league (PSAC) without more scholarship players. The school simply did not have the budget to award enough scholarships. Consequently, the team was outmanned by most competitors.

The consensus among alumni and townspeople was that Sharon Taylor wouldn't commit the necessary funds for football, spending money on women's sports instead. What Taylor's critics didn't know, or chose to ignore, was the fact that the Commonwealth of Pennsylvania would not allow their 14 institutions to use state money for athletic scholarships. Scholarship money had to be raised by the school itself. The Lock Haven University Foundation and the team members were responsible for fund raising. The football coaches did not feel that fundraising was in their job description.

Dixon could not believe the amount of telephone calls and personal visits she received about football, asking or begging her not to cut football.

Dixon remembers, "I had coaches and alumni from way back in the 1970s come in and beg me not to cut football. I got calls from...I couldn't believe it. I got a call from somebody at the Atlanta Falcons, the Chicago Bears, and the Indianapolis Colts. I thought holy smokes, what is this?"

Dixon decided against a switch to Sprint Football. Instead, she put the program on probation, so to speak. If the alumni could raise $150,000 or more per year, over the next three years, football would be safe. If not, the new president would be within his rights to eliminate football as a varsity sport.

During the 2010 season, LHU lost every game on its schedule by a combined score of 501-137. The losing streak expanded to 0-32. To make matters worse, the alumni and boosters failed the fundraising challenge set forth by Dixon.

Taylor's critics were right about one thing, she did favor the Sprint Football option. She held very little optimism that enough money would be raised to change the fortunes of Lock Haven's football program. Sprint teams featured no scholarship players. The funds going to football could be redistributed to men's basketball and wrestling.

The 2011 team lost all ten games on the schedule. The losing streak grew to 43 losses, only three losses shy of the record set by the University of Minnesota Morris in 2003.

Dixon describes her mission as the Interim President, "My job was to try to pave the way and clean up a lot of stuff for the new president." She knew that a decision to drop football would only surface again when the next president arrived.

During her brief tenure, Dixon solved an accreditation issue, managed the settlement of the remaining lawsuits, reworked the school's budget because of funding decreases by state government, and put a large bandage on the football question. As her one-year placement neared an end, she had not solved the Sharon Taylor situation.

Some of the trustees made it very clear that they would like to see a new director of athletics. Many alumni (predominantly men) harbored a strong animosity toward Taylor. Dixon found Taylor to be very capable and hard working, but she seriously doubted that Taylor could continue to operate effectively in the toxic environment that Lock Haven had become.

Dixon felt that a voluntary retirement on Taylor's part would be the best solution. The former student, successful coach and long-time administrator deserved better than to be driven out of Lock Haven by forces from outside the University. Fortunately, Taylor came to her first with a retirement plan.

She began to meet with Taylor to forge a retirement package that would acceptable to all parties.

As the final days of Dixon's contract arrived, only one issue stood in the way. Taylor was a plaintiff in legal action against PASSHE. In order to get the retirement package approved by PASSHE, her name would have to be withdrawn from the lawsuit. Taylor felt that she could not let down her fellow athletics directors by pulling her support.

Dixon recalls her final days at LHU: "I think the last day I talked to Sharon was the 28th of June. I was done on the 30th of June. We were so close and it was the one issue. In the end she wouldn't let go of that issue. And then I was gone. I had no more authority.

**Number Four: President Michael Fiorentino, Jr.**

With Dr. Barbara B. Dixon holding down the fort as interim president, Lock Haven University tapped Michael Fiorentino to take over in July of 2011. Fiorentino previously served as provost and vice president of academic affairs at Fitchburg State University in Fitchburg, Massachusetts. A 1971 graduate of Fitchburg, he returned in 1974 as an associate professor of special education.

Fitchburg shares a common history with LHU. Both universities began as state normal schools, Fitchburg in 1894 and Lock Haven in 1870. The purpose of a normal school was to train high school graduates to become teachers, adopting the educational "norms" of the time. Eventually, both schools began to bestow bachelor degrees and became state teachers colleges. In the 1960s their curricula expanded and brought about a name change to "state college" and eventually to "university."

Fiorentino's three-plus decades at Fitchburg provided him with both an educational and liberal arts background, making him a good fit with LHU.

With the many challenges facing the new president, he had time to make Sharon Taylor a priority. Within seven months, he "re-assigned" her to a teaching position.

The announcement of Taylor's removal from the athletics department did not go out under Dr. Fiorentino's name, but issued as a University statement. By late afternoon LHU emailed the announcement to the media. Taylor, for her part, handled media requests professionally, referring the questions to LHU's publicity department. Fiorentino, on the other hand, began a series of strange behaviors toward Taylor that would not become understandable until the Brock Parker story unraveled.

After 25 years as A.D. Sharon Taylor would again be known as Professor Taylor if the reassignment was not rescinded or modified in some way.

When the spring semester ended, Taylor had to move her office to another building, apart from her former associates in the athletics department. Fiorentino did not want Taylor in the athletics building at all. During the transition, her old office was kept locked. During this period, interim A.D. Peter Campbell and his staff were working on a project requiring files and information from Taylor's office. After unlocking and relocking the office door multiple times, they decided to prop the door open just a hair so they could enter and exit without a key.

Soon after, Dr. Fiorentino began to appear down the hall with no apparent purpose. Colleagues have surmised that someone walked by the office and assumed that she was in there accessing files that were no longer any of her business. Upon learning of the suspected breach of security, Dr. Fiorentino skulked about the building hoping to "catch" her violating his instructions.

Apparently, Fiorentino worried that Campbell and Barney were operating under Taylor's unseen hand.

Fiorentino, it seems, was hired with the quid pro quo that Taylor had to go if he wanted the job of president. More than a few LHU employees and former employees hold that view. One source requesting anonymity stated: "I think he knew he was hired to fire her. The search committee had been handpicked to include 'Sharon-haters.' One trustee (reportedly) said openly in a search committee meeting that they needed to find a president who will get rid of Sharon as A.D. I think they got to him on this before he was even hired. I heard he was the third choice, and needed three votes to get approved. I feel that he knew who hired him and why, so he had a mission to follow through. I don't think he is supportive of gender equity. Also, I think he is very insecure. He needs someone in the job who marches to his orders. Sharon is not that kind of person."

A former LHU administrator agrees with the previous assessment. "Certain trustees were disappointed with Miller for not being forceful enough with Taylor, or forthright enough with them. This time, in hiring Fiorentino, they were not taking any chances. These trustees absolutely had this (Sharon Taylor's reassignment) set up in advance when they hired him. There is no doubt about it. Fiorentino came in with that challenge."

Another anonymous staff member tries to make sense of the need to remove Taylor. "There is a cultural difference between men and women in power. Sharon Taylor is not awed by position and authority.

It's hard for men who need these things to accept women like Sharon. She scares men like that."

"Why do certain trustees hold such sway over Lock Haven University? I think it's the culture of the place; the culture of the community. This is a very conservative place. The priorities are very male. The ethos of the Council and the community is a very male oriented ethos. It's possible that a different university would have reacted differently, but here we have a confluence of very similar perspectives coming together."

If Fiorentino is seeking the respect of his staff, he seems to have some work left to do. If his goal is to be feared by his employees, he can check that off his to-do list. Both current and former employees hesitate to allow their names to be used when discussing LHU's academic leader. One source explains: "There might be other people who could go through the same thing as Sharon. There is a line that you should not cross. I have been warned several times not to say some of the things I do."

The handling of the Brock Parker investigation displays the kind of hardball Fiorentino is capable of playing in order to move forward and put his brand on Lock Haven University.

Machiavellian may be too strong a word to describe Fiorentino's strategy to prevent Sharon Taylor from receiving a well-deserved emerita honor, but his subtle instruction to council chair Guy Graham, to separate the names of the three emeriti candidates, got the job done quite efficiently, and without leaving his fingerprints at the crime scene.

Interim President Barbara Dixon met with her replacement and told him how close she had come to striking a retirement deal with Taylor. She thought that she had paved the way for Fiorentino to easily solve one of the biggest challenges of his new administration. But there were no further discussions on the issue of retirement.

Let it be said, finally, that Dr. Fiorentino had every right as the president to make a change in the athletics department, but to have executed that task with total disregard for the many contributions of Sharon Taylor was wrong. He could have negotiated a gentle departure for a long-time employee, and actually joined in the celebration of her retirement from Lock Haven University.

Chronology:

Craig Dean Willis 1982-2004
Keith T. Miller 2004-2010
Barbara Dixon (Interim) 2010-2011
Michael Fiorentino 2011-

Kathryn, Clarence and Sharon Taylor

Teenage Sharon Taylor in
AAGPBL-style softball
uniform

Sharon and Brother Geoff Taylor

Coach Taylor at Susquehanna University 1966-72

Sharon with Pat Bethea Bell, 4th grade
teacher and lifelong friend at 1996
Olympics in Atlanta

Taylor with Charlotte E. Smith

Taylor and Dr. Elizabeth K. Zimmerli

Mentor Bea Hallman introduced Taylor
to Lock Haven State in 1961 and
returned 35 years later for Taylor's
final National F.H. Championship.

Taylor with Diana Nyad

Taylor with Madeleine Albright

Taylor with Billie Jean King

1963 LHSC Field Hockey team -
Sharon Taylor in back row next to Coach Charlotte Smith.

First USFHA-AIAW National F. H. Championship in 1975. Current LHU
Coach Pat Rudy is shown in front row 5th from right. Smith (shown in top
photo), Taylor and Rudy are the only head coaches in Lock Haven's 70 years.

1st USWLA Div II Lacrosse Champions 1979

Last AIAW Div II National Champions in 1981

1982 NCAA Div. II National Champions

1992 NCAA Div. II National Champions

1989 NCAA Div. III National Champions

1994 NCAA Div. II National Champions

Coach Taylor's last team brings home the NCAA Div II Championship
with a perfect 21-0 record in 1995

Lock Haven University Marshal Sharon Taylor with
U.N. Ambassador Jeanne Kirkpatrick and President Craig Dean Willis

Honoring of the AIAW presidents by NACWAA at its Fall Convention
in St. Louis, in 2002 ... the 30th anniversary of both AIAW and Title IX (1972)
**Front, L to R:** Carole A. Oglesby, Carol Gordon, L Leotus Morrison,
N. Peggy Burke **Back, L to R:** Virginia Hunt, Donna A. Lopiano,
Christine H.B. Grant, Carole L. Mushier, Merrily Dean Baker, Charlotte West,
Judith R. Holland **Missing from the photo,** Laurie Mabry

Brock Parker wins another match for
Canton (PA) High School

Donna Lopiano – Past Director of
Athletics (U. of Texas), past president
AIAW, and founder and president of
Sports Management Resources

Diane Milutinovich – Former Associate
Athletics Director at Fresno State (CA)

Front Row: Diane Milutinovich, Lindy Vivas, Margie Wright
Back row: Linda Koch, Bernice "Bunny" Sandler, Sharon Taylor
National Women's Law Center Annual Dinner 2015

# Chapter Nine - Not the Only One

What makes the Sharon Taylor story noteworthy is not that she was the only woman to pay a price for advocating gender equality in athletics. Nor is it because she was the first. Others have suffered through similar struggles. Many had taken their turn before Taylor faced the "firing" squad. Her case certainly was not the most costly settlement or judgment rendered against an educational institution. Perhaps the payout from Lock Haven University represented one of the highest percentages of a school's annual athletics budget. But, no, her story is interesting because of the fact that, after 40 years, many school administrators still must learn the hard lessons of Title IX violations in a financially disastrous manner.

The law is quite clear and quite simple:

No person in the United States shall, on the basis of sex, be excluded from participation in, be denied the benefits of, or be subjected to discrimination under any education program or activity receiving federal financial assistance.

Title IX does not mention sports or athletics because its purpose is to provide for equality in all aspects of the educational process at every level, from kindergarten through graduate school.

University presidents, provosts, vice presidents, financial aid officers, admissions personnel, athletics directors and trustees should all be required to take a course called Title IX 101. One or two individuals holding strong beliefs in gender equality will not be enough if that attitude does not permeate the entire organization. Compliance issues commonly run into roadblocks before they reach the upper levels of a school administration. In some instances, the problem starts at the top and percolates down to athletics department leaders.

As a prime example of a university's failure to comply with the law, and compound that failure by later punishing the messenger, the case of Diane Milutinovich vs. The Board of Trustees of the California State University System illustrates the situation.

## Diane Milutinovich – Fresno State

Before proceeding with the events at Fresno State, a little history lesson is in order. In 1976, the state of California passed companion legislation to the Title IX statutes. Unlike the federal version of Title IX, the state specifically addressed intercollegiate sports. In 1993, the California National Organization for Women sued the California State University System for rampant violations of the state's gender equity laws.

**Sharon Taylor:** *After the passage of Title IX, a few states moved to support the statute with laws and legislative action of their own. I remember that the Florida legislature made specific grants to the University of Florida, Florida State University and other state institutions to secure the funding for intercollegiate athletics to permit those schools to move toward compliance. And, the California legislation was a signal of support for compliance coming from Sacramento.*

The result of the NOW lawsuit was a consent decree in 1996 that mandated specifically the percentage of women's participation in sports, the portion of expenditures going to women's teams, and the number of scholarships available to women. The California State University schools had until the 1998-1999 school year to come into compliance.

**Sharon Taylor:** *The Cal-NOW action, as it was known, should have been a lesson to other states that operated university systems; they were vulnerable targets if they didn't get their institutions into compliance with the law.*

Diane Milutinovich served as an Associate Athletics Director and Senior Woman Administrator for Fresno State, one of 23 campuses in the California State University System. She began her employment at Fresno State in 1979. She was promoted to Assistant Athletics Director/Senior Woman Administrator in 1983. In 1991 the title was changed to Associate Athletics Director/SWA.

167

In addition to supervising the men's and women's soccer, women's basketball, volleyball, wrestling, swimming and golf programs, she served as a Senior Woman Administrator (SWA). A generic NCAA job description for the position of SWA states:

The Senior Woman Administrator is responsible for assisting the university's intercollegiate athletics program and establishing policies and procedures that achieve the parallel goals of development of quality, competitive athletics teams and support of the individual education goals of female student-athletes. The Senior Woman Administrator assists in ensuring university compliance with applicable National Collegiate Athletic Association (NCAA), athletics conference, and university rules and regulations governing all facets of intercollegiate athletics programs. The individual serves as the sports administrator for women's sports programs and provides leadership with goal-setting, performance management, and budget planning and monitoring. [1]

Two particular itemized job functions stand out:

1. Acts as a key spokesperson for the needs and interests of women within the intercollegiate athletics department.

2. Keeps department of athletics informed of key information and/or changes relevant to Title IX

In essence, she was responsible for monitoring and reporting on the compliance with both federal and state gender equity requirements. To make her job more stressful, she performed under the microscope of the 1993 consent degree.

In October of 2001, Milutinovich met with interim Athletics Director Scott Johnson. She presented him with a handwritten memo outlining several Title IX problems. She advised him that grants-in-aid fell outside legal requirements. She also warned him that a pending NCAA decision would cost Fresno 11 female scholarships, a loss that would again put them out of compliance.

Continuing, she suggested that an upgrade to Tier One status was needed in three women's sports to stay within participation requirements. Next, she pointed out the disparity in travel arrangements between men's and women's sports.

She also informed Johnson that a men's basketball supervisor appeared to be retaliating against a female assistant for her support of women coaches advocating equal treatment.

Finally, she ticked off a half-dozen incidents where the media relations department provided less than adequate services to women's sports in contrast to the men.

Johnson, a former associate director like Milutinovich, must have felt like he just walked into a buzz saw. These problems could derail his prospects of ascending into the A.D.'s chair.

One month later, Milutinovich met with Jeannine Raymond, the vice president for administration and director of human resources, to discuss multiple problems. She complained that Paul Schechter, a former head trainer, received a higher salary than she, while doing a job for which he previously had no experience. Further, the position of director of football operations was not advertised before Schechter was selected. The situation created an increase in salaries for men's sports without a similar benefit to women's sports.

Two trainers were hired to replace Schechter. A women's head trainer was replaced with an assistant trainer. These moves represented two more compliance problems.

Milutinovich noted that the head softball coach had been made to comply with all of the university's policies and procedures in a similar scenario just two months earlier.

She also pointed out a disparity in which more men's coaches than women's were given university vehicles, despite her complaints to Scott Johnson.

Fresno State President John Welty officially hired Scott Johnson as the Director of Athletics on January 7, 2002. Milutinovich continued to apprise Johnson of current and pending Title IX problems during the early months of 2012. Obviously, he had to do something about these nagging compliance issues.

On April 16th, Johnson did just that. He summoned Milutinovich to his office. With Jeannine Raymond present, he informed Milutinovich that he was removing her from her position of associate athletics director and senior woman administrator. They told her that she had been terminated from her position due to budget cuts that required a reduction in personnel.

They demanded Milutinovich's keys and ID card and provided an escort to her office for the recovery of her personal belongings. She was forbidden to communicate with any other athletics department employees. The buzz saw was silenced. The Title IX problems would surely go away now.

Athletics department staff removed the uncollected personal items from Milutinovich's office. The items would be returned to her, she learned, when she accepted an alternate position at Fresno State, outside of the athletics department.

In the initial phase of the restructure, three new positions would be created. Milutinovich applied for two of them. The restructure was then "canceled." Her termination would stand. The athletics department ultimately retained other male administrators whose positions had been eliminated by the restructure. Only Milutinovich was left out in the cold. She ultimately negotiated a position as the Director of the University Student Union.

Following her dismissal, she had the right to meet with the president or his designee to appeal the decision. Welty sent a Vice President, Peter Smith, to the meeting. Milutinovich recalls the point in the conversation when they discussed the reasons for her firing. "Smith said, 'Well, it is spurious.' My witness at the meeting wrote that down. I couldn't believe it. He flat out said that."

In light of the shabby treatment she received from Fresno State, one might question Milutinovich's judgment in accepting the position with the student union. But she defends her decision: "I was 56 years old at the time. My family was in Fresno and my mother was elderly. I had to mitigate my damages. And, it was a good experience for me."

Surprisingly, Fresno put her back on the Gender Equity Monitoring Committee. She surmises they wanted to show that they really hadn't been discriminating against her. "I was still a thorn in their side," she confesses.

"It was not a tough decision for me to file a lawsuit. Nobody who really knows me thought I would not fight back." The toughest thing for her was finding an attorney in the Fresno area that did not have some ties to the University. The threat of conflict of interest made the search difficult.

**Sharon Taylor:** *No one could look at the Fresno State situation and be surprised that a lawsuit was filed. Diane Milutinovich was a strong woman who had been involved in intercollegiate athletics during the infancy of Title IX and under a governance structure of the AIAW (Association for Intercollegiate Athletics for Women) in pre-NCAA days. Women who came from those experiences knew what it meant to fight for an ideal and for equity, and they knew that they were expected to do so for the sake of girls and women in general.*

Milutinovich did file a sexual discrimination lawsuit in 2004 naming the following defendants: The Board of Trustees of the California State University (CSU), John Welty (President of Fresno State University), Jeannine Raymond (Human Resources at Fresno State) and Scott Johnson (Athletics Director at Fresno).

During the run up to the trial in 2006, Milutinovich's attorneys deposed President John Welty. Afterward, everything changed. "From that day on, my bosses at the student union changed the way they treated me. I kept telling my attorneys that they were about to fire me. My attorneys assured me that they wouldn't because they're not that stupid."

In 2006, Milutinovich's employment with Fresno State was severed completely. An amended complaint was filed with the Superior Court of California, County of Fresno Central Division. Said Milutinovich, "It was a blessing in disguise. It gave me enough time to prepare for my lawsuit as well as help with those of Lindy Vivas and Stacy Johnson-Klein."

The lawsuit alleged "Defendants ...engaged and continue to engage in practices which provide male student athletes with greater athletic opportunities than female student athletes at CSU, Fresno, in contravention of Title IX and thereby unlawfully discriminate against female student-athletes, their coaches, and programs." [2]

Why did Fresno University retaliate against Milutinovich? Why were they so determined to oust her from the athletics program? She believes, and asserted in her lawsuit, that they blame her as a whistleblower whose actions resulted in a Title IX compliance review by the Office for Civil Rights in 1995. The consequences of that review led to a corrective action plan that mandated specific requirements to be observed by CSU, Fresno.

Forced to leave the athletics department, Milutinovich could no longer speak up about Title IX violations that needed to be addressed. She pointed out that since her departure from athletics, expenditures on sports had increased by $3.4 million with 86% of it designated for men's sports.

In summation, Milutinovich claimed that, due to the defendants' conduct, she had "suffered harm, including lost earnings, loss of earning capacity, loss of professional status and reputation, loss of other employment benefits, humiliation, embarrassment and emotional distress."

Much like Sharon Taylor, Milutinovich distinguished herself with her efforts in gender equity and community relations. Very much like Lock Haven University, Fresno State should have been proud to have this kind of dedicated and decorated person representing their institution. She served as an executive committee member of the Western Athletic Conference Council. She initiated Fresno's celebration of National Girls and Women in Sports Day. She served as coordinator for "Kids Day" to benefit Valley Children's Hospital and was staff liaison for the Little Heroes Program where student-athletes were paired with patients at the children's hospital.

Milutinovich was one of two women to serve on the Fresno Athletic Hall of Fame Board of Directors. She is a member of the National Association of Collegiate Directors of Athletics (NACDA), the National Association of Collegiate Women Athletics Administrators (NACWAA), and a handful of NCAA committees. The NCAA honored her in 1991 for her contributions to softball and women's sports.

Instead of utilizing the talents, knowledge and connections of Milutinovich, Taylor, and others, certain university "leaders" seem to follow a perverse form of logic that calls for the removal of these employees. Why? Criticism from such people could be perceived to hold more water than that from a person with pedestrian credentials. Additionally, replacements can clearly view the danger in pushing too hard for gender equity lest they suffer the same fate as their predecessors.

The following Fresno State intra-net communication appeared in employees' mailboxes on October 11, 2007:

*You may read in upcoming media reports about a $3.5 million out-of-court settlement in the Milutinovich lawsuit. On Thursday, Oct. 11, the California State University did settle the case at that amount, which includes legal fees and associated legal costs. CSU believes that this positive resolution was the best course of action to benefit the community, the university, our students and the individual involved. With resolution of this matter, the university can put this past issue behind us to focus on the future. We've made great progress in gender equity. Fresno State will remain vigilant and continue to assure that we not only comply with the law but actually are leading the way. We pledge to continue to work with a sense of urgency and commitment to build on the progress we've made in gender equity over the past year.*

One year later, Fresno State settled another Title IX retaliation lawsuit with former volleyball coach Lindy Vivas and a sexual discrimination suit filed by former women's basketball coach Stacy Johnson-Klein. Also, in 2008, they settled with former men's basketball secretary, Iris Levesque, who claimed that she was fired for complaining about the hostile work environment in the basketball program.

So, what benchmark did Fresno State employ to justify the claim of great progress in gender equity? That is a hard question to answer. In a way, they did evolve into a leader in the fight for gender equity. They clearly led the nation in legal penalties. Counting an earlier settlement with former softball coach Margie Wright, Fresno State was on the hook for $16 million to clear litigation filed by women against the Fresno State athletics department. So onerous was the price tag that they negotiated for a payment plan on the Johnson-Klein settlement that stretched out over 25 years. [3]

**Lindy Vivas**

Lindy Vivas joined the Fresno State athletics department in 1991 as the head women's volleyball coach. She immediately encountered pushback when seeking equity for her program. After the Office for Civil Rights handed down a compliance order to Fresno in 1994, the atmosphere became even more toxic. Many of the male coaches and administrators took a very hostile attitude about the women's programs.

As the university gradually made concessions to the Title IX regulations, the animosity grew into a culture of resentment. As an example of that culture, Vivas sites an incident in which the athletics department hosted an "Ugly Women Athletes Day" lunch event.

Margie Wright, former softball coach, witnessed the luncheon that featured stick figures of female athletes with photos of male administrators' faces pasted on them. Wright also alleges that the members of the men's baseball team referred to her players as "dykes on spikes."

A Fresno trainer observed four administrators exchange high fives and smiles upon learning that Vivas' volleyball team had suffered a loss.

Lock Haven University had PLOW, Preserve the Legacy of Wrestling. Fresno State could have started an organization called PLOM, Preserve the Legacy of Misogyny.

Despite the lack of support and encouragement, Vivas was on her way to becoming the winningest volleyball coach in school history. She was honored three times as Western Athletic Conference Coach of the Year. Her Bulldogs appeared in the NCAA tournament and the National Invitational Volleyball Championship three times. She would finish her tenure with a career winning percentage of .612.

Vivas pressed the administration to elevate women's volleyball to a tier one status. Her request was refused repeatedly. She filed a complaint with OCR (Office of Civil Rights). She also agitated for long-term contracts for women coaches, a perk enjoyed by male coaches.

As Fresno State entered the new millennium, the OCR eased its pressure on the school to comply with Title IX sanctions. At that point, said Vivas, the school began to regress in compliance while the hostility against women's athletics escalated. In 2003, she asked A.D. Scott Johnson for a long-term contract. He denied her request and added performance clauses based on attendance, strength of schedule and tournament success. She became the only coach at the school with such requirements. She filed a grievance with the human resources department. [4]

In May of 2004, Vivas filed a complaint with the OCR citing retaliation. Seven months later she was fired for failing to meet the standards set forth in the performance clauses in her contract.

One month later, A.D. Scott Johnson announced the hiring of Ruben Nieves as head volleyball coach. Nieves had been the men's head volleyball coach at Stanford from 1991 to 2001. He led his team to a national championship in 1997.

In July of 2007, a jury agreed that Lindy Vivas lost her job because she spoke up loudly and frequently on behalf of women's rights as mandated by Title IX. They also agreed that she was discriminated against for her "perceived lesbian sexual orientation." [4a] The jury awarded her $5.85 million in damages. Fresno State promised to appeal. In 2008, Fresno withdrew the appeal and settled for $4.52 million to be paid out over 30 years.

The jury in any retaliation lawsuit must wade through a lot of contradictory evidence to find the truth. In some cases, employees have been terminated for real and legitimate reasons. In others, the causes for dismissal are spurious, yet difficult to prove. Jonathan Harr, in his non-fiction book A *Civil Action*, explains the challenge frequently put before a jury or judge with this profound observation: "The truth lies at the bottom of a bottomless pit." The Vivas jury had little trouble seeing to the bottom of the Fresno State pit. [5]

"Following the trial, attorney Dan Siegel approached the jurors to determine how they arrived at their decision. The five top Fresno officials who testified against Vivas displayed such a thorough lack of credibility that the jury began to refer to them as the "Fabulous Fibbing Five". John Welty, Scott Johnson, Human Resource Manager Jeannine Raymond and Provost Jeronima "Jeri" Echeverria were the four most prominent administrators to take the stand.

Echeverria's testimony provides the clearest window into the jury's perception of Fresno's mendacity on the stand. Vivas had gone to Echeverria out of desperation when she learned of her firing. The provost at Fresno has the responsibility for the athletics department. Vivas outlined in detail what had been transpiring.

Vivas appealed to her, "I have documentation. You have to do something about this. What did Echeverria say on the stand? She denied under oath knowing of any of the problems until my attorney presented 12 memos showing that she had been told. He walked each memo up to her and asked her if it contained her name and if she had been aware of the contents. She continued to deny everything until the fifth memorandum. She finally admitted that she did know what was going on in the athletics department."

"It's just amazing. Not only do they do their dirty work on campus, but they also lie in court to protect the university," said Vivas.

Vivas concludes, "The global takeaway is that they lied on the stand and the jury saw it."

## Stacy Johnson-Klein

Fresno State hired Johnson-Klein as head women's basketball coach in 2002. She had recently served as an assistant coach at Louisiana Tech. San Francisco Chronicle writer Ron Kroichick describes her as "attractive, charismatic and not averse to attention." Johnson-Klein hit the hardwood running, scoring endorsement deals and public billboards promoting herself as much as the team. She paced courtside in stylish outfits that highlighted her glamorous appearance. Her Bulldogs soon played in front of packed crowds. And they won games. It seemed that Fresno State had scored a slam-dunk with this hire.

The honeymoon ended when stories began to surface from the players citing abusive behavior by their coach. From minor complaints of the coach forcing players to carry her Luis Vuitton luggage, to walking out of a restaurant without paying for the players' meals, Johnson-Klein's behavior became more self-absorbed.

The line between rumor and fact soon became blurred. One story claimed that assistant coach Adrian Wiggins conspired with players to get her fired. Another had Johnson-Klein ordering the team bus to stop at a department store before continuing to a medical center with a sick player. [6]

Now it became Johnson-Klein's turn to complain to Scott Johnson that the women's team was not receiving equal treatment by the athletics department. On top of that, she complained of sexual harassment.

Then Johnson-Klein made a big mistake. In what she categorizes as a "poor decision," she requested and accepted a Vicodin from one of her athletes. Chantella Perera later testified that she gave her coach a half bottle of the painkiller, saying she couldn't say no to her coach.

Upon learning of this incident, the Fresno administration suspended her pending an investigation. Wiggins assumed the role of interim coach.

On March 2, 2005, Fresno President John D. Welty made this announcement:

*Today the university has notified Stacy Johnson-Klein of our intent to terminate her employment as head women's basketball coach at Fresno State. Johnson-Klein's termination is the result of findings made after a three-week administrative review into a series of allegations from team members and staff.*

The review confirmed that Johnson-Klein had inappropriately obtained pain medications from students and staff, engaged in deceptive and improper fiscal actions, lied, and was insubordinate. [7]

After disastrous and costly personnel decisions involving Milutinovich and Vivas, Fresno appeared to have a solid case against Johnson-Klein. She did not have a long and sustained history of advocacy of gender equality for which she had to forfeit her job. Fresno State felt that they were on terra firma with this firing. Then the administration took two very false steps that came back to haunt them in court.

The first poor decision was to hold a press conference and air all of the alleged dirty laundry in public. Mistake number two was the online posting of the 300-page report criticizing Johnson-Klein. She now had evidence of retaliation on the part of her erstwhile employer.

Johnson-Klein filed a lawsuit against the Board of Trustees of the California State University in 2007, claiming retaliation for her complaints of gender inequities and sexual harassment. During the eight-week trial, she described the hostile working environment in which her immediate supervisor made demeaning remarks about her appearance and clothing, and the athletics director sexually assaulted her and pressed her to spend time with him at his mountain cabin. Further, the press conference and online posting of the 300-page report crushed any chances for her to continue her coaching career.

The Fresno State administration presented a litany of wrongful acts on the part of Johnson-Klein. Her legal team presented Diane Milutinovich and Lindy Vivas to testify about the hostile conditions they experienced at Fresno. During one court session Johnson-Klein told the court how she had been groped, pawed, harassed, humiliated and patronized by athletics department officials. [8]

Diane Milutinovich was an early witness for Johnson-Klein. Milutinovich had earlier refused to allow a confidentiality clause in her settlement with Fresno State, hence allowing her to testify for Vivas and Johnson-Klein. When the lawyer for Fresno began his questioning, he asked her, "Miss Milutinovich, what did you think of Miss Johnson-Klein's attire?" The lawyer was looking to establish the fact that Johnson-Klein dressed in a provocative manner, compared to Milutinovich's conservative style.

Milutinovich recalls her response, "I never thought much about Miss Johnson-Klein's attire until they (the university) made a women's basketball poster where the athletes and coaches were on Harley motorcycles. The coaches wore leather vests with nothing underneath. I thought that was very inappropriate, but that poster hung outside President Welty's office for two years. Well, everybody in court started laughing. Welty put his head down and stared at his notes. The attorney couldn't scramble back to the table fast enough to find another question to ask me."

The defendant's effort to portray Johnson-Klein's appearance and demeanor as inappropriate backfired. The poster incident showed that Fresno State tried to promote the women's basketball team by using iconic sexual images: hot women perched on powerful masculine machines. The fact that the president of the university allowed the poster to be displayed in a prominent location suggested that the attitude went all the way to the top of the organization.

Athletics Director Scott Johnson emphatically denied grabbing Johnson-Klein's breast at a car wash or sexually propositioning her. Former athletics department secretary Doris Betancourt, described what she called an "obscene display of behavior" on the part of her boss, Scott Johnson. He and other staff members visited her hotel room on the road and viewed a pornographic movie. After the movie, the lights went out and Johnson had sex with a female co-worker in the bed next to her. The secretary feigned sleep and stayed quiet about the incident. [9]

The "Ugly Women Athletes" story was reprised for the jury of eleven women and one man.

The fate of the men's basketball coach was compared to that of Johnson- Klein. In the face of what turned out to be over 400 NCAA violations, and obstruction of a police investigation in a homicide case, Ray Lopes was allowed to resign and grab a $200,000 severance payment on the way out. [10]

The trial played out like a soap opera with both sides leaving the courtroom with sullied reputations.

On December 6, 2007, the jury deliberated only four hours before returning with their verdict. They unanimously found in favor of the plaintiff in the amounts of $634,254 for past economic damages, $4,440,419 for future economic damages, $3 million for past non-economic damages, and $11 million for future non-economic damages. [11]

The award amount was appealed and later settled for a total of $7.3 million spread over a 25-year period. Adding to that the damages from Milutinovich ($3.5 million), Vivas ($4.52 million), Wright ($605,000), and Levesque ($125,000), Fresno State will pay out $16 million for retaliation against female employees.

**Sharon Taylor:** *In one regard, the women employees at Fresno State were very fortunate: the administrators who were supposed to be running an institution of higher education were incredibly stupid...no other word describes their actions. They continued to blatantly disregard their obligations to equity and fairness and, in an environment already seething with recrimination for previous acts, they engaged in activities ranging from sophomoric to criminal--and all of it out in the open in front of soon-to-be-witnesses!*

Why Fresno State?

Lindy Vivas can pinpoint the beginning of the troubles at Fresno State. Following the OCR investigation in 1994, a lot of Title IX problems were uncovered. According to Vivas, Athletics Director Gary Cunningham told the male coaches that softball coach Margie Wright had filed the complaint that set off the investigation. That was not true, claims Vivas, "The placing of blame right off the bat on Margie as a female coach really accelerated the animosity. And it was a flat out lie."

The scope of the OCR complaint reached across five California schools, including San Diego State and Berkeley. The complaint could have been filed by any number of people across the California State University system.

Following Cunningham's accusation, the athletics department assembled the coaches to discuss the complaints. Vivas recalls, "There were a lot of meetings where the male and female coaches attended together. There was a tremendous amount of hostility against the female coaches; screaming and shouting and bashing Title IX and women (in general). It really could have gotten even more out of control, but Diane (Senior Woman Administrator, Milutinovich) told us, the female coaches, not to engage them further. 'Just don't,' she insisted."

"When he (Cunningham) told the men, 'She did this to all of us," it initially focused all of the hate on Margie. She took it on the chin in a lot ways. We all did eventually, but she was the lightning rod for a lot of resentment, not just among the men in the athletics department, but the boosters as well. Cunningham did little to stop or even tamp it down."

If Cunningham could be called the provocateur of the Fresno State uprising against women, then Scott Johnson, his successor, was the executioner. Editor Jim Boren opined, "If there is a hall of fame for sexual harassment, Scott Johnson has to be a first-ballot inductee." [12]

Although Johnson presided over the firing of Vivas, Milutinovich and Johnson-Klein, Vivas does not name him as the architect of the institutionalized misogyny. That honor goes to Fresno President John Welty. Vivas explains, "One reason is the person at the top always has control to dictate attitudes and culture. I didn't see any attempts to stop it. He operated very secretively. And he was a micro manager. Although he wasn't directly involved, I think he had his puppets out there. One of his puppets was the guy sitting in the A.D.'s office."

Diane Milutinovich agrees. "Why did things get so bad at Fresno? You look at the top. It was John Welty. He came in 1992 with an attitude toward women. His administrative strategy was to manipulate from behind the scenes and keep everything close to the vest. He thought that information was power and he didn't want to share it. I also believe that information is power, but I want to share it. I always gave my bosses all the information I had to keep them from going over the cliff. That was my management style. I gave them a lot of information on situations that weren't fair to women." She laughs before continuing. "For some reason they didn't like it and I don't know why."

**Sharon Taylor:** *Welty's departure from Indiana University of Pennsylvania in 1992 was just before their Title IX suit was resolved. He was part of the environment at IUP that resulted in success for the women student athletes in Favia (et. al.) v. Indiana University of Pennsylvania in 1993. So, he arrived at Fresno State "smarting" from what had just occurred at IUP.*

In the throes of a budget crunch in 1991, Welty and IUP made the decision to cut $350,000 from the budget of the athletics department. A.D. Frank Cignetti chose to eliminate four varsity sports, two men's and two women's teams. This seemed to be a fair plan on the surface, but the changes would throw the participation numbers of women way off the mark required by Title IX. Several students joined together and sued IUP, complaining that IUP's decision would cause them irreparable harm. [13]

The court found that while Cignetti had been making a sincere effort to balance men's and women's athletics, the elimination of women's gymnastics and field hockey would change the participation levels to 36% women and 64% men. The judge ordered IUP to reinstate the two teams and seek budget cuts elsewhere. For example, five members of the athletics department staff had golf memberships at the Indiana Country Club and several male coaches drove university-paid vehicles. [14]

The court also concluded that no irreparable harm would accrue to the plaintiffs if the teams were retained. [15]

By the time the case went to court, John Welty was gone and the new president had to deal with the fallout.

As for Scott Johnson, Vivas surmises that he was told by Welty to accelerate the mission to eliminate the three troublemakers, Wright, Milutinovich and Vivas. Stacy Johnson-Klein would later find her place in that target group. Vivas offers no documentation, but reports the rumor that the search committee formed to hire the new A.D. turned down Scott Johnson. Welty forced the issue and the avalanche of retaliation against women in the athletics department began in earnest.

Vivas continued, "We were the reason Scott Johnson was hired. Welty wanted him in there so he could fire everybody. He almost got away with it. He fired Diane. He fired me. He later fired Stacy Johnson-Klein. He was ready to fire Margie Wright when the Johnson-Klein lawsuit blew up in their face. That stopped the mission to get Margie out of there. She was the most successful softball coach in NCAA history. They had a hard time finding a credible reason to fire her, but I believe they were trying."

Stacy Johnson-Klein testified on Vivas' behalf in her court case. She informed the jury that Scott Johnson had plans to "get rid of lesbians in the athletics department." He preferred to hire women who were "straight and attractive."

Johnson-Klein testified further that Scott Johnson instructed other athletics department administrators to make life miserable for Lindy Vivas. Why? Because she was part of the group that Johnson referred to as the "other team," employees who made trouble. Diane Milutinovich and Margie Wright made up the remainder of the targeted threesome. [16]

Just as Lock Haven's new president, Michael Fiorentino, is thought to have carried out the will of the Council of Trustees to eliminate the "Sharon Taylor problem," so could Scott Johnson be seen as the instrument to help rid Fresno State of the cause of their Title IX troubles?

### Kathleen A. Bull vs. Ball State University

In 1988, Kathleen Bull accepted the position of head women's tennis coach at Ball State University in Muncie, Indiana. Court documents state that she had a "successful and celebrated career." She was also very verbal in her defense of Title IX and gender equality. She frequently reported incidents of unequal treatment of female coaches and student athletes.

Trouble began for Bull in 2006 when another female head coach lost her job. Like Bull, this coach advocated for the equality of female athletes. Assistant A.D. Patrick Quinn commented to another athletics staff member, "Kathy Bull should watch out or she will be 'next.'"

Bull's complaint to her boss resulted in no investigation of any kind. [17]

In 2008, the OCR (Office for Civil Rights) notified Ball State President Jo Ann Gora that an anonymous complaint had been filed with their office. One month later Bull received a negative performance review, her first such evaluation in her 20-year career at Ball State.

Bull "put two and two together" and quickly filed a complaint with the OCR citing the "she will be next" comment. Two months after that, she filed a second complaint based on her negative performance review and the athletics department's non-action on her recent discrimination complaints. [18]

In 2009, Bull composed a letter signed by eight other Ball State head coaches projecting serious Title IX consequences if the status quo remained in the athletics department. Three months later, she received a one-year renewal contract in which her performance was deemed "exemplary." Just as suddenly as she had fallen to a negative review, so did she now ascend to a very positive rating.

In September of 2009, Bull reported to her boss that she may have created an NCAA violation by holding a timed-run for her team prior to the official start of the tennis season. Bull ill advisedly asked three of her team members via text message if they would claim not to have "practiced" during the work out. Ball State administrators now had the ammo they needed to eliminate another Title IX pest. They reported the incident to the NCAA and filed a termination request through the president's office. [19]

Bull was accorded due process, a termination hearing before a committee with counsel. The committee interpreted the text messages as a request to "misrepresent practice activities." The committee recommended to President Gora that Bull be terminated. On Gora's further recommendation the Board of Trustees voted to fire Ms. Bull. She was terminated right in the middle of the 2009-2010 tennis season. She filed a retaliation case in July of 2010. [20]

Just as Fresno State shot themselves in the foot by publicly vilifying Stacy Johnson-Klein, Ball State erred by handing out a less forgiving punishment to Bull than to a pair of male coaches who committed alleged misdeeds. Both incidents took place during Gora's tenure.

Head baseball coach Greg Beals received a reprimand for an extra-marital affair. Basketball coach Ronny Thompson also received a reprimand for violating the same NCAA rule as Bull. Ball State later exonerated Thompson and apologized. Thompson quickly moved on and established a distinguished career in broadcasting.

Ball State attorneys filed a motion to dismiss the Kathy Bull case. Judge Jane Magnus-Stinson of the U.S. District Court Southern District of Indiana ruled in December of 2011, that Bull, indeed, had a prima facie case because she was able to demonstrate that the Ronny Thompson situation arose from similar violations but resulted in very different outcomes. Bull also noted in the suit that during a five-year period, 11 of 12 coaches of women's teams were fired or resigned. The judge did not agree that the Greg Beals case was comparable. The legal action could proceed. Ball State would have to prove that Bull was fired for reasons other than retaliation. [21]

In June of 2012, Ball State and Kathleen Bull settled the case with a $700,000 award. After the settlement, Bull stated, "Victories in retaliation lawsuits should send a message to administrators across the country. Our recent win is a victory for all women who advocate for gender equity." [22]

Yes, it was a win for gender equity, but it also signaled that many administrators had not learned a thing from the dozens of lawsuits that preceded it. The advocates for gender equity must be prepared to continue fighting a war with no end in sight.

**Sharon Taylor:** *I can't add much to that conclusion. Administrators that make these desperate decisions in such similar cases involving two coaches of opposite gender (1) certainly aren't paying attention to what is going on in the world around them, and (2) should be raising the question of whether they are fit to hold the positions that they do in institutions which purport to be places of learning and enclaves of fair treatment and safe environments.*

## Melissa Heinz vs. Winthrop University

If Kathleen Bull serves as a classic example of retaliation for gender equity advocacy, Melissa Heinz must be the "poster child" for egregious treatment at the hands of her A.D. and male counterpart. The environment at Winthrop, as described by Heinz, makes Fresno State look like a branch of the National Organization for Women. Some of the behaviors toward Heinz appear absolutely Third World in barefaced ferocity.

Winthrop University is located in Rock Hill, South Carolina, about 15 miles south-southwest of Charlotte, North Carolina. Heinz joined the coaching ranks of Winthrop in 2002 when she accepted the position of head women's soccer coach. She had previously held assistant coaching duties at Alabama, UAB, South Carolina, Clemson and Texas A&M. As a player, she earned Honorable Mention All-American in 1994 at William Carey University in Hattiesburg, Mississippi. Her strong credentials made her a perfect candidate to start a women's soccer program from scratch. [23]

By 2006, the women's soccer team had risen to the top of the Big South Conference, claiming the regular season crown and earning Heinz Coach of the Year honors. Her success did not come easily, however. From the very beginning, her program took a back seat to the men's program led by head coach Rich Posipanko. Her complaints to A.D. Tom Hickman went unheeded. As a recipient of federal financial support, Winthrop was under the mandate of Title IX regulations.

According to Heinz, by 2008, Winthrop was failing to comply with nine of the ten "laundry list" requirements for equal treatment of male and females athletes under Title IX. Despite the fact that the women's team had become a Division I entity, Posipanko's men held sway in scheduling and practice times, travel and per diem allowance, coaching assignments and compensation, facilities and equipment, medical and training services, publicity, support staff, and scholarships. [24]

The compensation disparity became a very hot issue. In 2009, Posipanko earned a base salary of $60,000, 27% more than Heinz. The additional income from soccer camps pushed his total earnings to around $90,000. Posipanko's camps included both men and women and reportedly earned $35,000 in 2008. University President Anthony DiGregorio refused to allow Heinz to run her own camps for women players. As a palliative gesture, Winthrop paid Heinz around 10% of the soccer camp profit, bringing her income into the $50,000 range, 44% less than her male counterpart. [25]

When Heinz approached Posipanko directly to complain of the inequities, she claimed that he responded with insults and verbal abuse.

She requested a meeting with Athletics Director Tom Hickman to discuss the harassment. On August 22, 2008, she met with Hickman and Posipanko. She brought up the camp issue and described the abusive behavior by Posipanko. [26]

Hickman turned to Posipanko and asked him if her accusations were true. He admitted as much, and insulted her again with "a bathroom expletive." Heinz then continued by relating sexual misconduct on the part of the soccer coach and his team on road trips. [27]

Hickman summed up the meeting by stating, "If these accusations continue, someone is going to get fired."

At the conclusion of the 2009 season someone did get fired. It wasn't the coach with the following rap sheet: allowed a bench-clearing brawl in conference championship game resulting in a forfeit; suspended by the Big South Conference for a game; received a conference reprimand for unsportsmanlike conduct; handed multiple red and yellow cards during games; and led the 2005 team that received 90 game suspensions for party misconduct, bringing national attention to the university. No, the fired coach was Melissa Heinz. When she asked Hickman why, he said, "I can't explain it. And I don't have to tell you the reason." [28]

Winthrop did not renew her contract going into the 2010 season. Hickman thanked Heinz for getting the women's soccer program started, but told USA today that it was time for a change. [29]

Heinz began a job search and interviewed for several openings, but she was not getting offers. During the interviews, she could not explain the exact reasons for her dismissal at Winthrop. She could sense that interviewers were uncomfortable about her inability to answer that question. Heinz recognized the unspoken suspicion that Winthrop had eliminated a malcontent or troublemaker from their coaching ranks.

"I really didn't feel like I was complaining. I was just asking for some help. I don't feel I'm a troublemaker. When your program is new, you're not going to get everything right away. I worked very hard to fundraise and find other ways to get our program up to where it should be. But when the program began to grow, and things didn't change I began to understand it wasn't going to. At that point you complain or keep pressing forward. I did a little of both."

With no job and diminishing optimism to find another position, she decided to go to court. She decided to file the lawsuit before landing the Valdosta position. "I just felt that things were unfair. I didn't want it to continue for anyone else. Nothing was going to change about my position, clearly. If I did something wrong it would be justification. But I didn't do anything wrong"

I'm sure that people think that when you sue (your school) that you are a troublemaker. But that wasn't the case. I was more of a problem solver. I gave them the solutions.

In November of 2010, Heinz filed her lawsuit claiming that she was fired as a "direct consequence of her complaints to Winthrop about inequitable treatment of her program, which came to a head in 2008 and 2009." She further asserts that Rich Posipanko pressured A.D. Hickman to fire her due to her complaints about inequities and his conduct toward her. [30]

Heinz claimed that Winthrop retaliated against her for complaints that the university failed to comply with Title IX regulations as they related to the women's soccer team, sexual harassment and a hostile work environment brought on by Richard Posipanko. Posipanko regularly heaped abuse on her by calling her "shit," "crap," "moron," and "idiot." He often concluded with "because you are a woman." [31]

Winthrop's retaliation extended beyond Heinz's employment at the school. She interviewed with several other Division I schools but did not receive an offer. Hickman's refusal to cite a reason for her dismissal severely handicapped her when she was asked the reason for her termination.

During Heinz's tenure, Hickman got rid of four female coaches; three were fired and the fourth pressured to resign. Two were replaced by men. At one point, Heinz was the only female head coach among 13 male coaches. The vast majority of assistants were men, as well. This seemed odd in a school that began as a women's college and still had a predominantly female student body.

Her lawyers wanted her to go to trial. She says they described the case as a "no brainer." Heinz felt differently. Her research demonstrated that judges and juries in the South were reluctant to favor young females railing against the male establishment. When Winthrop offered a settlement that included a positive recommendation and a non-toxic explanation of their decision not to renew her contract, she accepted the offer.

At this time, the Winthrop University website proudly displays a news event announcing a settlement in the lawsuit filed by former soccer coach Melissa Heinz. The webpage states that Heinz received a cash amount of $35,000 and a reference letter. The statement further reports that the money is being paid by their insurance reserve fund. Winthrop admitted no liability in the case. University President Anthony DiGregorio said in the release, "I am pleased that no wrongdoing was established in this lawsuit. We understand and respect that for business reasons, insurance companies sometimes have to settle lawsuits." [32]

When asked to comment on the arrogant tone of the Winthrop statement, Heinz laughed and said, "I know. I know. That was a good jab." She went on to add that another clause in the settlement required a pledge by Winthrop that they would look into Title IX problems and do better in that area.

A man, Spencer Smith, currently coaches the women's soccer team. Both assistant coaches are male, as well.

What a painful irony it would be to learn that women's athletics at Winthrop University could only progress when men coach the teams.

# Chapter Ten – Worse Than Fresno State?

In 2008, Florida Gulf Coast University joined the list of schools in legal hot water over gender equity issues. Although FGCU trailed Fresno State in the number of lawsuits, they quickly became a "player." The Ft. Myers, Florida school appeared in a doubleheader of sorts when the women's volleyball coach and the women's golf coach filed as co-plaintiffs in a court action claiming retaliation under Title IX as well as defamation.

Plaintiff number one was former Head Volleyball Coach Jaye Flood, who brought over 20 years of coaching experience to Florida Gulf Coast when they hired her in 2003. She quickly compiled the best won-lost performance in the school's history and was named Atlantic Sun Conference Coach of the Year for the 2007-2008 season. Her team won the ASC title with a 23-3 record. FGCU rewarded her with the decision not to renew her contract the following year. In other words, they fired her. What could cause such a disconnect?

Flood played volleyball for Central Michigan University while Fran Koenig served as director of women's athletics. Flood received one of the first scholarships ever bestowed on a female athlete. Koenig, who later became very active within the AIAW structure, created an environment that was very conducive to the growth of her women student athletes. Said Flood, "We had a pretty good experience there as female athletes."

After graduation, Flood accepted the position of assistant volleyball coach at Elmhurst College in Elmhurst, Illinois. She was promoted to head coach and led the Division III Blue Jays to a national championship and one runner-up finish. Flood recalls, "My A.D. was excellent and I got along very well with him."

After her family moved to the Naples area, she followed them and quickly put her volleyball coaching and playing knowledge to work by launching a successful junior volleyball program.

A newly created university soon began to expand its athletics department. A head coach would be needed to start a varsity volleyball program. The parent of one of her junior volleyball players was an FGCU trustee and lobbied for her to be interviewed. She may not have been A.D. Carl McAloose's first choice, but her credentials were impeccable.

When she accepted the head volleyball coaching position at Florida Gulf Coast University in 2003, she may have been somewhat naïve to expect the level of support she had enjoyed at Central Michigan and Elmhurst.

Coach Flood wanted to elevate her program to the same status enjoyed by the men's programs at FGCU. She succeeded in moving her program from Division II up to Division I.

According to her lawsuit, she requested a better marketing program, locker room upgrades such as hot water and an end to pooled donations. Even when volleyball boosters earmarked gifts for the women's team, A.D. Carl McAloose funneled the money into a general fund. Another sore point for Flood was the multi-year contracts provided to the male coaches while the women had to re-sign a new contract each year. [1]

She sought a second assistant coach to help prepare the team for its foray into Division I competition. Another request concerned revenue guarantees for visiting schools to motivate the better teams to schedule visits to FGCU. [2]

One by one, all of her requests were denied or ignored, despite the fact that men's programs enjoyed such resources. Finally, Flood issued a request that she believes constituted the proverbial straw that broke the camel's back. She wanted to budget a raise for her assistant coach. The salary for the assistant was so low that Flood had to supplement the assistant's income with money from her non-university junior volleyball program in order to raise her above the poverty level. In this case, the camel was A.D. McAloose, and the result was a decision that Flood had to go.

According to Flood, McAloose would frequently call her into his office, but not to discuss her requests for program upgrades. Flood explains, "He would ask me, 'Do you like it here?' He was trying to goad me into saying I didn't like it (at FGCU). I would always answer that I love my players and I love the program."

Plaintiff number two was former Head Women's Golf Coach Holly Vaughn. Vaughn came to FGCU in 2000, tasked with the mission of building a women's golf program. She graduated from Mercersburg Academy (PA) in 1980 where she was the only female on the golf team. She starred at Southern Methodist University and joined the Futures Tour right after graduation. She advanced to the LPGA Tour in 1988. The pinnacle of her professional career occurred at the U.S. Women's Open in 1994 where she turned in a sub-par round. A shoulder injury cut short her Vaughn's career as a tour golfer. [3]

In Vaughn's first year at FGCU the team captured first place in three of the eight tournaments they entered. After four years, the women golfers had 11 tournament victories and rose as high as third in the country in Division II. Despite her early success, the program remained in the shadow of men's athletics.

One of the first discrepancies she noticed was that men's assistant coaches were offered additional duties to elevate them to full-time status. Women's assistants did not receive similar opportunities.

Men's assistant coaches had their own offices, while women's head coaches did not. When Vaughn raised this issue with A. D. McAloose, his response was, "If you don't like it, you can get the hell out." Vaughn felt threatened and intimidated. In 2006, McAloose escalated his harassment when he moved Vaughn out of the Alico Arena and into an outdoor trailer that she shared with several other staff members and a construction crew. [4]

By May of 2007, it was abundantly clear that gender equity was not a priority of Carl McAloose. Title IX compliance would not be allowed to complicate the difficult job of managing a university athletics department. Flood and Vaughn decided to try another tack. They decided to seek an ally to help present their case directly to Interim President Richard Pegnetter. Joining forces with two other women's coaches, they enlisted the services of former Interim Athletics Director Merrily Baker.

Why had they chosen Baker as an ally? FGCU's first president, Roy McTarnaghan, had called Merrily Dean Baker out of retirement to initiate the university's athletics program. Her credentials were formidable. She had been the Director of Women's Athletics at Princeton University after the Ivy League school went co-ed. She served in that capacity from 1970- 1982. She held the same position at the University of Minnesota from 1982-1988. She moved to Kansas City in 1988 to become the Assistant Executive Director of the NCAA.

In 1992, Michigan State tapped her to be the Director of Intercollegiate Athletics. She then held authority over all programs, both men and women's teams. She was a great choice to launch FGCU's athletics programs, and a perfect mentor for Jaye Flood, Holly Vaughn and the two assistant coaches. Baker was accomplished, knowledgeable, and obviously highly regarded by Florida Gulf Coast University.

According to newspaper reports, the four female coaches sent a letter to Baker outlining the Title IX violations and shabby treatment they had suffered. Baker was credited with summarizing the complaints and forwarding them to Interim President Richard Pegnetter. [5]

The media reports and court documents tend to characterize Merrily Dean Baker as a "casual" player in the Flood/Vaughn case. There is, however, much more to this story. Merrily Baker played a much larger role than most people realize.

Here is the back-story in Baker's words:

"This was a very odd situation. I was giving a speech to the Naples Women's Bar Association. It was a luncheon in Naples. When I arrived, I was told that (all four) of the female coaches from FGCU were there and they wanted to sit at a table with me. So that is where they seated me. I was meeting three of these women for the first time. After the speech, the women asked if they could talk to me and I said, 'Sure.' We went outside and had a half-hour conversation. I was absolutely appalled at what they were telling me; the issues and realities they were dealing with. They asked me if I could help them. I told them I could but we needed to talk more specifics. I said, 'Let's arrange a time next week.' Then they began to leave in four different cars. I said, 'I don't understand. You didn't come together?' They said, 'Oh, no, if they (FGCU) knew we were coming to hear you speak, we would have been fired.' When they called to arrange another meeting we held it at a very remote restaurant. They drove in four separate cars again so no one could trace that they were coming."

Later in the evening, after Baker's speech to the Women's Bar Association, she received a call from Jaye Flood. Flood told Baker that she needed to discuss something with her. Out of respect to Baker, she did not want to put her in a bad position. Flood told her, "I'm gay, and if you don't want to help me, that's okay." Baker assured her that her sexual orientation would make no difference, unless she was already being harassed because of it. Since Flood had not experienced any negative consequences to date, Baker repeated that she would help all of the women.

Baker met with the women three or four times, allowing them to pour out what they were experiencing. From these meetings, the so-called Baker letter was composed. She tried to research the validity of their claims as best she could from an outsider's position. Baker had made it clear to the women that her approach was simply to represent them in communicating with the university, and attempting to bring all parties to the table. This was not to be a formal Title IX complaint. The Office for Civil Rights would not be involved. Baker only wanted to alert Interim President Pegnetter that some issues in the athletics department needed to be addressed.

Baker recalls what happened next:

"Now, much to my shock and surprise, and to the shock and surprise of the women coaches, they went ballistic when they received the letter. They went into instant denial that any problems existed. They pegged me as a troublemaker, and immediately began retaliating against the coaches in very real and substantive ways. I worked with them to get through the initial accusations. The university was hell bent on destroying both of them."

The "Baker letter" would set off a chain of events that would change the lives of several people. President Pegnetter soon distributed an email throughout the campus reporting the allegations set forth in Baker's letter. He made two very curious contradictory statements. First, he announced that an internal investigation would be forthcoming. Then he declared that the Title IX allegations were "unsubstantiated." The result of the internal audit would not be hard to predict.

To no one's surprise, the audit of alleged Title IX violations, announced in July of 2007, cleared FGCU of any failures to comply.

Jaye Flood's subtle warning to Baker about the consequences of helping a gay woman, proved to be sadly accurate. In Baker's words:

"As soon as the retaliations started, they (FGCU) went after her sexual orientation where they hadn't done it before. It was brutal. I don't know how she got through it emotionally. Her parents lived in town (Naples), as did her brothers, nieces and nephews. The university was absolutely brutal to her, openly, and in the press."

In August of 2007, Wilson G. Bradshaw became the third-ever president of FGCU.

In September, both Flood and Vaughn filed official complaints through the university's grievance system citing inequity and discrimination. Both alleged that FGCU discriminated against them on the basis of their sex and retaliated against them for their efforts to seek gender equity in the athletics department.

How can an athletics director rid his school of a successful, pain-in-the-ass coach? The athletics director's standard playbook features two very important moves. First, performance reviews must be quickly executed, highlighting the failures of said coach. The team's winning record must not be allowed to influence the evaluation. After the Baker letter, Flood's performance was rated as "below expectations." She was put on probation as a result. Vaughn fared slightly better, receiving a grade of "marginally meets expectations." Her previous review categorized her performance as "outstanding."

Court documents claim that coaches who did not press for gender equity were not evaluated in the same categories, such as NCAA rules observance, travel authorization paperwork, and subjective areas such as social and communication skills.

According to Brad Kane of the Naples News, Associate A.D. Kathy Peterson told an investigator that "she would find it hard to give Flood a good evaluation because she didn't like the volleyball coach." [6] That may have been a misguided attempt to deflect any possible suggestions of Title IX retaliation. After meeting with her boss, Peterson explained to the investigator the next day that "she didn't mean to imply she gave Flood a bad evaluation because she didn't like her." [7]

The next step in the playbook requires that an act of moral turpitude must be discovered or invented. A particularly effective accusation involves a student or student athlete. In the case of Stacy Johnson-Klein at Fresno, it was borrowing a controlled substance from a team member. In the case of Jaye Flood, she was accused of inappropriate behavior toward an athlete.

In October of 2007, she was placed on administrative leave because of "issues involving student welfare." Her leave was made effective prior to anyone from the administration speaking to the victimized student or the assistant coach who was said to have witnessed the inappropriate act. The exact nature of her alleged offense was not revealed to Flood. She later learned that she had inappropriately tugged on the jersey of a volleyball player during a practice game.

One ploy that should definitely be avoided is to release personnel records to the public, either directly or through the media. Fresno State made that mistake with Stacy Johnson-Klein, first with a press release, then by posting a 300-page report on the school web site. FGCU made the same error by releasing Jaye Flood's personnel file to the media, including the "facts" behind the negative performance review. Even if the contents of the file were factual and accurate, the act of subjecting the employee to public humiliation hints strongly at retaliation. If the employee can credibly refute the charges, the university has literally handed prima facie evidence to a prospective legal team.

Newly minted president Wilson Bradshaw apparently concluded that the first audit of potential Title IX violations had not looked deeply enough into the matter. Public opinion ran strongly against Pegnetter's quick report absolving FGCU of any wrongdoing. Accordingly, he hired an outside law firm to study the allegations. FGCU chose the firm of Littler Mendelson to perform the investigation. Littler Mendelson enjoys a reputation as one of the largest and most respected firms dealing with employment and labor law. They assigned attorney Robert Clayton the case.

Clayton soon became involved in the Flood investigation. He eventually informed Flood that if she issued an apology to the volleyball team everyone would be happy. Flood refused.

Perhaps because the uniform tugging incident may not have carried enough gravitas, two more investigations were launched to look into Flood's activities. Both inquiries dealt with potential violations of school policies. Clayton continued to be involved. He notified Flood of the impending investigations but refused to indicate what activities she may have engaged in and what policies may have been violated. [8]

Flood eventually learned that investigation number two involved an incident during a road trip. Flood explains, "I had an old friend of mine visit me at the hotel while I was doing laundry. She was sitting in my room and we were chitchatting. I had my leg up, icing my bum knee on the couch.

Apparently one of my players thought that was a little too cozy. So that was brought to the attention (of Carl McAloose or Kathy Peterson)."

The third investigation involved the so-called inappropriate relationship. A non-playing staffer made the accusation after being dismissed from the team. For the first time, Flood publically describes the story:

"The point is, I've never made it a secret that I'm gay. If they had asked me I would have told them. I didn't go volunteering that. I'm actually married now. I was dating someone and they (FGCU) tried to pin this inappropriate relationship on me. I was prepared to defend myself. (The student) basically lied, was very deceitful and very disruptive. She was so disruptive to my program that I dismissed her, and she didn't like that. She came forward after I was suspended (for the shirt-tugging incident) and tried to put salt in the wound. (FGCU) said I abused her time as a student. She was a volunteer, so I didn't pay her because it wasn't a paid position. She claimed she had an internship through the business department but I (obtained) a letter from the business department (stating) that she never had set up an internship."

Flood has declined to identify the young woman. Merrily Baker has likewise opted to not reveal her name because the woman was dealing with psychological and emotional problems. According to Baker, "Her emotional instability makes it difficult and risky to reach out to her."

The young woman allegedly later recanted her accusations to friends of Flood, but no corroborative evidence has been presented to confirm this. Flood, herself, claims no knowledge of such an event.

Also in October of 2007, Holly Vaughn threw in the towel and resigned. When she handed her resignation to Carl McAloose, he allegedly replied, "Good." [9] Jaye Flood decided to soldier on.

On November 14, 2007, the Atlantic Sun Conference named Jaye Flood Coach of the Year. FGCU made no public mention of the award. Flood was not permitted to participate in a program honoring the team.

About two weeks later, Robert Clayton gave Flood a heads-up. Her contract for the next year would not be renewed. This decision had been made prior to the completion of the investigation against her, and prior to Flood even receiving the courtesy of an interview to discuss her alleged transgressions.

In January of 2008, President Bradshaw announced Flood would not be returning to coach the 2008 season. He then released on the university web site the results of three investigative reports for public consumption. He also announced that the latest inquiry into Title IX violation found no difference between resources allotted to women and those to men. Most athletics directors would admit that even in a university program truly dedicated to gender equity, a few disparities will occur from time to time. FGCU, however, was 100% in compliance, according to the Littler Mendelson report.

The Littler Mendelson report also found that there was no wrongdoing by Flood in the shirt-tugging incident. More importantly, Clayton's investigation determined that the two performance evaluations given to Flood and Vaughn were problematic. As a result, Carl McAloose and Associate A.D. Kathy Peterson received letters of reprimand in their personnel file. Clayton did not agree that the reason for the negative evaluations was due to Title IX retaliation. The evaluations were simply not supported by any evidence. Missing from the report was an explanation for creating negative reviews with no justification. [10]

Peterson previously worked in the admissions department prior to her promotion as Senior Woman Administrator in the athletics department. Said Vaughn, "She had no prior athletics experience as a player, coach or administrator. Women's golf was under her umbrella. She never once attended a practice, meeting or tournament while I was coaching, until after the Baker letter. She and Carl both admittedly falsified my annual evaluation during this turmoil. All of my previous evaluations were graded 'outstanding'. They (Peterson and McAloose) were quietly reprimanded and given a slap on the wrist."

One might speculate that Kathy Peterson would display some empathy for the plight of women trying to advocate for the rights of FGCU's female student athletes. She was, however, just as aggressive as the males in pursuing punishments for Flood and Vaughn.

How can one explain Kathy Peterson's zeal in going after the female coaches? Merrily Baker has no problem analyzing the Peterson situation. She explains, "She had never been in, and knew nothing about, athletics. Carl (McAloose) brought her in because he was dating her. She was working in another department at the university. He brought her in (to athletics) and made her senior woman administrator, which ostensibly is the second highest-ranking person in charge of the athletics department. She didn't know the first thing about Title IX. She had no background, no training and no preparation. Of course, that frustrated the coaches.

Finally, the Littler Mendelson report stated that FGCU fired Jaye Flood because of an "amorous" relationship with a student intern, the third of the three investigations launched into Jaye Flood's alleged misadventures involving "student welfare." Flood denies the accusation, stating that this was one more attempt to "manufacture grounds for her removal." [10a]

The first and second charges were dropped because the student in the shirt-tugging case was not offended, and the incident that occurred in the hotel room did not involve a student.

In the meantime, the local media had a field day with the Flood story. The university reported initially that her suspension was related to "student welfare" issues. Subsequent newspaper and Internet articles in the Naples Daily News and NaplesPress.com soon began to report that Flood was being investigated for an "inappropriate relationship." Dana Caldwell, who, according to Merrily Baker, seemed to be on a mission to destroy Jaye Flood, wrote most of these articles. When asked to explain why Caldwell took a particular interest in her, Flood explained, "Caldwell played poker with Carl McAloose and they were big buddies. Every article he wrote hammered the hell out of me. He was very biased."

On January 22, 2008, the Naples Daily News reported: *SPIKED: FGCU volleyball coach fired for having inappropriate relationship with student.* A high school newspaper writer could have immediately pointed out the missing word "alleged." Four years later the online version of the story began to display an editor's note: "This article was edited on July 18, 2012 to correct that Jaye Flood allegedly had an inappropriate relationship with a student, not a student-athlete." [11]

The article then paraphrased President Wilson Bradshaw's accusation that Flood violated FGCU's rules against sexual harassment. [12]

The public never heard Jaye Flood's side of the story. Not wanting to throw gasoline on the fire, she refused to speak to the press, even when they "door-stepped" her. "I never talked to the press. Never. They used to show up at my door but I never made a comment. So my story never came out. Oh, well."

Flood feels that the other local news outlet, the Ft. Meyers News-Press, has been fair to her. She deems their coverage of her as "excellent."

Following the onslaught of accusations against Flood, Baker recommended that she and Vaughn needed to seek legal counsel. The situation had flamed out of control and had grown beyond Baker's ability to be of assistance. After the coaches met several times with a women's law center, Public Justice agreed to take on the case pro bono.

Jaye Flood filed her lawsuit on January 18, 2008. In May, Holly Vaughn joined the complaint as a co-plaintiff. Each plaintiff cited two counts, retaliation in violation of Title IX and defamation. Merrily Baker recalls that FGCU, to her astonishment, would not admit any culpability in Title IX violations. Said Baker, "They finally had a state attorney tell them that they had better settle (the case) or they will be looking at $18 million awards or settlements."

The decision to file the lawsuit was not a difficult one for Jaye Flood. Said Flood, "I figured I was going to lose my job anyway."

The case eventually went into mediation and a settlement was reached on October 10, 2008. Florida Gulf Coast University would pay a total of $3,400,000 to Flood and Vaughn in two installments. [13]

The first installment provided $1,965,000 to a trust for Flood and $435,000 to a trust for Vaughn. [14]

The second installment provided for $480,000 to a trust for Flood and $20,000 to a trust for Vaughn. Additionally, Flood received another $500,000 to fund a monthly payment of $4,859.44 for the rest of Jaye Flood's life. [15]

Because Flood suffered the greater retaliation, including termination, she received the greater payout of $2,945,000 compared to Vaughn's $455,000.

FGCU also agreed to complete a Title IX compliance review to be handled by an independent expert agreed upon by the court. The court suggested that the Baker letter should be used as a starting point in the review. [16]

Finally, the defendants got to state officially that they did not admit to any wrongdoing. The plaintiffs retained the right to claim that FGCU's actions violated Title IX laws pertaining to retaliation. [17]

The court settlement gave both plaintiffs and defendants the right to hold a press conference to discuss the results of the settlement. Flood and Vaughn wasted no time. Flood began, "This was all part of a witch hunt that was launched on me after I was put on administrative leave. All the allegations are unfounded."

Vaughn revealed that she labored over the decision to join the lawsuit, but believed she did the right thing. She said that she missed coaching and wanted to get involved in it again. [18]

As Flood and Vaughn looked out at the attendees, they saw no one from the FGCU administration, no one from the athletics department. They did, however, see Dana Caldwell. Flood remembers well Caldwell's first question: "He asked me if he could borrow some money from me."

Flood characterized Caldwell's attitude following the settlement as "snarky." The beginning of his article reporting the settlement tends to bear her out: "Two former Florida Gulf Coast University coaches received $3.4 million to settle a federal discrimination lawsuit against the university. This, however, didn't keep them quiet during a press conference Wednesday held at the Holiday Inn Historic District in downtown Fort Meyers." [19]

When FGCU President Wilson Bradshaw had his turn in front of a microphone, he recited language from the court settlement document: "By entering into this settlement agreement, defendants do not admit any wrongdoing." He stated further that no foundation or booster funds would be spent paying the settlement. Insurance would handle "some of it." [20]

In response, Merrily Dean Baker, the author of the Baker letter, said, "Why would you give up $3.4 million? I know the university broke laws." [21]

Two days after FGCU announced the settlement, Carl McAloose resigned his position in protest. When she was asked about this, Flood laughed softly and replied, "You don't really believe that do you? I don't think anybody I ever talked to really thought he resigned in protest. I think the administration obviously felt that he needed to leave.

McAloose later assumed the role of CEO of Athletics Staffing and Consulting. In 2012, he accepted the position of athletics director at Clayton State University in Morrow, Georgia. [22] On February 14, 2014, he was announced as the new athletics director at Edison State College in Ft. Myers. [23]

Just when it appeared that Florida Gulf Coast University could not keep up with the pace of discrimination and retaliation cases established by Fresno State, former FGCU general council Wendy Morris filed her lawsuit. Morris claimed that Interim President Richard Pegnetter conspired with an assistant to obstruct the investigation of discrimination set forth in the Baker letter by creating a false report and retaliating against the female coaches who authored the Baker letter. [24]

Morris, at first, was not apprised of the Baker letter. When she learned about the charges and Pegnetter's response, she complained to him and was subsequently fired with 60-day notice. [25] FGCU settled with Morris in 2008 for $800,000. [26]

In June of 2009, the former provost at FGCU filed a lawsuit of her own alleging that she was the victim of a hostile environment created by former President William Merwin. He allegedly made degrading and inappropriate comments to then Provost Bonnie Yegidis, including the statement that she displayed "too much boob." [27]

After Merwin's resignation, Yegidis repeatedly informed FGCU officials that the firing of Morris was legal quicksand. When Wilson Bradshaw took over the presidency in the fall of 2007, he spoke on the phone with Yegidis who warned him that the Title IX investigation of the athletics department was a 'whitewash'." [28]

Shortly after he settled into the job, Wilson met with Yegidis and asked for her resignation. She responded by telling Bradshaw that she was being punished for her advocacy of gender equity. According to Yegidis' court filing, Bradshaw told her she had to be "out by Friday." [29]

In February of 2011, a jury found for the defendant, Florida Gulf Coast University.

The Flood/Vaughn settlement called for a gender equity assessment of Florida Gulf Coast University to be performed by an outside expert. The court reserved the right to select the individual to conduct that audit.

Public Justice attorney Linda Correa suggested the name Dr. Christine H. B. Grant. Dr. Grant was born, raised and educated in Scotland. She taught school in the U.K. for six years before immigrating to Canada where she coached field hockey at the collegiate level for a decade before moving on to the University of Iowa to earn a Ph.D. in physical education. She became the Director of the Women's Athletics at the University of Iowa in 1973 and held the post until she retired in 2000.

She testified before Congress in support of Title IX. She has written, spoken and testified in court about gender equity many times. She served as the ninth president of the Association for Intercollegiate Athletics for Women (AIAW).

To no one's surprise, the court selected her to perform the assessment.

On July 21, 2009, she released a 30-page report. Dr. Grant's executive summary took many people by surprise. Grant wrote, "Overall the institution is to be commended for being in compliance with Title IX in most areas. Rather than discriminating against female student athletes in the allocation of athletic scholarships, the institution has been overly generous to women. In the second major area, that of participation, the FGCU is in compliance with Prong 1. Women are being provided equal opportunity to participate in intercollegiate athletics at FGCU. The lack of uniform and consistent policies in the third area has inadvertently caused some discrepancies in the treatment of male and female student-athletes. With the creation and implementation of such policies, the disparities should disappear."[30]

What are the implications of this report?

Following Carl McAloose's departure, Associate Director of Athletics Jo-Ann E. Nester was chosen to guide the athletics department on an interim basis. She had previously served as Senior Woman

Administrator at San Diego State. Kathy Peterson was retained as FGCU's Senior Woman Administrator.

McAloose's successor, Ken Kavanaugh, took over in June of 2009, just one month prior to the release of Grant's report. Kavanaugh had virtually no time to effect any major changes in policy. Did the interim staff right the ship in eighteen months?

The first thought is that FGCU might not have been greatly out of compliance leading up to the culmination of the Jaye Flood termination. Perhaps Carl McAloose had not left the athletics department in defiant violation of Title IX regulations.

One person who was not surprised by the Grant report was Merrily Baker. She categorized FGCU's response to the Baker letter and Flood/Vaughn settlement as a "classic cover-up/clean-up" pattern. Over a two-year period they quietly cleaned up all, or most, of the problems while employing a diversionary tactic of attacking the messengers.

As the Grant report continues, the kind of issues that bothered Flood and Vaughn appear to remain unresolved. Coaching salaries/contracts, travel expenses, uniform allowances, and practice time/facility issues appear as areas still in need of attention. Grant issued recommendations to rectify these imbalances.

On page 26 of Grant's report, she lists the results of a coaches' survey. The question involves the commitment of the athletics department to gender equity. Survey responses were broken down into Strongly Agree, Agree, and Neutral. There was no choice for Disagree or Strongly Disagree. The men coaches answered 83% for Strongly Agree and 17% Neutral. The women's coaches posted just 38% for Strongly Agree, 50% Agree and 12% Neutral.

How, then, does one reconcile the Grant report with the Baker letter? One possible answer is that the women's teams coached by males probably received more resources than teams coached by females. The compliance issues suggested to Richard Pegnetter by Merrily Baker following her meetings with the female coaches undoubtedly had some substance. Was this caused by sexism on the part of Carl McAloose? Holly Vaughn describes him as a "good ol' boy." Merrily Baker calls him a "typical ol' boy." Jaye Flood would not venture a description, but she definitely felt he did not like her. Furthermore, she has no doubts that her sexual orientation played a large part in the way he treated her.

McAloose was not verbally abusive to her, but he essentially ignored her and froze her out of the athletics department "family." He met daily with the male coaches, including their regular poker game. She received no credit from McAloose for the successes of her teams. Her requests for better or additional resources were just ignored.

The "cover-up/clear-up" strategy identified by Merrily Baker most likely took care of the most blatant Title IX violations that existed prior to the Flood/Vaughn settlement.

Had Richard Pegnetter gathered Baker, Flood, Vaughn, McAloose and Peterson in his office to discuss the issues contained in the Baker letter, some of the complaints might have been addressed to the satisfaction of the women coaches. Title IX regulations are very clear and specific. Mutually acceptable remedies could have been found. The more subjective topics relating to the way Flood and Vaughn perceived their treatment at the hands of McAloose and Peterson could have, at minimum, been aired and discussed. A show of concern by the university president may have softened the attitudes of the A.D and his assistant. That was not what transpired, to put it mildly.

Several years later, Merrily Baker is still puzzled by Pegnetter's reaction. "This is a guy that I liked. Suddenly he was presented with a challenge and he became a whole different person. World War III erupted and nobody anticipated that reaction. He (Pegnetter) went into "defend, protect, and attack mode." I saw behavior in both men that I had never seen before. It was close to misogynistic behavior. He fired eight women in about three months on that campus."

After the Flood/Vaughn settlement, McAloose was gone, and Interim President Pegnetter gave way to new President Wilson Bradshaw. It would not have been difficult for the new players to clean up the lingering compliance problems. When Dr. Grant came on the scene, she would find a relatively clean program.

# Chapter Eleven - The Price They Paid

Diane Milutinovich loved her job at Fresno State. She had risen to the position of associate athletics director and senior woman administrator. Taking her responsibilities quite seriously, she reported the various discrepancies between the resources allocated to the men as compared to the women. Title IX legally gave her the right to do so. Her job description gave her a mandate to monitor gender equity. When she was fired from the athletics department, she later accepted the position of director of the student union, not to fulfill some burning ambition, but to stay employed and remain a part of Fresno State. Also, she hoped to someday win her way back into the athletics department.

"I was so good at my job that I thought they would want me back (laughs). I thought they would see the error of their ways. People told me it was wishful thinking."

After her termination from the student union completely severed her ties with Fresno, she sued for retaliation. She intuitively knew that her career in athletics was over. "I didn't think I could get a job at any other school. The lawsuits have marked me. "

What price did she pay? "Except for seven years, I have spent my whole life in Fresno. I went to Fresno State. My family lives here. I am well known in the community with Rotary. I am on the Hall of Fame board. I loved my position and what I did there. It was a real blow to me. Emotionally…everything. I can hardly talk about it today, ten years later, without getting choked up."

What about the large settlement she received? Many people would be willing to trade a career for a $3.5 million payout. The reality is somewhat different. One third of the money went to the lawyers, and another third to the taxman. Yes, it's a large sum, but she would gladly give it up for an opportunity to have remained a happy and respected employee at Fresno State. What price can be placed on the days, weeks and years of harassment and humiliation by her superiors?

Today, Milutinovich has resigned herself to the reality of being a whistleblower. She does speaking and counseling on Title IX and gender equity issues. "A lot of coaches call me to learn how to get help from their administration without getting fired. If they think their job is in jeopardy, I work behind the scenes to advise them how to shore up their position and where to be careful. If a lawsuit is being considered, I consult there, as well. I also address coaches at their conferences on how not to get fired. After being fired twice, I think I have a handle on it. The work I do now is totally rewarding. It's what keeps me going."

Lindy Vivas exited Fresno shortly after Milutinovich. "It was very traumatic. For two years prior they had done nothing but put obstacles in my way. All I was doing was defending myself against a hostile environment. When they finally found reasons to fire me, it wasn't much of a surprise. It was exhausting trying to fend off their attacks. The new senior woman administrator worked hard to get my best player to quit the team. And she succeeded. But the team still had a good year, and I felt that I had done a good job."

The price Vivas paid began well before the trauma of her termination. Following the termination of Diane Milutinovich, Fresno State hired Desiree Reed-Francois as the SWA. Just as Sharon Taylor is convinced Lock Haven President Michael Fiorentino was hired with the mandate to fire her, so did Vivas come to realize that Reed-Francois carried the same mission. Reed-Francois began by trying to ferret out any possible NCAA violations committed by the volleyball program. Vivas had a good won-loss record and her team's graduation rate was 100%. Each year for 14 years Vivas completed and submitted an "outside income form" designed to gather information on monies earned from activities related to the position other than salary. A coach who received payment for appearing on a radio or TV show, or money earned from running a summer camp, had to include this on the form.

Vivas describes what happened after she was summoned into Reed-Francois' office. "Desiree pulled out a piece of paper and held it up. 'You have a violation! You have a violation. You didn't report that you had a university courtesy car and that is a violation.' I explained that I filled it out the same way every year and never listed the car before. Scott Johnson signed off on the report the previous year. She told me she was going to report me to the NCAA. Then she showed me her copy from the previous year. It had been altered and was different from the original that I had in my office."

The public might imagine that a university athletics administrator would fudge paperwork to avoid NCAA trouble. In this case, a school official was willing to bring possible embarrassment to her employer in order to build a case for termination.

The internal grievance procedure offered by Fresno's human resource department proved to be another source of frustration and anxiety for Vivas. When she first began to fight the alleged violations and complain about the pointless meetings scheduled during her team's practice times, she began to understand that the process was rigged against the individual. "HR is only there to protect the president and the university. The conflict of interest is outrageous. Even after I was fired, I still had to go through their system. They told me they were there to help me but that wasn't true. When I hired (attorney) Dan Siegel, he told me we would not be using that (human resource). He said that it never works. He instructed me to drop my claims and begin to fight in the legal arena because the system is always stacked against someone who is being treated unfairly."

For Vivas, the decision to file a lawsuit was hard in some ways, but easy in others. "I pretty much knew, everybody knows, if you do something like this your career is over. It's very likely that no one else will take a chance on you. Right after I was fired, I applied to a few schools and was turned down. That was the point when I should have had the best chance to get a job. I had just completed a successful career at Fresno State so I should have been able to seriously compete for one of the positions. I didn't get any. I didn't get a sniff of anything. I expected to be blackballed forever. On the other hand, the decision was easy because I knew what Fresno State did was wrong. I felt that it was illegal. Clearly, they were not going to change and operate above board without intervention by someone who could make them change."

The $4.52 million before legal fees and taxes will be spread over a 30-year annuity. The jury's award has not made her wealthy. The money has not changed her, but the anger has, at least for the first few years. She concludes, "I paid a price. The athletes paid a price. My family also paid a price. My parents sat there every day of the five-week trial. It was hard for them to listen to their daughter being bashed at every turn. It was hard on my friends, too, because I was not the same person for a number of years. I was angry. I held a lot of anger until recently. There were after-effects that I didn't realize until later. I was 48 years old when I got fired. I would have been vested after spending over 17 years in the system. They (Fresno State) knew what they were doing. They wanted to take everything away from me."

Why can't women who file lawsuits or blow the whistle get another job? Donna Lopiano's answer is very blunt. "That's self-explanatory.

Eighty percent of all A.D.s are guys; a very tight small club and most of these programs are not compliant with Title IX. Would you hire someone who blew the whistle somewhere else?" Lopiano has testified as an expert witness in dozens of Title IX retaliation lawsuits. She has witnessed the damage left in the wake of these cases, even the successful ones, like Milutinovich's. Fortunately, there are some rare exceptions.

Melissa Heinz, unlike many other women, did not file a lawsuit that resulted in hundreds of thousands, or even millions, of dollars, then experience a sudden end to her career. Heinz traded the big payout and the satisfaction of proving wrongdoing for a chance to get a fresh start. Winthrop University paid out a mere $35,000 that covered her legal costs and put some food on her table. What she wanted even more was the piece of paper signed by Athletics Director Tom Hickman that certified her as a competent, knowledgeable soccer coach. She was hot on the trail of a coaching job at Valdosta State University in Valdosta, Georgia, and she needed to escape the gravitational pull of an apparent failed tenure at Winthrop. Valdosta needed a coach with her start-up experience. She needed a second chance.

During the 2013 season, Heinz led her Blazers to a 9-5-3 record. She couldn't be more thrilled about her happy landing at Valdosta State. "Our AD here is just fair across the board. Every program is treated the same. It reflects in the sports because there is winning across the board. It's refreshing. From the start-up at Winthrop I learned a whole lot so I knew what I wanted to do the same or, do differently. The program here was funded better, which made everything easier. It shows when you support your programs you will have winning."

Perhaps Mel Heinz did not pay such a heavy price for advocating gender equity in sports. The Winthrop years could be viewed as a steppingstone to a better job. And yet, there is a hint of hurt in what she says, and more so in what she doesn't say. When asked if Winthrop A.D. Ton Hickman intentionally tried to sabotage her chances of finding another coaching job, she declined to comment. When asked to provide the names of other former women's coaches from Winthrop, she likewise declined, saying that she didn't think that many people in the South would want to "stand up against that sort of thing."

She does genuinely sound like she is in a good place at Valdosta, but a subtle form of post-traumatic stress disorder may be at work. She fears that some kind of bad juju spell might reach across the border from South Carolina and mess up her good thing in Valdosta, Georgia.

The shock, sadness, and public humiliation of losing the Winthrop position have not been totally exorcised. "I started to feel sorry for myself for a little while. But then I just got going and made calls, resumes, etc. I'm just a doer. I was blessed to get a call from the A.D. here. It wasn't easy. It takes a lot of motivation. It was a hit both personally and professionally. It doesn't taste good. It starts to make you doubt your coaching abilities. When I was offered this position I pulled my boots up and went after it. Luckily, I was able to get my confidence back and show that I am the kind of coach that can be in a winning program, be successful and help these athletes perform on and off the field."

Jaye Flood received a settlement of almost $3 million. The vast majority of Americans would gladly trade places with her. After all, she has financial security for the rest of her life. But she looks at her life a little differently. Flood explains, "I would have had security if I had fulfilled my career. My biggest regret is not being able to work with my student athletes. When you take that away, you leave a void in the life of someone who has done that all her life. You leave a void; a huge void."

Flood admits that she had been advised that she would most likely be blackballed from finding another coaching job after filing the lawsuit, regardless of the outcome.

What did surprise her, however, was the reaction of local high school administrators that would not consider her for a coaching position. That disappointment stemmed from the public humiliation that she received at the hands of FGCU. With her family situation requiring her to stay in the Naples area, she had to seek work in a job market tainted by the media stories of her alleged inappropriate relationships and incidents of sexual harassment.

Said Flood, "When you put in the newspaper something like sexual harassment, that is very damaging whether you win a settlement, or not. Those allegations were completely out of control. I believe they coached (the complaining students). They tried to make something out of nothing. They couldn't prove anything." She had no forum to explain to the public that her student-athletes were her number one concern.

Flood applied for several jobs, received just one interview, and had to watch as recent college graduates were chosen over her. One could make the argument that younger coaches could be hired at a lesser salary, but that would be ignoring the fact that Flood had financial security and could work for a nominal pay level. "So I figured," she concluded, "that my career was pretty much done."

Before joining the Atlantic Sun conference, Flood's teams had been to the NCAA South Regional Tournament four times and made it to the finals in three of those appearances. In their first season competing in the ASC, her Eagles wove a 23-3 record, which placed them first in the conference. Flood was named Coach of the Year. A high school volleyball program would have gained a great deal under her direction. Realistically, though, no one could blame a school board or athletics director for steering clear of Jay Flood. She was damaged goods.

Her public persona hurt her in another area, as well. Her successful and lucrative junior volleyball program suffered because local parents began to pull their kids out. She was forced to sell the program before it lost all remaining value.

### The Role of Homophobia

Both Fresno University and Florida Gulf Coast University demonstrated a bias against lesbian coaches and/or administrators. Debra Blum, in the Chronicle of Higher Education, states that "Women in college athletics are finding that homophobia is widespread and that identification as a lesbian can damage their careers." She cites the case of Tanya Tyler, the basketball coach at Howard University. Tyler, like many female coaches around the nation, complained of grossly unequal treatment of women's teams. Rumors soon floated around campus that she stole money and "ratted out" Howard to the NCAA. The additional rumor that she was a lesbian proved to be the most damaging, in Tyler's opinion. [1]

Homophobia as defined by the Merriam-Webster dictionary is the irrational fear of, aversion to, or discrimination against homosexuality or homosexuals. This word today is tasked with too many functions. Literally, a phobia is a fear of something. But homophobia as we view it in the 21st century seems more like a hatred of homosexuality, as one would detest a mortal sin, or sinner.

When a male athletics director or coach is accused of homophobia with regard to a female coach, it seems unlikely that he fears the person or her sexuality. More likely, he is illustrating a hatred for the person's life style. Moreover, it's possible that he does not fear or hate homosexuality at all. If he can portray the coach as homosexual he can appeal to the actual homophobia in others. This represents an even more deplorable act, the cynical strategy of using the homophobia of others to cause damage to a woman who may or may not be a lesbian.

Did the Fresno A.D. or president really fear or hate the perceived lesbians in the athletics department? They would surely deny it. They most likely did not fear the coaches' alleged homosexuality. What they most feared was the bonding of other female coaches and administrators into a larger coalition of women pressuring the university to work toward gender equity. Retaliation against Milutinovich and Vivas, for example, would discourage the others from joining the chorus of criticism.

Pat Griffin, in her book *Strong Women, Deep Closets: Lesbians and Homophobia in Sport*, reveals the true nature of homophobic treatment of females in athletics: "The purpose of calling a woman a lesbian is to limit her sport experience and make her feel defensive about her athleticism. As long as women's sports are associated with lesbians, and lesbians are stigmatized as social deviants, the lesbian label serves an important social-control function in sport insuring that only men have access to the benefits of sport participation and the physical and psychological empowerment available in sport." [2]

Griffin did not garner her understanding by sitting on the sidelines and observing the male and female roles in college athletics. She lived the experience as a lesbian athlete and coach.

The Duke (University) Journal of Gender Law and Policy calls homophobia in sports "a weapon in the service of sex discrimination" and a way to continue the celebration of masculine domination of sports. [3]

This technique of devaluing women in athletics has been around since before Title IX, and today remains basically unchallenged by society. Women, both heterosexual and homosexual, have been collateral damage in this diabolical gambit to retain the spoils of athletics for men only.

Sharon Taylor doubtlessly paid a price for being Sharon Taylor. Unlike Diane Milutinovich and Jaye Flood, she was not deprived of future opportunities in her chosen field. She has built up a mountain a goodwill with university administrators and sports associations around the country. As she neared retirement, various organizations were still conveying honors on her. Where she paid the biggest price was right near home in Lock Haven. Her accomplishments as a coach, teacher and administrator should have created an enduring legacy at LHU.

She followed in some important footsteps. Elizabeth Zimmerli has been honored with a building named for her. Charlotte Smith has been memorialized with a sports field that bears her name. What of Sharon Taylor's legacy? What will the incoming freshmen know of Sharon Taylor in five years? As it stands now, perhaps little or nothing.

Former president Dr. Craig Dean Willis is very blunt about Taylor's contributions. He said, "She has certainly left a bigger legacy than Elizabeth Zimmerli or Charlotte Smith, and they were both important. I hope that it comes to pass (that she is rightfully recognized)."

There is no doubt that her shoddy reward for 40 years of service has hurt her deeply, especially the insult of being ignored for emeriti status. In discussing all that has transpired in the past few years at Lock Haven, she remains consistently upbeat and almost completely devoid of any desire for sympathy. The support from her former players, coaches, faculty members and colleagues is very much appreciated, but not exploited.

In fact, the only crack that has appeared in her stoic demeanor took place when discussing a proposed celebration of her career that former associates have attempted to organize. In reporting that Pat Rudy and Karen Weaver are upset with her for steadfastly refusing to be a part of such an event, Taylor broke down emotionally, unable to speak for a few moments. Her next words were a tongue-in-cheek threat to publicly deny any such emotional weakness. To allow a consolation prize of appreciation for her career and life is akin to giving in to the forces that worked for years to bring her down. She refuses to "give the bastards any satisfaction." Her protective armor must not be compromised.

Taylor was not the only person at Lock Haven who paid a price. Peter Campbell left a law practice in Ohio to pursue a career in athletics. The former professional soccer player came to Lock Haven in 1999 when offered the opportunity to coach the women's soccer team.

Campbell led the Lady Eagles to the program's first NCAA Division II National Tournament appearance in 1999, and returned again in the 2000 season. He guided the team to its first-ever PSAC title, also in 1999, and the Lady Eagles defended that title in the 2000 campaign. Overall, his teams recorded a 31-6-4 mark in his two seasons at the helm. Campbell was named PSAC and Northeast Region Coach of the year in both his seasons as head coach.

In 2002, he was named assistant athletics director and soon given the title of associate athletics director. He had aspirations of becoming the director of athletics at LHU when Taylor retired. He always had Taylor's back, and vice versa. Serving under Taylor both as coach and assistant, he felt that she was a top-notch athletics director.

When Michael Fiorentino reassigned Taylor to a faculty position, he named Campbell as interim A.D. But Fiorentino never trusted Campbell, going so far as to lurk around Campbell's office trying to catch him allowing Taylor access to the athletics department facilities.

After the Brock Parker incident was uncovered, Campbell realized that the investigation was a sham and he asked to be reassigned out of the athletics department. He is now a professor in the Department of Sports Studies. His sense of loyalty to Sharon Taylor cost him a shot at a career goal that he had worked toward for 13 years.

**Many more victims**

Vicki Dugan, the women's softball coach at Oregon State, protested the school's attempt to eliminate softball. She was fired after six years as head coach and was replaced by a man. She claimed retaliation and won a million dollar settlement after four years of legal wrangling. [4]

Deena Deardruff Schmidt, Olympic gold medal swimmer, coached the San Diego State swim and dive team beginning in 1974. When SDS closed the campus pool in 2000, she had to find off-campus facilities, consistently substandard compared with all other schools in the Mountain West Conference. She lobbied hard for her employer to build a new pool, while at the same time battling cancer. In 2007, San Diego State completed their new $12 million swim facility. Shortly after it opened, she was informed that her contract was not being renewed. Schmidt, like Dugan, was replaced by a male. She filed a lawsuit and reached a settlement for $1 million plus legal fees. [5]

Robyn Handler sued Nova Southeastern University in Ft. Lauderdale, Florida, after being terminated for her complaint to the OCR that she received lower pay than "similarly situated" male coaches. The former head softball coach reached a confidential settlement with NSU in 2003. [6]

Lorri Sulpizio served as head coach of the women's basketball team at San Diego Mesa College for eight years. Her domestic partner Cathy Bass held the title of director of basketball operations. Supizio complained of inequities in the women's programs. Sulpizio and Bass were publicly identified as domestic partners by a local newspaper. Despite their records of success at Mesa, the university terminated them both in 2007. [7]

OCR investigated and found disparities significant enough to produce negative conditions for the female athletes. The California State court found for Sulpizio and awarded her one year's salary. [8]

Amy Draper, head volleyball coach at the University of Tennessee-Martin, approached the athletics director to point out several discrepancies in the way women's programs were treated vis-à-vis the men's teams. She was told that if she persisted with her complaints he would "bring the curtain down" on her. She was later fired without a hearing for poor performance. She filed a retaliation lawsuit in 2008. [9]

Surina Dixon accepted the position of women's basketball coach at Texas Southern University. She quickly discovered that her contract terms varied greatly from the contract of the men's basketball coach who had also been recently hired. When she pressed for equal treatment, she was fired three months into her contract. She never coached one game for the Tigers. She sued and won a $700,000 verdict. She is currently coaching in the high school ranks. [10]

Not all of the victims of retaliation have been women. Mike Burch was hired as head wrestling coach at the University of California-Davis, also known as UC-Davis. Burch inherited a team that had finished the past two seasons without a dual-meet victory. Burch led a resurgence in the wrestling program and was named UC-Davis coach of the year. Female wrestlers were permitted to train with the male wrestlers and seek NCAA certification to compete in tournaments. Upon learning that the female wrestlers could no longer participate for liability reasons, Burch campaigned to have the decision reversed. Burch soon learned that his contract would not be renewed. He sued in 2005 and subsequently settled for $725,000. [11]

Three of the UC-Davis female wrestlers also filed suit and won a $1.35 million verdict. [12]

Most commonly, the retaliation lawsuits do not result in reinstatement, although there are exceptions. Iowa State University women's Softball Coach, Ruth Crowe, won her case for reinstatement and also received back pay and emotional damages, totaling just under $300,000. [13]

California-Berkeley settled with women's swim coach Karen Moe Humphreys and was forced to reinstate her, formally apologize to her, and pay out $3.5 million in damages. The Olympic gold medal winner complained that the athletics department treated women unfairly. She spent three uncertain years getting her case through the court system. [14]

In addition to those who chose to fight back is the legion of coaches, athletes and administrators who remained quiet and suffered under presidents and athletics directors that paid little or no heed to the precepts of Title IX. Many of these silent victims have felt helpless to buck the establishment, perhaps because they had decided it was more important to protect their job and income. They endured the pain of knowing that equitable treatment of female athletes and coaches was being ignored while they were incapable of doing something to correct it. Not everyone can be, or should be, a whistleblower.

Most of the courageous men and women who have sought a legal remedy for inequitable treatment of women have been successful. The dollar amounts of verdicts and settlements continue to rise as the litany of Title IX actions grows longer and longer. So, this question must be asked: Why aren't university leaders learning vicariously from the costly mistakes of their colleagues at other schools?

# Chapter Twelve - Lessons Learned (Or Not)

All across the country, Title IX retaliation lawsuits are costing universities six and seven-figure verdicts and settlements. Legal counsels for universities must surely be advising presidents and athletics directors how to prevent these situations from happening at their institutions. University presidents must be monitoring their athletics departments for potential problems. Athletics directors at schools that have senior woman administrators certainly must be meeting regularly to ascertain that gender equity is being maintained within their sports programs. All of the above assumptions are probably true, yet the retaliation cases continue.

Why? How do individuals intelligent enough to rise to lofty positions in education fail to avoid these costly and embarrassing failures?

Title IX is more than 40 years old. The concept of providing equitable programs for women athletes should not be alien to universities' upper echelon administrators. Clearly, the schools that run into big-time trouble suffer from a top-down failure. This failure can take many forms: complacency, ignorance of Title IX regulations, personal vendettas, pressure from booster groups, anti-feminism, and homophobia. Sometimes the problems stem from over-protectiveness of men's sports; other times from a resentment of women's athletics in general.

As an athlete, a coach, an administrator and now as a consultant, Donna Lopiano has seen it all in the fight for gender equity in sports. Lopiano has testified in twenty-some Title IX retaliation cases. If you ask her how many cases have resulted in a verdict or settlement for the plaintiff, her answer is, "All of them, so far."

She then asks a question that initially sounds rhetorical. "Why are A.D.s and other administrators not learning from history?" But she quickly volunteers the answer. "Title IX isn't a case of Machiavellian athletics directors out to get women athletes. It's just a case of dinosaurs fighting to keep the last bastion of male power. I don't see most of these guys hating women. It's a matter of keeping their power base and way of life. Anyone who advocates for gender equity is questioning the priority of men's sports. It's a fight to preserve this privileged sports culture where men get paid more than women and treated better than women. It's the Penn Sate mentality (pre-Jerry Sandusky scandal). They're above the law and they don't see that in themselves."

Lopiano also points the finger at the financially successful programs. "The arrogance of deep-pocket higher education institutions is incredible. The same is true of deep-pocket athletics departments. They're in a different world. A world of special treatment, (where) they get whatever they want. And they're going to (continue to) get whatever they want. It's not a matter of who is right or wrong, but who is more powerful. It's depressing when you think about it."

Lopiano continues, "All of them were egregiously out of compliance. The measure of arrogance. What struck me about those programs that went to court was not the fact that they were out of compliance but they arrogantly denied that they were. They were just committed to fight them in court to the end."

Lopiano served as the Director of Women's Athletics at the University of Texas for 17 years. Her athletics department budget during her first year was $70,000. When she left, the department had a budget of more than $4 million. [1] When asked how she managed to get the University of Texas to commit more and more resources to women's athletics, she answers with a slight tinge of bitterness, "It was a fight every year."

One thing that helped greatly was that her department produced winning teams, claiming 18 national championships in that 17-year period.

**A Zero-Sum Game**

What is a zero-sum game? It is a contest in which one side's loss is equal to the other side's gain. In a healthy university setting, athletics should not be a zero-sum game. If the men's basketball team claims a league championship, the entire athletics department grows in stature. The same should, and often does, hold true when the women bring home a championship trophy from their softball tournament, for example.

At Lock Haven University, the success of women's teams during the past three decades appeared to bring little joy to many of the male alumni, the community at large, and sadly, to a key group of trustees. In wrestling, football, and men's basketball, the LHU teams struggled

217

during the same period in which several women's teams flourished. These failures by the men did not increase the "winnings" of the females. Conversely, the success of the women should not have been perceived as a diminution of the men's programs.

The LHU field hockey program produced national championships in 1981, 1982, 1989, 1992, 1994, 1995 and 2000. The women's lacrosse team won it all in 1979 (under coach Sharon Taylor). The women's softball team claimed titles in 2006 and 2009. The last men's title belonged to the 1980 soccer team.

To many of LHU's male boosters, the success of the females has created a black hole that has sucked the men's programs into an abyss from which there has been no return. In their eyes the strong gravitational pull of Sharon Taylor's alleged pro-female agenda has not allowed a spark of light to escape.

Taylor particularly catches blame for abandoning the football program. Dennis Therrell served as defensive coordinator for the LHU football program for three years before ascending to the head coach position from 1990 to 1995. On his watch, Lock Haven went 14-51-1. The temptation to blame the A.D. for this lack of success would have swayed some coaches, but not Therrell. When asked if he felt the football program suffered because of her disregard for men's sports, he answered, "Lord, no. Sharon did everything she could to support the football team. I have the highest regard for her as an administrator and as a person." During Therrell's second season as head coach, Taylor oversaw an upgrade to the Bald Eagles' football facilities.

Therrell currently serves as defensive coordinator at Murray State in Kentucky, a position he has also held at UNLV, Army and Illinois State. He played linebacker at Tennessee Tech and had a tryout with the St. Louis Cardinals.

About Taylor, Therrell added, "She was very honest. She tried to get us as much money as she could. She was unjustly accused of hoarding money for the women's teams. She even found money to pay for our travel expenses so we could use the transportation funds we had for scholarship money. Her hands were tied in a lot of situations."

LHU professor Gayatri Devi put a very personal spin on the subject of women and men in sports:

*"At the 2012 Olympics, I think the women athletes brought home more gold medals than the men. America was proud of its women athletes, but LHU does not seem proud of its women champions. This is a very strange disconnect and very misogynistic, I feel. How can you love your daughter, your sister, or your wife? How can you claim to love all these women in your life and not want the best for them; and consider them inferior, or feel they are taking something away from you? It's very unfortunate that Sharon Taylor has been on the receiving end of that attitude. To some extent it frightens me, in a very different way. I don't mean afraid. But it frightens me how there can be so much hostility and animosity toward a woman. I would never be able to possess this level of hostility toward a person."*

When interviewed by USA Today writer Erik Brady, Patrick Guerriero, a former assistant athletics director at LHU and litigant against the university, summed up the problem very simply. "Sharon Taylor hates men." On the contrary, most of the people in a position to observe Taylor's modus operandi over the years strongly dispute any bias for women, or against men.

The inter-gender animus seems to be emanating from the male side of the equation, and not just at LHU. The world of sports has always been a male domain. Title IX forced the issue. Many efforts have been made over the years to reverse or weaken Title IX. All have failed, but many schools pay lip service to the formulas for measuring gender equity.

More than a few people, both men and women, have been persecuted for asserting the legal rights of female athletes. Women have been allowed to live on the fringes of athletics. What happens when the women consistently claim the bragging rights for success in sports? Lock Haven University clearly provides an answer to that question.

Pat Rudy, current LHU field hockey coach, is feeling the backlash from the decision to reassign Taylor. "Our program (field hockey) has been the most successful at LHU in terms of championships, producing U.S. Team players and even World Cup players. My alums are supposed to raise money and generate interest in the program. But they are furious about what happened to Sharon Taylor and how she is being treated. It's been very difficult and I don't know how you turn it around."

With Taylor gone, the wrestling boosters are once again contributing but the boosters of women's teams are holding back. LHU now has a zero-sum situation measured in dollars.

Rudy compares the downgrading of LHU wrestling over the years to a similar situation in field hockey. "When I started college, Lock Haven, West Chester and Ursinus (a private college in Collegeville, PA) were the top field hockey programs in the East. Any one of us could have beaten the big schools like Penn State. Now, I understand that we will not be competing against the likes of Penn State or the University of North Carolina."

Rudy feels that the PLOW organizers are living in the past. "They just cannot change. They still think that Lock Haven wrestling can be as good as Penn State. When wrestling doesn't return to its past glory, who are they going to blame? Sharon Taylor won't be there."

Diane Milutinovich, former associate director of athletics at Fresno State, views the male attitude as a matter of historical status quo. "People with privilege, whether it's civil rights or gender dominance in sports, feel that whenever anyone else gains something, they have to give up something. That is not necessarily the case."

She also ascribes the generational influence to the reluctance of established male administrators and presidents to share the resources. "Older males didn't play with girls. The generation coming up today has seen the girls on the soccer field, for example, and in many cases have joined them in playing the game. They don't necessarily see it as strange and undeserved. When men and women are in the training room and both have a leg in a bucket of ice water, or are being taped to be able to continue, they are both in the same amount of pain. When they see women playing hard, working hard, and suffering as much, they hold no lack of respect."

A scenario in which male athletes perceive their female counterparts to be deserving might lead to the conclusion that the fight for gender equity will become easier. Milutinovich fears otherwise. She worries that the younger women athletes take Title IX for granted because they do not know what it was like not to have that legal umbrella protecting them. When the advocates for gender equity have been purged, and fewer people are left to promote women's rights, the John Weltys (Fresno State) will have a better chance of prevailing.

Even though Fresno State got rid of Diane Milutinovich, she did not stop monitoring their athletics expenditures. "In the first three years I was out of athletics at Fresno, they dropped a number of sports and cited Title IX as the reason. (During that period) the spending per male athlete went up $17,000 while the spending per female athlete went up $1,800." Bear in mind that she was allegedly removed because of a reorganization plan designed to ease budgetary stresses.

Another threat to Title IX, according to Milutinovich, is "big time" football. As more and more money is spent on football programs, people have begun to believe that football pays for everything else in the athletics departments. She wants the public to know that it does not. She reports that only 22 of 120 Division I-A schools made income over expenses. Coaches making multi-million dollar salaries at educational institutions have made the problem worse. As football expenditures ramp up, so do the allocations due to female programs. The rule of thumb holds that women's programs should demonstrate a participation rate within 5% of male student athletes' programs. The spending in dollars for the women should be within 10% of men's programs. The number of scholarships for women needs to fall within 5% of the grants given to the men. Sharon Taylor reports that the courts are beginning to lean closer to a 1-2% variance in the distribution of program resources.

Milutinovich feels that the January 2007 Fiesta Bowl, one of the best bowl games ever, has become one of the worst things that could have happened to the mid-major programs like Fresno State. Mid-major Boise Sate ambushed Oklahoma University 43-42 in overtime. Many other mid-major schools thought that they could become another Boise State success story. All they had to do was sink more money into their football programs. Schools that adopted this mentality made it much more difficult to maintain a semblance of equity in the women's programs.

Judy Sweet has fought the gender equity war from the trenches as well as from the sidelines. She served as the director of athletics at UC-San Diego from 1975 through 1999. During that tenure she also served as the NCAA membership president for three years. After leaving San Diego she became a senior vice-president for the NCAA from 2001 until 2006. In 2011, she founded the Alliance of Women Coaches.

Sweet agrees with Milutinovich about big time football programs, and adds men's basketball as well. At too many schools, these programs are the top priorities and other sports, ironically men's as well as women's, are not fairly supported.

But Sweet goes further in her indictment of universities. She has observed an arrogance that drags presidents and athletics departments into legal fights that they cannot win.

"Unfortunately, there are too many universities that have demonstrated an attitude that suggests that they think they are larger than the law. They made decisions that are contrary to the moral imperative of gender equity and legal employment policies, and are willing to face the consequences, if there are any. Many believe that the party who has been discriminated against won't pursue legal channels, or they can provide a modest severance package to get rid of the gender equity advocate. The sad bottom line is that they don't have a commitment to gender equity 42 years after the passage of Title IX."

Barbara Dixon, a former university president, has an interesting theory to explain the failure of university presidents to stay on top of gender equity issues. "A lot of presidents, around 75%, come out of the academic tradition. When you become the president, you soon realize that you must spend most of your time with non-academic issues, such as Title IX. I think that some of them do not want to do that." We live in a litigious society. After gender equity lawsuits have been filed, it may be too late to exercise oversight of the athletics department. Presidents should make the effort to gain a basic understanding of Title IX and recognize the importance of tracking their school's adherence to the law.

To quote Barbara Dixon, "I think most presidents would agree that there is too much that can go wrong (in athletics) and be so public, so fast, if you don't have your hands on it."

In April of 2014, the Women's Law Project of Philadelphia filed a Title IX complaint with the Office for Civil Rights claiming that nine of the fourteen PASSHE schools were not providing equal opportunities to female students. The nine schools named were Bloomsburg, Cheyney, Clarion, Kutztown, Lock Haven, Mansfield, Millersville and Shippensburg. [2]

Two years after Sharon Taylor's departure from the athletics department, Lock Haven landed on the list of alleged violators. As recently as 2010, Taylor was accused of favoring female students over males in terms of athletics opportunities. Either that claim was grossly unfair, or Taylor's successor allowed Lock Haven to fall rapidly out of Title IX compliance.

One PASSHE school not on the list was Edinboro University near Erie in the northwestern part of the state. To their athletics director, the balancing act known as Title IX compliance can be tricky, but not impossible. Bruce Baumgartner, A.D. at Edinboro, cites two keys to success in this area. The first is based on personal philosophy: treat all students the same way. The second is based on a practical perspective. Baumgartner elaborates, "At Edinboro and other PSAC schools, it's all about the balance between sports and education. More than 99% of PSAC graduates will use their education rather than their sports experience to make a living. It's not like that at the big schools."

If the name Bruce Baumgartner rings a bell, it's because he competed as a heavyweight wrestler in four Olympics, winning a medal each time. He captured gold twice (Los Angeles 1984 and Barcelona 1992), one silver (Seoul 1988), and one bronze (Atlanta 1996). He also earned gold medals at three World Championships and three Pan American Games.

Beginning with his senior year at Indiana State University he went 44-0. Baumgartner never lost a match to an American wrestler through his retirement in 1997. [3]

Baumgartner came to Edinboro as an assistant wrestling coach in 1984. He accepted the head coach position in 1990 and was promoted to athletics director in 1997. He is currently in his 17th year as A.D. at Edinboro.

Edinboro University's athletics department fields seventeen varsity sports, seven men's and ten women's teams. Unlike Sharon Taylor, nobody at Edinboro seems to be after his head despite the unbalanced array of sports teams. With a student ratio of close to 50% men and 50% women, Baumgartner stays legal with a distribution of scholarship money that mirrors the student male/female population.

In addition to his philosophical approach to gender equity, his department's organizational structure speaks volumes about his commitment to fairness. Even though Edinboro has a senior woman administrator (S.W.A.), Bruce retains the informal responsibility as chief administrator for Title IX compliance. He also oversees a committee that reviews Title IX and Clery Act reports. The Clery Act requires colleges and universities to report campus crime. Baumgartner feels that Title IX is "taking a turn" toward preventing sexual harassment and sexual assault on campus.

Baumgartner credits Sharon Taylor for helping him develop his philosophy toward gender equity. While still serving as head wrestling coach, Baumgartner received some sound advice from his boss, A.D. Jim McDonald: call Sharon Taylor with any questions about athletics. When Baumgartner became athletics director in 1997, he turned to Taylor several times for guidance. Said Baumgartner, "I found her to be a very logical thinker, and never with an agenda."

Baumgartner cites one more reason why Edinboro has successfully avoided serious Title IX troubles. During his 30 years working for Edinboro, Baumgartner served under several presidents that have shown a strong attitude toward fairness in opportunities toward all students. The Fresno State and Florida Gulf Coast University stories clearly illustrate the devastating cost of a top-down philosophy against women's athletics.

What is the future of Title IX? Donna Lopiano does not see any serious threats on the horizon, despite the occasional bill in Congress. She does, however, predict that the retaliation court cases will continue.

No future scenario will feature the male dominated world of sports inviting women into the fold with open arms. Gender equity, if it ever arrives, will come about because women have continued to demand their rights and use all of the remedies available to them when the scales begin to tip in the wrong direction.

Mariah Burton Nelson wrote a book in 1994 with a title that nicely sums up the attitude of many men toward women athletes: *The Stronger Women Get, The More Men Love Football*. Nelson lays out a game plan for women to follow: "We need to keep challenging sexual harassment, rape, statutory rape, college and high school gender discrimination...and the myriad ways men try to preserve sports and heroic ideals and physical power for themselves." [4]

Nelson, who led her Stanford University basketball team in scoring all four years, also calls for more legal actions when institutions fail to uphold the law, and more pressure on the media to expose flagrant incidents of sexism and misogyny. [5]

**Sharon Taylor:** *Lessons Learned... or, Not: Hmmm, so many lessons to consider... and, from so many sources ... one could never cite them all, but a few do stand out.*

*In 1977, Jimmy Carter told us "there are many things in life that are not fair;" I guess we should have believed him.*

*And, Richard Attenborough's documentary films have shown us how few jackals it takes to bring down a noble lion(ess). Each time we see it, we are saddened; but we know that, in the end, the jackals will be somebody else's dinner.*

*Perpetrators of injustices and misogynistic acts against women, the "discriminators," the weak characters who allow themselves to be manipulated, the jealous and spiteful in the world of athletics who would keep a woman from taking her rightful place in "their" world of college sports... these individuals never seem to learn. The same boorish behavior and costly outcomes ... costly in both financial awards and in institutional prestige ... have continued to occur far too regularly these 43 years since the passage of Title IX.*

*I saw these kinds of injustices and their outcomes many times and in many programs. I don't believe I was ever so naïve as to think that it could never happen to me, but none of that made it any easier when it did.*

*I don't know that I learned any new lessons, but two thoughts occur to me in retrospect:*

*Without question, the most rewarding response for me was the outpouring of love and support from so many professional colleagues, friends, and, most importantly, from present and former students and student-athletes, both women and men, with whom I had worked over decades. Some stood up and were heard publicly; others called, or sent letters, cards and emails with notes of personal support. All of them were wonderful, were so very much appreciated, and I will never forget the sentiments.*

*The second thought is a quotation that I'd come across in 1977 or '78, and I have written it and quoted it dozens of times in articles and presentations since that time. It came from a speech that political activist Jill Ruckelshaus delivered to the 1977 California Convention of the National Women's Political Caucus; it is as true today as the day she said it, and it continues to guide me to this day:*

*We are in for a very, very long haul...*
*I am asking for Everything you have to give*
*We will never give up...*
*You will lose your Youth, your Sleep,*
*your Patience, your Sense of Humor*
*and occasionally ... the understanding and support*
*of people that you Love very much*

*In Return, I have nothing to offer you but...*
*Your Pride in being a Woman, and*
*all your Dreams you've ever had for your daughters,*
*your nieces, and granddaughters...*

*Your Future*
*and the certain Knowledge that*
*at the end of your days*
*you will be able to look back and say that*

*Once in your life*
*You gave Everything you had*
*For Justice.*
[6]

# Chapter Thirteen – Most Proud

Looking back on her career, Sharon Taylor does not have a difficult time deciding which accomplishment stands out as her proudest. The reader, however, may struggle to guess what that accomplishment might be. The most obvious answer would be her magnificent career as a coach —of tennis, lacrosse, and, especially, field hockey. Twenty-eight years, seven national championships, and 390 coaching victories adorn her biography. There can be little doubt that she is proud of those successes. In fact, the Pennsylvania license plate on the back of her car reads ST-390.

So, a good guess, but no prize. What about her career of 25 years as the director of athletics at Lock Haven University?

Taking into consideration the years of criticism heaped on her for allegedly favoring women's sports over the men's programs at Lock Haven, one could logically point to the Dixon Trophy awarded to Lock Haven University three times between 2000 and 2007. Beginning in 1996 through 2012 the Pennsylvania State Athletic Conference based the award on the six most successful men's sports and six most successful women's sports at each of the sixteen PSAC member institutions during an entire school year. This award recognized the value of broad-based athletics programs and would seem to be out of the reach of any program that wasn't reasonably balanced in its approach to gender equity.

The three Dixon Trophies, as well as averaging top five finishes for LHU over all of those years, provide Lock Haven and Taylor with an objective measure of her performance as A.D. (Since Taylor's reassignment out of athletics, and her subsequent retirement, Lock Haven has finished thirteenth in the two ensuing years). Again, a good guess, but incorrect.

Perhaps the answer lies in the long list of awards that have been bestowed upon her? Within one year after LHU President Fiorentino removed her from the school's athletics department, and the same year the LHU Council of Trustees shamefully failed to support emerita status recommended by LHU, Taylor was honored by no fewer than four national organizations, including the National Association of Collegiate Women Athletics Administrators (NACWAA). This

Lifetime Achievement Award means a great deal to her, as do many other honors, but is not her crowning accomplishment.

If you guessed Taylor's contributions to the creation of play-offs and championships for women's teams you're wrong but getting "warmer," as we used to say as children when playing "hide the button." Taylor has already stated how proud she is to have helped lay the foundation for female student-athletes to extend their season until a champion is crowned.

One last guess would have to be supporting and preserving Title IX legislation. If that's your final answer, you are "getting hot." But, as important and vital as this civil rights legislation has been to the development of women's athletics, it is an accomplishment shared by thousands over decades, not any single individual's personal achievement.

Taylor cites her role and experiences in the growth and development of the AIAW and the opportunities that organization created for young women as the correct answer. The Association for Intercollegiate Athletics for Women formed in 1971, just one year before the passage of Title IX. The confluence of those two events changed the face of educational and athletics opportunities for girls and women forever.

The vast majority of men and women currently in sports have little or no knowledge of the AIAW. Those who had been exposed to AIAW while taking a course in the history of women in sports likely have not been able to retain much about this one acronym in a sea of many. To understand Sharon Taylor's feeling about this organization, a short primer is in order.

### The Association for Intercollegiate Athletics for Women

In 1969, the NCAA had rebuffed women educators who had come to them about offering championships for women. As a result, the AIAW was created and began offering those championships in the same year that Title IX was passed, 1972.

The AIAW did not just materialize out of thin air in 1971. Plenty of women's athletics organizations existed, many representing a single sport, such as the United States Field Hockey Association (USFHA). Instead, it grew out of the Division of Girls and Women's Sports (DGWS), which was part of the American Association of Health,

228

Physical Education and Recreation (AAHPER). DGWS was the first national organization focusing on collegiate women athletes.

**Sharon Taylor:** *A group of physical educators was concerned that the "highly skilled" woman athlete was not being served by the PE class, intramural, playday, sportsday offerings that were prevalent for college women in the first half of the 20th century. DGWS did not write rules; it offered "guidance" in how programs were to be run, and published sport "Guides" (rules without any enforcement mechanism) for women's sports.*

*To address this void, the DGWS organized a committee chaired by Katherine Ley from SUNY-Cortland. The women wanted championships and the NCAA, headed then by Walter Byers, saw no benefit to their organization and had turned down every request in the past. The DGWS committee contacted the NCAA one last time to no avail.*

*The stage was set for women to create an organization of their own to govern collegiate competition. The AIAW was thus born in 1971. Carole Oglesby was named as the first president.*

The AIAW bylaws called for a new president each year. The list of presidents below could also serve as a "Who's Who" in the development of women's athletics:

AIAW Presidents:

Carole Oglesby, 1972-73, Temple University
Carol Gordon, 1973-74, Washington State University
Leotus (Lee) Morrison, 1974-75, James Madison University
Laurie Mabry, 1975-76, Illinois State University
Peg Burke, 1976-77, University of Iowa
Judith Holland, 1977-78, U.C.L.A.
Charlotte West, 1978-79, Southern Illinois University
Carole Mushier, 1979-80, SUNY-Cortland
Christine Grant, 1980-81, University of Iowa
Donna Lopiano, 1981-82, University of Texas, Austin
Merrily Dean Baker, 1982, Princeton University (Served half her term; AIAW ceased operations in June, 1982) [1]

Anyone who referred to the AIAW as the women's NCAA was wrong in many ways. The philosophy behind this new governance body emphasized strong educational values in sports and concentrated their focus on the female athlete as a student.

Christine Grant explains how the organization set out to reach this objective: "To achieve this goal, it was necessary to try to create for student-athletes a non-exploitive approach to the sport experience. The rules pertaining to students, which included the Student-Athlete's Bill of Rights, were examples of this attempt to create a non-exploitive approach. Moreover, since the AIAW had encouraged all institutions to create Student-Athlete Advisory Committees on each campus, the student-athlete voice should not have been lost in the debate on policies."

Nationally, AIAW was required to allocate 20% of its committee positions to student-athletes. Grant compares this to the NCAA: "It is ironic that today student-athletes are demanding representation on NCAA committees, when female student-athletes had these opportunities more than 40 years ago with the AIAW. "

Grant adds one more AIAW tenet adopted in 1980. All national committees had to allocate 20% of their seats to minority persons. Title IX has always been about civil rights. The AIAW realized this 35 years ago, unlike the NCAA that even today has no comparable policy.

Taylor represented Lock Haven State College to the AIAW Delegate Assembly throughout the organization's lifetime. She served on the AIAW Executive Board for five years, two as "Small College VP" and three as Division III VP after divisions were adopted.

She is especially thrilled that she was selected as one of the six reps to travel to Washington D.C. in 1979 to visit Secretary of Health, Education and Welfare, Joseph Califano, to make the case for Title IX.

**Sharon Taylor:** *Within 10 years, the AIAW offered 43 championships in 19 different sports; had a membership of nearly 1000 institutions (many more than the NCAA, as we included NAIA and NJCAA women's programs, too), serving about 6000 women's teams.*

*Administratively, the AIAW was the most effective "affirmative action" program ever created as it offered 1200 administrative roles, committee assignments, and leadership positions... nearly all of which were filled by women*

*I ran for President (of AIAW) in January 1982 and lost by seven votes to my dear friend Ginny Hunt. Neither of us would have served, as the organization closed its doors in June of that year.*

*The AIAW was the first multi-sport organization that I was involved with. I learned strategizing skills and cut my "political teeth" on the floor of the Delegate Assembly in serious debating...then went to dinner, often with my "opponents."*

Grant shares Taylor's sense of accomplishment in the growth of AIAW. "Looking back, I am astonished by what we achieved in one short decade .... An organization built from nothing to become in ten years bigger than the NCAA...and we did so in spite of the fact that we were repeatedly fighting off almost annual attempts of take-overs by the NCAA. But the thing that we should all be most proud of is the fact that we built an organization that truly did put the welfare of the student-athlete as its core principle. "

To cite a few statistics, during the AIAW's brief lifetime, athletics budgets for women jumped from 1% of the men's budget to over 16%. Female participation in sports rocketed from 50,000 to 120,000. The number of schools offering women's scholarships jumped from 60 to 635. [2]

The growth of the AIAW occurred contemporaneously with the first decade of Title IX, when various interest groups were taking aim at destroying the new law. The AIAW already had an organized and highly engaged army willing to counterattack opposing forces.

During the 1970s, the NCAA and the American Football Coaches Association (AFCA) waged an all-out blitz to kill or weaken Title IX. They attempted to win this battle by playing the fear card. Football revenues, they testified, provided the income to support the non-revenue producing sports. If universities had to fund women's athletic teams, football would suffer. As a consequence, many other men's programs would be harmed or eliminated by a budget crunch. Lobbying the U.S. Congress, they testified that football should be exempted from Title IX. Besides, they contended, women just weren't that interested in varsity sports.

How did the AIAW manage to fend off the all-male NCAA from influencing the predominantly male U.S. Congress? Donna Lopiano, a former AIAW president and long-time A.D. at the University of Texas, explains:

*"Key to the success of AIAW was the educational training of its leaders, former physical educators, many of whom held doctoral degrees, who masterfully rolled out research that supported arguments critical to parents and Congress, exploding these NCAA and AFCA myths and supporting the proposition that equal opportunities for sons and daughters in sport mattered. The NCAA's data was used to reveal that few football or basketball programs generated revenues that exceeded their own expenses, countering the myth that these sports supported other sports. Despite running huge deficits, NCAA data also showed the continued explosive growth of football programs with regard to team size and expenditures, undermining the football death prophecy. United States General Accounting Office and NCAA data showed that the elimination of men's minor sports was about institutional decisions to fuel football and basketball rather than support wrestling or men's gymnastics or choices related to supporting the growth of more popular men's sports such as soccer and baseball. These data showed that the richest athletic programs were cutting men's minor sports while Division II and III programs successfully added women's sports programs while maintaining existing men's sports offerings."*

**Sharon Taylor:** *To those on the outside looking in, it did not appear to be fair fight. The NCAA had endless financial resources and powerful allies at all levels of government, both in the states and in Washington, DC. What the AIAW had was a membership committed to opportunities for young women at the collegiate level; a strong network of women, men and students who stood up for Title IX; and, as it turned out, a supportive Congress led by Title IX advocates within their ranks such as Birch Bayh, Patsy Mink, Jacob Javits, Claudine Schneider and others. And, when HEW Secretary Patricia Harris promulgated the Final Policy Interpretation of Title IX on December 11, 1979, the NCAA knew that it had lost the battle over Title IX. Against all odds, the AIAW position had prevailed.*

*For seven years, the NCAA and the AIAW found themselves in direct conflict over Title IX, with the battleground being the Congress and the*

*Executive branches of the government. The NCAA attempted to gut the law or, at the very least, keep it from applying to athletics. The AIAW championed the statute that would ensure endless opportunities for girls and women in sport long into the future.*

Would Title IX have survived without the AIAW? Donna Lopiano pulls no punches in her answer to that question. "During the 1970's, if the NCAA was in control of women's athletics, the defense of Title IX's application to athletics would never have occurred. AIAW's success was only possible because of the fact that the organization was separate from men's athletics, an oasis of powerful female independence. "

**Sharon Taylor:** *Yes, the AIAW had won this battle, but soon learned the cost of their victory. Shamelessly, only a month after the release of the Final Policy Interpretation, the NCAA, at its annual convention, passed legislation to offer championships for women in Divisions II and III; the next year, 1981, it included Division I women's championships, and adopted a governance plan for women's athletics.*

*The NCAA sponsored championships for women in Divisions II and III in 1981. The AIAW was still in existence then. So both NCAA and AIAW offered championships in the '81-'82 scholastic year.*

*NCAA ran the whole shootin' match by 1982-'83.*

Why did the NCAA suddenly flip-flop on the subject of bringing women's sports under their governance? Did their leaders finally see the moral and ethical rightfulness of providing athletic opportunities for women? Lopiano answers both questions with one statement. "The primary purpose of the NCAA's takeover of AIAW in 1982 was to silence this powerful women's voice. "

Christine Grant agrees. "The result was that women, who had for a decade enjoyed the leadership opportunities in the AIAW and who had built a different type of organization, were now forced to live, without vote, in an organization for which they did not vote and with a structure and a value system with which many did not agree. This was a heartbreakingly sad time for women in sport."

The 1981 NCAA convention should have been an open forum for men and women to explore the practicality of merging the two entities, but that did not happen.

**Sharon Taylor:** *The 1981 Convention was the most hostile and unprofessional gathering that I ever attended in my 45+ years in higher education. While some, relatively few, women supported the NCAA position, the vast majority of women continued to support the AIAW. Women were treated rudely and were shouted down on the floor for expressing opinions counter to the prevailing NCAA "line."*

NCAA had lost the battle against equity for women with the survival of Title IX, but it had won the war to control the programs for those very same women. The AIAW, the organization without which the fight for Title IX might well have been lost, ceased operations at the end of the 1981-82 academic year.

Candace Hogan covered the 1981 NCAA Convention for the New York Times. Her takeaway from the event mirrors that of Sharon Taylor. "Believing that most NCAA delegates were motivated by a general good will toward women, female delegates came to the National Association's convention microphones to urge the NCAA not start women's championships. In more than one instance they were hissed and booed after calmly and logically suggesting that the AIAW and the NCAA executive board meet and plan together what was best for the future of female student-athletes."

The NCAA announced that they would pay the expenses of all of women's teams who participated in the championship tournaments under the NCAA aegis. This offer, surprisingly, converted many nays to yeas among the male voting delegates.

Using parliamentary chicanery, the men succeeded in getting the vote they wanted. Frank Boyles of the University of Arkansas rose and addressed the group: "I have never seen such a power play, such a blitzkrieg against women who have worked so hard." [3]

Hogan continued, "The upshot? Against the will of the majority of women in athletics, the NCAA voted itself chairman of the board of the business of women's college sports. Whatever the National Association's intentions – whether to reap financial benefits or to dismantle women's athletics piece by piece - it was clear by the end of the day that the motivation did not stem from good will to women." [4]

Christine Grant, among others, felt that the NCAA bought their way into women's athletics. After the convention's important motions had been adopted and the NCAA had won the day, Christine Grant addressed the assemblage:

"You have bought your way into women's athletics with the lure of big money and other luxuries, but you haven't bought it from those most directly affected. As certainly as I stand before you, you will find that you have also bought the philosophy and expectation of organizational responsiveness that those in women's athletics have held dear. AIAW is a governance organization, but it is also an idea. And, while I do not know what the future may hold for that organization, I do know that the idea will never die."

**Sharon Taylor:** *Christine's comments were prophetic in so many ways. The NCAA "bought women" in every sense of the term! Women's programs came under the NCAA and the sensitivity to educational values and student-athlete welfare that women brought to the NCAA wrought dramatic changes to the rules system of that organization. Flexibility for both men and women was improved by changes to the transfer rule; protections for student-athletes were built into financial aid provisions; inclusion of voices of student-athletes in the governance system came about through their own advisory councils; and, realized in the enlightened presidency of the late Myles Brand, was a full-throated support for implementation of Title IX on NCAA campuses, and a strong voice for the statute when outside attacks were mounted to change or weaken its provisions.*

*Christine was right. Title IX was the law of the land and remarkable changes came about in sport opportunities for girls and women over the next few years.*

Donna Lopiano has observed another lasting legacy of the AIAW. "The AIAW should be credited with the fact that the American public now understands the relationship of sports and physical activity to girls' and women's health and success. Because of AIAW, it is now common knowledge that regular participation in physical activity during childhood and adolescence results in the development of positive body image, confidence, and self-esteem."

Former AIAW president Charlotte West made a discovery while serving as the Director for National Championships. "Once college women were given the opportunity to compete and were successfully coached, the level of skill soared. The improvement was obvious in all of the championships but in those sports like swimming and track and field, the objective times proved the point!"

**Sharon Taylor:** *The loss of the AIAW and the vitriol of that time were very emotional and difficult for many of us. In retrospect, Title IX had thrown open the gates to unlimited opportunity for collegiate women athletes, and the battle that women engaged over the AIAW or the NCAA was, for most, a disagreement over which road would get us there quicker and more certainly. There was never a disagreement about Title IX! And NCAA leaders like Dick Schultz, Judith Sweet and Myles Brand knew that and did much to change the climate and the public face of the NCAA for the benefit of both women and men.*

*During the battle of AIAW vs. NCAA, the "NCAA women," (a small group of about a dozen women) formed an organization, in 1979, and called themselves the CCWAA... the "Council of Collegiate Women Athletics Administrators."*

*After the NCAA took over, women who had stayed loyal to the AIAW felt a need for ALL women to get together for networking and just general support of each other within the male-dominated NCAA system. The second "president" was a woman who had served in AIAW and, from 1983 on, the group opened up to others. So, we all joined the CCWAA! In fact, Christine Grant became the 2nd president elected as soon as the membership was 'open'.*

*We felt that the term "Council" sounded too narrow ... too limited... and a bit 'elitist' so, in 1992, the name was changed to the National Assn. of Collegiate Women Athletics Administrators, NACWAA. I'd served on the Board from 1985 to 1988 and became the 10th president for the year 1997- 98.*

*The highlight of my year as president was that we negotiated a three-year commitment with NIKE to sponsor the Lifetime Achievement Award and we inaugurated the first class of eight women that year.*

236

*When I got the award [in 2013], I was proud to tell the gathering that NIKE was in the 12th year of our three-year agreement!*

*The point of this is that NACWAA really took up the charge that the AIAW had borne for a decade: to see that women in all aspects of intercollegiate athletics had opportunity to succeed in their chosen field. At the beginning, the women were almost all from the AIAW experience. As time went on, there was a true commitment to pass that experience ... without the negatives of the end of it ... on to younger colleagues, and it is simply a part of the fabric now. As a result, women have developed a true base of power inside the NCAA and that has been a positive for both women and men student-athletes.*

Charlotte West recently reflected on her AIAW experience. "Since the fledging AIAW initially had only one paid administrator to oversee the activities of the association, the workforce was essentially a group of volunteers. These volunteers were in large part physical educators who had full time college positions. Their commitment to providing wholesome competitive experiences for college women was impressive. Sharon Taylor is a perfect example of the talented group of volunteers who led and served the AIAW."

# Chapter Fourteen - Perspective

**Sharon Taylor:** *My career of 47 years in higher education and intercollegiate athletics ended abruptly on February 3, 2012, when the President of Lock Haven University told me that my expertise, experience, and life-long devotion to student-athletes, and to my alma mater, was no longer required or desired. As a tenured faculty member, I could have remained at Lock Haven University, but not in the career that I had built and to which I had committed my life. That was a very difficult and emotional day...a time that one might think was a singular and devastating memory that would forever color my career in a negative way, since it was the final act, so to speak.*

*But, that was not to be the case for a couple of reasons. It certainly would not be the case as I considered the hundreds, even thousands, of students and student-athletes whom I had taught, coached, assisted with their athletics and lifetime careers, and been a part of their lives and their families' lives. And, it certainly could not be the case as I considered, and as I was to be reminded of over the next months, my small part in the wonderful "ride" that had been the effort to give girls and women athletics opportunities in the final decades of the 20th Century. No, I had been too fortunate, and I'd had too long and memorable a career, to allow one petty and misguided act to be permitted that kind of impact on my life.*

*Instead, when I think of a single incident at the beginning of 2012, I think of something that happened to me in the three weeks preceding that ugly day in February.*

*The second week in January found my colleagues and me at the NCAA Convention in Indianapolis. Other than our Division II Business Session, at which voting on legislation occurred, I confess to attending only sessions that really interested me. For that reason, finding myself in a ballroom awaiting the Division II General Session was odd because the published program indicated neither the topic nor the presenter(s). Perhaps my being there was just serendipity.*

*The session featured Dr. Sandra Magnus, a former Division II soccer student-athlete from the Missouri University of Science and Technology at Rolla. Dr. Magnus did a masterful job of melding together lessons learned in her undergraduate college athletics experience with the*

238

*characteristics and tools she found to be necessary for the very successful career she had pursued. Dr. Magnus spoke of competition, commitment, dedication, perseverance, cooperation, etc., all of the qualities that we espouse in athletics and that she had honed in her own athletics career. The significant factor was that she was able to use those qualities as a successful woman, and in a career that had held the imagination of all Americans for the past 50 years ... that of a NASA Astronaut!*

*The program was exceptionally well received. When it ended, delegates hurried off to lunch, though I was pleased to see many of the students from the Student-Athlete Advisory Committee go to speak to Dr. Magnus. When the students left, she was to be escorted to a luncheon by the NCAA's Jennifer Fraser, and I asked Jenn if I might have a moment with her. I thanked her for a truly wonderful program and we chatted briefly about the impact of sport on women's opportunities in other aspects of their lives. As I was about to leave, I realized that I was wearing a silver Title IX 40th Anniversary commemorative bracelet, which had been created by Maui Divers Jewelry in Honolulu and was marketed to benefit the Women's Sports Foundation. I took the bracelet off and gave it to Dr. Magnus; she didn't want to take it at first but when I said to her, "You are one of the women for whom the women of my generation did what we did," she graciously accepted it, with appreciation.*

*I returned to campus from what was to be my last NCAA Convention and, about a week later, a package arrived at my office from the Lyndon B. Johnson Space Center in Houston. In the package were several items, including a letter from Dr. Magnus. She thanked me for the Title IX bracelet, and the message continued:*

*"Thank you for that kind and spontaneous gift. Speaking to you, only briefly, made it clear to me how much it meant to you. Talking with Jennifer Fraser afterward I learned more about the efforts and dedication that you have committed to women's athletics. I was very impressed and very thankful...The women of my generation owe a debt of gratitude to those of yours for the vision and hard work that you have applied to opening up opportunities for us. I feel that this is not only true in athletics, but also in my chosen career paths of science and engineering."*

*In addition to the letter, the package contained a crew patch from the 2002 Space Shuttle Atlantis' mission (Dr. Magnus' first mission; she also flew on the final shuttle mission of the U.S. space program); a certificate of authenticity attesting to the fact that the patch had flown in space and explaining the mission and, a photo of herself with the other two women who were part of that historic mission. All items are beautifully framed and prominently displayed in my home.*

*So, when I consider the first five weeks of 2012, and the end of the career in athletics that brought me so much pride and satisfaction, I prefer to recall meeting a brilliant and successful young woman who not only experienced and appreciated opportunities open to her in athletics, but who used some of them to make her mark in a most profound way in science, engineering, and in the space program of the United States of America.*

*I also think of hundreds of thousands of young women for whom, since 1972, opportunities in athletics have paved the way to success in so many other fields of endeavor or, perhaps, have just allowed them to see themselves as strong and accomplished women, up to any task before them.*

*That is the legacy of 47 years...so many working together to make opportunities in athletics not just a privilege for a few, but a right for all girls and women. The model of Dr. Sandra Magnus, Astronaut, on that day in 2012, simply put an exclamation point to it all.*

*So, the lesson to young girls and to women of all ages might be: "Reach for the stars; you never know just how close you might get!"*

# Appendix A

Field Hockey Coaching Career - Sharon E. Taylor
Source: NCAA & PSAC web sites

| | | | | |
|---|---|---|---|---|
| 1966-67 | Susquehanna | 2-3-1 | .417 | |
| 1967-68 | Susquehanna | 4-4-1 | .500 | |
| 1968-69 | Susquehanna | 2-5-2 | .333 | |
| 1969-70 | Susquehanna | 0-7-2 | .111 | |
| 1971-72 | Susquehanna | 1-6-2 | .222 | |
| 1973-74 | Lock Haven | 6-2-0 | .750 | |
| 1974-75 | Lock Haven | 7-2-2 | .727 | |
| 1975-76 | Lock Haven | 18-2-1 | .881 | |
| 1976-77 | Lock Haven | 17-5-1 | .761 | |
| 1977-78 | Lock Haven | 23-3-1 | .870 | |
| 1978-79 | Lock Haven | 13-4-3 | .725 | |
| 1979-80 | Lock Haven | 12-3-1 | .781 | PSAC Champion |
| 1980-81 | Lock Haven | 12-5-4 | .667 | PSAC Champion |
| 1981-82 | Lock Haven | 18-1-2 | .905 | AIAW & PSAC Champion |
| 1982-83 | Lock Haven | 16-1-0 | .941 | NCAA & PSAC Champions |
| 1983-84 | Lock Haven | 17-2-0 | .895 | NCAA Runner-Up |
| 1984-85 | Lock Haven | 12-5-1 | .694 | |
| 1985-86 | Lock Haven | 13-6-0 | .684 | |
| 1986-87 | Lock Haven | 12-7-2 | .619 | |
| 1987-88 | Lock Haven | 12-5-2 | .694 | |
| 1988-89 | Lock Haven | 7-12-1 | .375 | |
| 1989-90 | Lock Haven | 17-4-2 | .783 | NCAA & PSAC Champions |
| 1990-91 | Lock Haven | 12-7-2 | .619 | PSAC Runner-Up |
| 1991-92 | Lock Haven | 16-7-0 | .696 | PSAC Runner-Up |
| 1992-93 | Lock Haven | 15-5-2 | .727 | NCAA Champions |
| 1993-94 | Lock Haven | 17-5-0 | .773 | NCAA & PSAC Runner-Up |
| 1994-95 | Lock Haven | 18-3-0 | .857 | NCAA & PSAC Champions |
| 1995-96 | Lock Haven | 21-0-0 | 1.000 | NCAA & PSAC Champions |

| | | | |
|---|---|---|---|
| Career | Susquehanna | 9-25-8 | .417 |
| | Lock Haven | 331-96-27 | .759 |
| | Total | 340-121-35 | .721 |

# Appendix B - We have Title IX. Now what?

Title IX has been labeled as a "stealth bill." It sailed through Congress with very little resistance because Congresswoman Edith Green wisely kept it in the shadows. President Richard Nixon quickly signed it into law.

The next step was to turn the 37 words into a comprehensive law that covered all facets of the educational experience. Myriad regulations had to be created and approved. Athletics became a very important and controversial aspect, particularly when the NCAA woke up and realized the potential monster that had been created while they slept.

The next several decades would see desperate efforts to weaken or kill Title IX. The guardians of women's athletics greatly appreciated the opportunity that had been handed to them. They rallied forces to help define and protect this landmark legislation.

How Title IX fully developed and survived has been beautifully chronicled in an article written by Sharon Taylor in observance of its 40th anniversary. Entitled Perspectives of Title IX, it was published on the Pennsylvania State Athletic Conference (PSAC) website June 23, 2012.

**Perspectives of Title IX by Sharon Taylor**

In the summer of 1972, I had just left my first teaching and coaching position at Susquehanna University in order to assume a new position on the faculty of my Alma Mater, Lock Haven State College. I was hired to teach in the professional preparation program in Health and Physical Education, and to coach, of all things, tennis! My teacher and mentor, Dr. Charlotte Smith, was within a year of retirement, and coaching the field hockey and lacrosse teams loomed large and exciting in my future. After completing a Master's degree the spring before, I had stayed on at the University of North Carolina-Greensboro to take a summer seminar from a highly respected visiting professor, Dr. Katherine Ley. Dr. Ley spent three weeks revealing and detailing for us the promise of a newly-formed organization that she had guided into being: the Association for Intercollegiate Athletics for Women (AIAW). For the first time, college women athletes would actually play for championships, and the future in coaching was bright, indeed.

The AIAW would conduct its first national championship, in the sport of golf, in the spring of 1972. A few months later, on June 23, the Congress of the United States passed Title IX of the Education Amendments of 1972. The short, one-sentence statement, that decades later would be called "the 37 words that changed everything" (Steve Wulf, ESPN-W) declared: No person in the United States shall, on the basis of sex, be excluded from participation in, be denied the benefits of, or be subjected to discrimination under any education program or activity receiving federal financial assistance.

A colleague from Susquehanna University, the Dean of Women Dorothy Anderson, contacted me in late summer and asked if I would be willing to make a presentation to the Intercollegiate Association of Women Students (IAWS), a national conference that she was chairing. The conference was to be in Harrisburg, PA, in October, and she asked me to talk about "Title IX and Intercollegiate Athletics."

I immediately said, "Yes!" And then, it occurred to me that I really didn't know much about Title IX!

Oh, sure, it was in the papers and in the Chronicle of Higher Education, and I had discussed it with colleagues; we speculated about how it would affect sports for girls and women. We were all very optimistic and were looking forward to its application to athletics and to seeing all of the benefits that, we thought, would accrue to women students. Finally! Our daughters would have the same opportunities for teams and championships and scholarships as our sons had, and everyone would embrace and celebrate that achievement ... right?

So, in mid-October I became the "expert" on Title IX in athletics and did a convincing job, I guess, explaining in my presentation what the impact of the new law might be on college sports. The late morning session ended and I answered a few questions from folks that came up to me afterwards. In addition to the many students present were also some advisors and mentors...professionals from various colleges and universities, faculty members and deans.

But, there were two women who really wanted to talk further about the athletics issues. We had lunch together, talked for much of the afternoon instead of attending other sessions, and shared dinner conversation. When I left for Lock Haven late that evening, I never anticipated how many more times my life would come into contact with

Bernice "Bunny" Sandler and Margaret Dunkle, or for how many decades the focus of that year would consume our personal lives and professional efforts. Sandler had worked with Rep. Edith Green (D-OR) in drafting the Title IX legislation (Bunny is now referred to as the "Godmother of Title IX"), and Dunkle would write the first guide to Title IX in Athletics for the Office for Civil Rights (OCR) under the Department of Health, Education and Welfare (HEW), the soon-to-be source of the original Title IX Regulations some three years later.

As the sponsors of Title IX readily acknowledged, then and now, there was no consideration of athletics during the passage of the statute. The purpose of Title IX was, largely, to open to women access to professional programs at colleges and universities...medicine, the law, engineering, architecture, etc....programs closed to women, or severely limited by quotas, and Title IX would, for the first time, make that discrimination on the basis of sex/gender illegal. But, Rep. Green insisted that there be no lobbying for the amendment, dissuading women's groups from testifying before Congressional hearings on its behalf so that there was no opposition incited; she prevailed, and Title IX passed the House with little debate. In the Senate, the primary sponsor was Birch Bayh (D-IN), a continuing supporter and advocate to this day. Sen. Bayh did say the word "athletic" when he mentioned "athletic facilities" in his comments, assuring his colleagues that "Title IX will not mean co-ed football."

The omnibus bill, the Education Amendments of 1972, passed easily and was signed into law by President Richard M. Nixon on June 23, 1972. Three years later, in the summer of 1975, the Final Title IX Regulations would be published in the Federal Register by the Department of HEW under Secretary Casper Weinberger. The "Regs" would detail the scope of the law and the procedures for enforcement that would be used by OCR. But, in that interim period (1972-1975), a firestorm of opposition erupted from individuals and groups representing men's athletics interests and, primarily, football. Unfortunately, the face of that opposition was the NCAA and their supporters in Congress, and their goal was to seriously weaken Title IX's coverage or to remove athletics from its scope, entirely.

Women's efforts to support the statute coalesced around the newly formed AIAW, now a strong and viable governance organization, soon to be the largest such organization in the nation; the men rallied under the banner of the NCAA. Although not a level playing field based on money, power and access to power, it turned out to be all right!

Men's athletics interests, through the NCAA, hired one of Washington's most visible law firms and, eventually, sued the Secretary all the way to the Supreme Court (which denied 'cert') to keep Title IX from applying to athletics in educational institutions.

Universities contributed institutional funds to a lobbying effort to get Congress to exempt various items: athletics, revenue-producing sports, football, etc. In fact, during this interim period, "no fewer than nine amendments were introduced that would have weakened the law" (Nancy Hogshead-Makar, USA Today, June 2003).

Football coaches like Darryl Royal provided access to the Oval Office to make the case against Title IX's application to intercollegiate athletics.

Through the AIAW, women had two things going for them: a network for organizing letter-writing campaigns and for contacting and lobbying their legislators, and the activism of their student-athletes who were mostly, though not all, women; both groups proved to be invaluable.

In Congress, proponents of strong, fair and broad coverage of Title IX as it applied to all aspects of educational programs, including athletics, prevailed. Led by Sen. Birch Bayh in the Senate and by Rep. Patsy Mink (D-HI) in the House, Title IX emerged unscathed. Well-reasoned concepts, such as considering the nature of different sports when looking at the relative costs of football and women's sports, suggested by Sen. Jacob Javits (R-NY), prevailed over the potentially disastrous suggestion of Sen. John Tower (R-TX) to exempt football from coverage of the law, altogether.

In June of 1975, Gerald Ford had replaced Richard Nixon as President, and Casper Weinberger continued at HEW. When the "Regs" were published in the Federal Register, the Department received 9,700 comments ... virtually all of them on athletics! This phenomenon caused Sec. Weinberger to say, "I had not realized until the comment period that athletics is the single most important thing in the United States." [1]

The Title IX Regulations were published and provided most of what women's groups, including women's athletics proponents, hoped they would, and they were the nightmare that men's athletics leaders feared. In other words, they were designed to end discrimination on the basis of sex in educational institutions.

In a move that reflected the level of importance that athletics had assumed around this law, HEW's Office for Civil Rights took the unusual step to publish, in September 1975, a special Memorandum to state school officers, superintendents of educational entities, and presidents of colleges and universities entitled: *Subject: Elimination of Sex Discrimination in Athletic Programs*. The document became known as the Holmes Memorandum, for Peter E. Holmes, the OCR Director who signed it.

After three bitter years, efforts to weaken the regulations had failed. The Congress ... yes, really, the U.S. Congress ... showed compassion, restraint, and a great deal more attention to Title IX and its purpose than they had back in 1972. As per an earlier directive by the Congress, the Regs were sent back for a 45-day "review", an action that nearly caused a Constitutional crisis based upon the "separation of powers" doctrine. In a bi-partisan effort, Congress quickly released the Regs and approved them "by not disapproving" them. This action of review should have had an impact nine years later when the Supreme Court ruled in the Grove City decision; regrettably, it did not. (I don't know whether anyone else shares the irony that I find in the fact that Richard Nixon and Casper Weinberger emerge 40 years later as the good guys, heroes in this struggle for equality and justice; they do, and we should recognize it.)

From 1975 until 1978, a three-year compliance period was provided for high schools and colleges/universities to come into line with the law; elementary schools had a single year to comply. At the end of the compliance period in 1978, additional comments were invited from the public and from anyone or any group that cared to comment, prior to HEW's issuing the "Final Policy Interpretation" for Title IX, at some point in 1979. By this time, Jimmy Carter was President and Joseph Califano had replaced Sec. Weinberger at HEW. It had become very important to all of us who advocated for women's athletics that the Final Policy Interpretation, the last regulatory step, would be as broad and as strong as possible.

In the closing days of the contentious struggle over final approval of the Title IX Regulations, I can remember a conversation with my long-time colleague and newly-elected President of AIAW, Carole Mushier. Carole said, "On the way in (to D.C.) this morning, I thought to myself, 'what if we save Title IX and lose AIAW in the process?'" I have never forgotten her words, and they would prove to be prophetic!

The AIAW was extraordinarily fortunate to have as its legal counsel a very successful D.C. communications attorney named Margot Polivy. Through Margot's legal efforts and advice, as well as her connections in and out of government, the positions taken by AIAW ... in actions of advocacy and in testimony before congressional committees ... were respected and given due consideration.

In early 1979, Margot was able to arrange a meeting for a small group of us from the AIAW with HEW Secretary Joseph Califano. The Carter White House's liaison for Women's Issues, Sarah Weddington (prevailing counsel, Roe v. Wade), was a friend of Margot's and made it happen. So, in April, along with Margot and Sarah, Christine Grant (U. of Iowa), Kaye Hart (Temple U.), Donna Lopiano (U. of Texas, Austin), Nell Jackson (U. of Michigan), Charlotte West (Southern Illinois U.) and I (Lock Haven State C.), went to see the Secretary.

I would love to say that Sec. Califano listened and agreed with everything that we said and that he committed to the strongest and most widely encompassing policy possible. He did not. Instead, he expressed concern for some of the arguments that our opponents made: he "wasn't sure" how football should be handled; he gave little comfort on a few specific items of coverage; and, he indicated that there would need to be "adjustments" in the reforms that AIAW and its supporters advocated. We left the Secretary's office with great concern for the progress we had made and for the commitment we were seeking.

BUT, there was a happy ending to this part of the story! In July, President Carter fired Joseph Califano and replaced him with Patricia Harris. In December 1979, Secretary Harris promulgated the strong and sweeping Final Policy Interpretation that was supported by AIAW and other women's advocacy groups. That Final Policy Interpretation was decimated by the Supreme Court's Grove City decision in 1984 (Orwell was right!), but it was the basis of the Civil Rights Restoration Act of 1987, and the Final Policy Interpretation of 1979 guides the application of the law today!

After 1979, the remainder of the 1972-1982 decade saw the battles over Title IX shift away from the Congress to the courts and, with less success, to OCR. Including lawsuits, some of the most significant developments/cases were:

- 1979, Cannon v The University of Chicago: established the private right of action (to sue) under Title IX;

- 1980, Haffer v Temple University: the first athletics suit brought under Title IX; interrupted by the Grove City decision hiatus, it was successfully concluded in 1988;

- 1982, North Haven v Bell: prohibition against sex discrimination in employment in education;

- 1982, the dissolution of the AIAW; after the NCAA failed to prevail against Title IX, its decision to provide championships and a governance structure that included women spelled the end for the AIAW.

(In reflecting on Carole Mushier's comment of so many years ago, I am certain that I speak for every woman and man that ever supported the AIAW and its efforts when I say that, given the choice, every one of us would choose the survival of Title IX!)

**After the first decade:**

- 1984, the Grove City decision: based on the legislative history of the act, Justice Byron White wrote for the majority that coverage of Title IX was restricted to those areas of educational institutions that were direct recipients of federal funds, i.e., virtually never athletics. (I often wondered if he missed the specific actions of the Congress in passing clarifying amendments during the period that the Regs were being written, or the 45-day review wherein the Regs were "not disapproved." I spent about 10 days in the company of Justice White and his family at a field hockey World Cup in 1979; had Grove City occurred before that time, I certainly would have asked him that question!);

- 1988, the Civil Rights Restoration Act of 1988: in a bi-partisan show of support for the statute, Congress passed the Act...see, they really did mean it! ... over the veto of President Ronald Reagan, fully restoring the broad coverage of Title IX that prevailed in 1979;

- 1992, Franklin v Gwinnett County Public Schools: unanimous ruling of the Supreme Court established the right of the plaintiff (in this sexual harassment case) to monetary damages under Title IX when it is established that defendants were aware of the discrimination; [NOTE: It was determined that in athletics cases, because claims of discrimination involve teams separated by gender, all findings of discrimination are seen as intentional as a matter of law and, thus, are subject to monetary damages);

- 1993, Favia v Indiana University of PA: predicted plaintiffs' ability to prevail in an action based solely on discrimination in athletics [106.41.(c)], the so-called laundry list;

- 1993, Cohen v Brown University: landmark case involving most aspects of Title IX athletics coverage;

- 2005, Jackson v Birmingham: the Supreme Court ruled that retaliation constituted intentional discrimination, and established protection for individuals who challenge and report discrimination (i.e., "whistleblowers"). [2]

Allow me a few final and personal thoughts that I offer with a great deal of certainty. In terms of scope and impact, Title IX was the single most important piece of legislation affecting education passed in the United States in the 20th Century; the only statute that comes close to that assertion might be the education component of the G.I. Bill of Rights after World War II. Also, the value of the AIAW to Title IX is incalculable; without the existence of the AIAW in the eight years after the passage of Title IX, the law, as we know it, would never have survived. Finally, just as threats to Title IX have recurred over the past 40+ years, it is clear that new generations of women and men, especially those who have received the benefits of Title IX for themselves or for their loved ones, will need to stand in its support!

**The Promise of Title IX:**

"When female athletes are not forced to resort to the courts to vindicate their rights, and colleges and universities, high schools and middle schools, conferences and governing bodies choose, on their own, to come into compliance with the law, Title IX will truly have achieved its promise." Ellen J. Vargyas, J.D., Former Chief Counsel, Equal Employment Opportunity Commission (EEOC). [3]

# Appendix C –Andrea Myers Report

## Lock Haven University - Dr. Keith Miller

Athletic Program Review

April 2005

Prepared by
Andrea L. Myers

PURPOSE: A program review for the intercollegiate athletics department at Lock Haven University.

PROCESS: Prior to the campus visit the following Lock Haven documents were reviewed:

    I.   Strategic Plan: A Framework for the Future, 2003- 2008

    II.   Student Athlete Handbook, 2004-2005

    III. Department of Athletics Operating Manual

    IV. Director of Athletics Position Description, 2005

    V.   Sample of athletic performance reviews.

    VI. APSCUF Non-Faculty Athletic Coaches Agreement

A number of groups were invited to provide input for this review. Those groups included: University Trustees, Community Representatives, Athletic Administration, Senior University

Administration, Student Athletes, Head Coaches and University Administrative Personnel. At the completion of the campus visit and exit interview was held with President Keith Miller and University Trustee Guy Graham. All groups were asked the same series of questions. After introductions each group was asked to name something about LHU athletics that gave them pride. Each group was also asked about recommendations for improvement and the final question was, "If you could whisper in the ear of President Miller what would you tell him"? This report will summarize those comments and perceptions that were shared by multiple interviewees. The report will not include perceptions that were not widely shared unless otherwise noted

LOCK HAVEN PERCEPTIONS

Every group that was interviewed was asked to name something about LHU Athletics that gave them pride. The list that follows is perceptions that were widely shared by the interviewees.

Points of Pride

Athletic Success:

- Wrestling tradition
- Success in PSAC and winning the all-sports award
- Broad-based athletics program
- Success of athletics very important component of admission decisions.
- Overall athletic success (several commented that success was due to A.D. Taylor's leadership)
- Pride in Small College Athletics

Planning and Management
- Concern for student athletes is always the first priority for Director of Athletics
- Good relationships with academics.
- Academic success of athletes is admired.
- Development of women's sports, attention to Title IX.
- High retention rate and graduation rate of student athletes.
- Quality of young coaches
- Trustees believe there is sufficient funding for athletic scholarship while coaches do not.

Athletics Administration

- Respect Ms. Taylor's ability to make tough decisions
- Director of Athletics has open door policy – very good at listening.
- Newly implemented (February 2005) development of strategic plan in athletics.
- Director of Athletics is good administrator, impeccable credentials, concerned about the welfare of entire department. (mostly internal comments)
- Athletics Director has high expectations but trusts you to do your job; A.D. doesn't look over your shoulder.
- A.D. investigates any questionable matters and takes appropriate actions as required.

Concerns about LHU Athletics

Each group was offered the opportunity to list concerns about LHU athletics, the following lists were perceptions shared by multiple interviewees.

Funding and Resources:

- Quality and maintenance of athletic facilities, concerns came from both student athletes and coaches.
- Coaches being evaluated and perhaps retained based upon fundraising (there was not universal dissatisfaction among coaches on this point, this comment came from only two coaches)
- New athletic development officer will infringe upon coaches' ability to raise funds.
- Need better communication from the foundation regarding scholarships.
- Long-term financial stability

Planning and Management:

- Need coaches representation on search committees (some said this was happening, others seemed unaware, some said it had been resolved through the union)
- Each team needs to be on the same competitive level within the department. (I believe this was related to scholarships)

- Anxiety about change – fundraisers, new president, implications of union
- Community and trustees indicate a lack of knowledge about competitive goals for LHU athletics

Athletic Administration:

- Needs an articulated vision, some believe should be more emphasis on football and men's basketball.
- Director of Athletics needs to be more involved in fundraising.
- External groups felt there is too much attention to gender equity.
- Lack of management (trustee & two community members, two coaches) As a group the coach's spoke positively about management in athletics.
- Serious deep-rooted problem in community and alumni against Ms. Taylor. (This comment came from only one member of the community but was very adamant)
- Coaches would like more staff meetings.
- Many external constituents believe Director of Athletics should be removed (consensus among trustees was that A.D. not be "blatantly" fired, but they believe a change is needed)

Observations

Based upon the information gathered during the review it appears that the athletics program is very sound and well balanced. The fact that Lock Haven has won the PSAC All-Sports Award on numerous occasions would seem to support this observation. Numerous individuals throughout the campus visit spoke about the commitment and integrity of the athletics director.

Upon my review of the University's Strategic Plan it was observed that there was no mention of athletics. Involving athletics may have helped in articulating the goals and vision for intercollegiate athletics at Lock Haven University. It is impressive that athletics has begun to prepare a strategic plan and is involving the coaches in gathering information and making recommendations. It will be important to gain the support of others by continuing to seek broad based input throughout the preparation of the plan. I have offered suggestions on this process later in this report.

The coaching staff and athletic administrators seem very dedicated and committed to excellence. This commitment is reflected in the overall success of LHU athletics program. Most of the coaches feel that A.D. Taylor does not micromanage, in fact the comment was that she let's them do their job. Several coaches said the fundraising expectation was articulated when they were hired and therefore it was expected that it be a part of the evaluation process. Others (3 coaches) felt that the fundraising requirement would take away from game preparation, recruiting, and general sport oversight. The coaches communicated openly and several followed up by phone or e-mail after I left LHU.

As the campus session with the head coaches was ending, I was provided several letters of support for Ms. Taylor that had been sent from athletics directors in the PSAC. None of the letters indicated or any way suggested that Ms. Taylor had solicited them. Without exception the letters spoke to Ms. Taylor's concerns for student athletes, her honesty, professionalism, knowledge and the respect she has among her peers within the conference.

There is great misunderstanding among the trustees and the community about the requirements and implications of Title IX for intercollegiate athletics. Associate AD Campbell seems to have a good understanding of Title IX and the requirements to address inequities. As all of us who have dealt with Title IX realize, compliance is an institutional issue, not just an athletics problem. There is some belief among community constituents that a Title IX plan was written approximately 10 years ago and that plan has been abandoned.

A comment from the community group suggests that there is a great deal of incorrect information in the community regarding past NCAA issues and some personnel matters. There were accusations that NCAA violations had not been investigated. As I queried these matters in follow-up meetings it appears there is no merit to those accusations.

Negative impressions of the athletics director's management of athletics may be the result of the myriad of rules she is required to enforce including the University, PSAC, NCAA, Title IX, and now union policies. It became clear that the external constituents have a lot of misunderstanding about the internal operations of an athletics department. I also believe it would be helpful to educate both the coaches and the trustees (maybe even the community) about the manner in which scholarships and other athletic budgets are allocated.

The majority of the concerns and negative comments came from the trustees and a limited number (two) of the community representatives. Internally Ms. Taylor is held in high regard and many speak of her integrity. Two coaches did speak of concerns about evaluations and allocation of scholarships.

It seems as though Ms. Taylor does not have the support of the trustees; perhaps she could meet with them independently and seek their input on issues of concern. An educational session for the trustees may help to answer many of the questions about the athletic director's leadership ability.

While the trustees expressed dissatisfaction with the leadership of the athletics director they indicated they would support the President and asked for that statement of support to be included in this report.

Recommendations for Improvements

I. "Athletics 101" presentation for the trustees. I recommend the A.D. be a participant and deeply involved in preparation and presentation of these materials. Indications are that she is extremely knowledgeable. It may also be helpful to involve Associate A.D. Campbell and/or vice presidents to assist in the presentation involving their areas of administrative oversight.

Suggested topics might include:

Membership or structure of PSAC conference.

Membership requirements for NCAA Division II participation.

Comparison of scholarships, budgets, staff sizes and athletic fundraising to other PSAC member institutions.

Competitive goals for PSAC athletics.

Title IX and its implications in administering athletics. (What it takes/means to be in compliance with Title IX)

A brief explanation of the challenges of administering athletics program that includes both D-I and D-II sports.

II. It will be important to have broad based participation in the development of the strategic plan; the coaches need to have an integral role in the adoption of final plan. It appears the strategic plan for athletics will focus on facility needs. A head coaches meeting where all facility requests could be listed and a group prioritization of these needs would help all of the coaches to understand each others needs and the priorities for the entire department.

III. Consideration should be given to holding monthly athletic staff meetings, if agenda driven. Head coaches actually requested more staff meetings. Some agenda topics might include:

A. Educational sessions with further explanation of the union agreement between APSCUF and Non-Faculty Athletic coaches.

B. It was a recommendation by both the financial aid director and the director of admissions that they provide in-service workshops for the athletics department. This had been past practice and it is believed that it would be helpful to the coaches to have a better understanding of the way financial aid and admissions decisions are made.

C. Meeting with new athletic development person to explain coach's expectations vs. development expectations.

D. Meeting Vice President, University Advancement to explain scholarship allocations.

IV. The establishment of a University Athletics Committee/Board. This committee functions on many campuses as an advisory board, which has responsibility for advising or establishing athletics policies. The NCAA Division II Operating Manual should have information about the composition of this committee and it's role. The NCAA does not require this committee but most institutions find it helpful in recommending and setting athletic policy.

V. Develop a public relations initiative, which will address the success of LHU athletics and the value of a broad-based athletics program. Try to involve the student athletes in purveying the information. Your student athletes are knowledgeable, passionate and articulate.

VI. A coaches' retreat in conjunction with the preparation of the strategic plan. This retreat could include a SWOT (Strengths, Weaknesses, Opportunities and Threats) analysis. Once each of these areas has been listed the department should prioritize them. This is a proactive approach to building consensus.

# Appendix D - Judith Sweet Report

## Review of Lock Haven University of Pennsylvania Department of Athletics January 2010

Judith Sweet and Ronald Strattan

In an effort to assist Lock Haven University of Pennsylvania (LHUP) in making policy decisions regarding intercollegiate athletics at the university, the following document suggests several courses of action.

We were charged with identifying how LHUP can best plan for the future of its intercollegiate athletics program. We were also asked to identify strengths, weaknesses, and opportunities, as well as to make recommendations for continuous improvements that will ensure that LHUP is well positioned in the future. We are pleased to assist LHUP in its review of its intercollegiate athletics program.

During the process, we examined numerous documents, held more than 30 individual meetings with campus representatives over a three-day period, reviewed comments submitted by various individuals in response to a request from President Miller to the LHUP community, and researched policies and processes that could be of assistance to LHUP. Documents reviewed include the LHUP university strategic plan, the athletics department strategic plan, the Equity in Athletics Disclosure Act (EADA) report for LHUP, the recommendations from Andrea Myers (who evaluated the LHUP athletics program in 2005), the gender equity report that was completed in 2002, union policies, financial information for the athletics department, the operating manual for the athletics department, gender equity surveys completed by head coaches, and other resources provided by the Athletics Department and President Miller's office. We are appreciative of the cooperation we received from all parties and the information provided by each individual with whom we met.

We have attempted to categorize the comments we heard, information we received, and suggestions provided into themes or topic areas and thus submit the following recommendations based on our assessment of strengths, weaknesses and other observations, which are included in the Appendix.

## Recommendations for the Future

1) It is our belief that the President and Council must take a serious look at the role athletics will play at LHUP in the future and how much they are willing to support its growth and health. In a world of competing priorities, these are not easy decisions and must be evaluated carefully. Following are several recommendations.

A. Develop a clear philosophy about the role of athletics at LHUP and establish specific realistic expectations and a process to assure accountability. Athletics department policies should be consistent with the established philosophy.

B. Identify priorities for the athletics program and ways of funding those priorities. This may include sports sponsorship (number of sports, possibility of tiered sports, divisional affiliation), level of university support, fundraising expectations and strategies. Sample questions that need to be answered:

1. Is the intent to have a broad-based program and stretch resources, which could impact the competitiveness of all programs, or 2. Should there be fewer programs with a higher amount of support to increase the potential for those teams to be successful to a greater degree, or 3. Should sports be tiered, or 4. Should all sports be at the same divisional level, or 5? Some other new well-defined model?

C. Clarify the role and sphere of authority for the athletics department staff. The specific skills and experiences required of administrators should be consistent with the defined goals for the program. There should be a team approach, inside and outside the athletics department, to supporting the mission of the athletics program. Diverse experiences and skill sets are important to the strength of the team and should be valued.

D. Keep the athletics department aligned with the academic mission of the university and the vision expressed by the President for technology, diversity, and engagement of students in the learning process. Consider the appropriate reporting lines for athletics in light of these goals.

E. Review guidelines established by the Association of Governing Boards (AGB) with respect to the role of campus boards. (April 3, 2009 Document attached)

F. Review the Models for Success for a Division II Athletics Program developed by the NCAA. (Division II Model program document attached)

2.) Establish university committees to assist in addressing internal governance issues and the gathering of information to determine feasibility of various sports sponsorship models and their funding.

A. Establish an Athletics Advisory Committee to offer assistance to the athletics department and campus. Composition of this committee should be diverse and include faculty and administrators from across campus, as well as athletics department administrators, coaches and student-athletes, alumni and possibly community representatives. This committee could assist with the development of a Five-Year Strategic Plan outlining the role of athletics on campus and corresponding needs. Athletics department personnel should be actively engaged in this process as the experienced experts.

B. Review financial information from conference schools and other Division II programs that might be considered peer or model programs consistent with the LHUP philosophy and assess how this information may help develop a road map for the future of LHUP athletics. Spend time on those campuses that might serve as model programs to evaluate what processes, strategies and actions might be appropriate for LHUP.

C. Establish a Gender Equity Committee to monitor Title IX and gender equity compliance within the athletics department. Suggested committee members include men and women (both in the athletics department and across campus), athletics department representatives (male and female administrators and men's and women's coaches), athletics department Senior Woman Administrator, Title IX Coordinator, university legal counsel, faculty, President's office designee, students (male and female student-athletes, campus student representatives, and possibly alumni athletes). Develop a gender equity plan that is a living document and is reviewed on a regular basis for progress and action needed.

D. Develop criteria for assessing sports sponsorship to identify sports that are consistent with university priorities and resources, including a cost analysis of where the break-even point might be for making any changes (cost per student-athlete/tuition generated), including adding new students to campus. Consider the place of club sports teams in this evaluation. Be willing to make changes if it makes sense for the future.

E. On an ongoing and regular basis, evaluate participation opportunities and interests of male and female student-athletes and benefits to each gender, and make adjustments if warranted to ensure compliance with Title IX.

F. If a goal is for all sports to be competitive at a high level, determine steps to be taken that will result in increased competitiveness for sports that have not enjoyed success recently.

G. Given the ongoing lack of competitiveness of the football program and the large financial investment, determine at what level football can be realistically supported or other options that might be more appropriate. Options might include sponsorship of sprint football, which would be less costly but retain football participation opportunities. If the philosophy is to support a broad- based athletics program with an emphasis on a high number of participation opportunities, consider the possibility of other sports such as men's and women's rugby, which are now Olympic sports, or other conference, regional or club sports not currently available at LHUP.

H. There should be a clear and equitable funding philosophy for all sports. Establish a coordinated fund-raising strategy for the athletics program and clearly define the individual responsibilities of the athletics department administrators, coaches, and university development office. Determine a cooperative means to involve alumni and community members.

3.) There is a need for enhanced communication, cooperation and collaboration surrounding the athletics department within the LHUP campus and externally. The President and Director of Athletics need to assume primary leadership to make this happen.
A. Develop strategies and programs to strengthen community outreach efforts. Identify alumni and community representatives to assist in promoting the program and encouraging more community engagement. One common theme needs to be adopted that stresses a positive relationship between the university, community and athletics. The focus should be on educational experiences for student-athletes in the classroom and on the playing fields.

B. There should be an expectation that athletic administrators, coaches and staff members be positive ambassadors for the university and relate well with other campus groups, as well as the university's external support groups. Administrators and coaches should work well together, be collaborative, and mutually support the goals of LHUP athletics. All administrators and coaches should be willing participants in the athletics department's fundraising strategies. All job descriptions and performance evaluations should reflect these expectations.

C. The athletic support groups need to have their roles defined in light of NCAA institutional control guidelines and the role of the President. Loyalty from those alumni and community members who truly care about LHUP needs to be exhibited, and appreciation should be shown for their support.

D. Create a public relations and marketing plan for LHUP athletics (possibly donor funded) that includes student body engagement.

E. Provide Title IX education to the athletics department coaches, university and community members, and student-athletes.

F. Provide professional development/team-building experiences for coaches and administrators to promote a more unified department.

G. Stop tolerating negative attitudes and behaviors from coaches and supporters, pitting men's sports against women's sports. Relationships and trust must be restored, which will require collaborative, constructive efforts internally and externally.

H. A communication plan should be developed immediately to deliver a clear message to all concerned constituents with regard to the lines of authority, the role of the athletics program, and the decision-making process utilized by athletics and the university.

I. Keep demonstrating strong loyalty to LHUP, supporting gender equity for men and women, compliance with NCAA and conference rules and policies, providing positive experiences for students and striving to perform at high levels.

## Summary Recommendations

We believe that intercollegiate athletics serves an important role at LHUP and can have an even greater positive impact on campus and in the community. We suggest that an important step in making this happen is a review of the Association of Governing Boards (AGB) of Universities and Colleges April 3, 2009 document on Board Responsibilities for Intercollegiate Athletics with special attention to questions listed on page 5 for boards to consider pertaining to the athletics department mission. The questions identified should be addressed by the suggested athletics advisory committee, and their recommendations should be presented to the Council of Trustees to provide a roadmap for the future of LHUP intercollegiate athletics. It is our belief that this process will address some of the identified weaknesses and provide for developing appropriate strategies and directions for LHUP.

1. Are the mission, values, and goals of the athletics program compatible with those of the institution?

2. Does the administrative structure of the institution and the athletics department allow the institution to achieve its mission and goals?

3. What benchmarks should be used to gauge the success of the athletics department? Are they consistent with the institution's mission and values? Are they achievable given the resources, culture, and history?

4. What is the impact of intercollegiate athletics on the campus climate? How does athletics affect admissions, social life, academic values, and the composition of the student body?

5. What degree of autonomy should the athletics department have? In comparison with other co-curricular activities, is the athletics department appropriately integrated into the general administrative structure in terms of finances, employment practices, operating procedures, and accountability?

6. Is an annual risk assessment conducted to evaluate the internal controls of the athletics department? Is the institution's internal audit program engaged in the evaluation?

7. Is a comprehensive compliance program and review in place for the athletics program?

The AGB document states, "The measure of success of an intercollegiate athletics program should be the degree to which the program contributes to the institution's mission and academic reputation. The board should be certain that its institution has established and promotes a definition for success for the athletics department that goes beyond wins and losses and net revenue. To that end, boards should insist that there is a clear mission statement for the athletics department."

## Appendix

The LHUP athletics program has demonstrated success in the Pennsylvania State Athletic Conference (PSAC) and nationally in various sports throughout its history.

LHUP student-athletes perform well in the classroom and in their respective sports, as evidenced by team GPA's and the overall high ranking of LHUP teams in their conference and nationally.

Student-athletes appear to be having positive experiences at the university and in the athletics program.

Student-athletes add to the diversity of the university and the athletics program enhances the campus climate, particularly when teams are successful and the campus, alumni and community share pride in such successes.

There is great passion for LHUP athletics, both within the university and in the external community, and a rich history that is frequently referenced by alums, community members and campus personnel. The athletics program would be further strengthened if this passion were directed in more constructive and cooperative ways.

Coaches and athletic administrators are dedicated to excellence at LHUP, and for the most part, they have been successful beyond what might be expected given the limited resources available.

A review of the Equity in Athletics Disclosure Act (EADA) submitted by LHUP in 2009 shows that there is equitable financial support for men's and women's athletics. Ongoing evaluation of participation opportunities consistent with Title IX requirements should continue.

In the past several years, as Title IX requirements were more consistently met, the LHUP women's teams have enjoyed increasing success. While most people have applauded this success, it has also been viewed incorrectly by individuals not knowledgeable about Title IX as the reason for some men's teams not being successful in recent years.

**Strengths and Weaknesses**

The mission statement for athletics should be consistent with the university philosophy and the defined role for athletics at LHUP. It is not clear what the expectations are for athletics and whether the level of financial resources is appropriate for the expectations.

The absence of a clear mission statement for LHUP athletics as it relates to the university vision and an appropriate structure for accountability and communication has led to confusion with regard to the program and its direction.

There is a lack of understanding outside the athletics department about the requirements of Title IX, the federal law that addresses gender equity in all university programs, including athletics. A Title IX report was completed in 2002, but it does not appear that there have been ongoing reviews and follow-up action based on the report.

There are some sports that have not been as successful as others in recent years. These sports should be reviewed to determine specific reasons for the decline and constructive steps that should be taken to enhance their competitiveness. Compliance with Title IX has been viewed incorrectly by individuals not knowledgeable about Title IX as the reason for some men's teams not being successful in recent years.

The report submitted in 2005 by consultant Andrea Myers, which included many relevant recommendations, was provided to President Miller and the Council of Trustees, but there was no follow up. Several of those recommendations addressed issues that appear to have continued to be problematic since the report was submitted and correspond to issues that we have also identified. It is unclear to us why there was no follow–up to this 2005 report.

**The lack of follow up to the 2005 Myers report has led to questioning the administration's commitment to both intercollegiate athletics and to the Director of Athletics.**

Relationships among the university, athletics administration and some alumni and members of the community are fractured.

There is an unhealthy divisiveness within the athletics department that appears to be delineated by sport and gender of teams and may be influenced by pressures from outside the university.

**Other Observations**

Like many universities today, LHUP faces serious financial challenges. There is increasing pressure on the coaches and athletics department to generate funding for scholarships and operating costs. This is even more pervasive with the economic downturn and reduced funding from the state. This pressure creates a high degree of frustration and perhaps unrealistic expectations within the athletics department and the community. What might have worked for LHUP athletics in the past might no longer be appropriate or doable.

There is not a universal understanding of how athletics is funded, the source of funds, and how they can be used. The various changes in university policy pertaining to summer camps and the associated funding have created additional misunderstandings and financial pressures.

Athletically related financial aid is dependent upon funds generated through fund- raising and other external means. This creates uncertainty on availability of scholarship support from year to year. Given the large number of football student-athletes, fund-raising a reasonable number of scholarships for this sport is more challenging and may be a factor in the lack of competitiveness of the football program. In addition, athletically related financial aid should be within 1% of participation numbers for men and women.

There is great interest from alums and community members in having a voice in the direction of LHUP athletics, including the hiring and firing of coaches and staff, and some individuals believe that because decisions have not been consistent with their stated recommendations, they are not being heard. It must be made clear that while input is welcome, decisions are to be made by university personnel with the professional expertise and designated authority, and that those individuals will be held accountable for their decisions.

We are concerned that there is a counter-productive influence from outside parties. This has been distracting to moving the athletics program forward and is detrimental to the university. One student stated "Stuff going on is nuts. There are personal attacks by the community while they are saying that they want to build things up." Clearly, this is a concern to the university, as well as the community.

Reporting lines are unusual, with the Director of Athletics formerly reporting to the Provost and now reporting to the Vice President for Finance. The previous reporting line to the Provost seemed to be consistent with LHUP athletics being tied to the academic mission of the university. It is our understanding that on most other PSAC campuses, the Director of Athletics reports to the Vice President for Student Affairs.

It appears that there is limited direct communication between the President and Director of Athletics. The Director of Athletics has direct line accountability to the Vice President for Finance, and before that, the Provost, but it seems that all-important decisions regarding the athletic department require the President's approval. Without regular contact and discussion between the President and Director of Athletics, the decision-making process is slowed and healthy dialogue is limited between those closest to the athletics department operations and the President who ultimately has decision-making authority. In light of the need to overcome tensions that currently surround the athletics program and critical decisions that need to be made for its future, more direct dialogue needs to take place. It is common practice at many universities that the Director of Athletics reports to the President, and in many instances the Director of Athletics is a member of the President's Cabinet. The Division II Model Program document attached to this report suggests that the Director of Athletics should report to the University President. We understand that union regulations do not allow for such a direct reporting arrangement at LHUP. The impact of union contracts creates added challenges for the administration. Although the Director of Athletics has input, it is highly unusual for the Director of Athletics to not have greater decision-making responsibility for the program and hiring and firing authority for department coaches and staff.

It is not clear to us what the role and authority of the Faculty Athletics Representative are at LHUP. This individual should help enhance communication on athletics matters between the faculty, University

President and athletics department, assist with NCAA compliance procedures, and participate in conference and NCAA dialogue and decisions.

We heard varying and conflicting reports about athletics department management, decision-making, and actions. There is praise, support and criticism of administrators at all levels of the university structure involved with decision-making for athletics from both internal and external sources. Recognizing that there are always at least two sides to every story (and we heard significantly more sides than that) we did not feel that with our short time on campus and the information provided to us it was possible for us to determine the actual circumstances.

# Notes

### Introduction

*[1] "Too Strong For a Woman"- The Five Words That Created Title IX by Bernice Sandler at www.BerniceSandler.com*

*[2] Ibid.*

*[3] Ibid.*

*[4] Ibid*

*[5] National organization for Women Website: http://www.now.org/history/founders.html "Honoring NOW's Founders and Pioneers*

*[6] "Too Strong For a Woman"- The Five Words That Created Title IX by Bernice Sandler at www.BerniceSandler.com]*

*[7] Females Athletes, Thank Nixon by Allan Barra New York Times Sunday Review June 18, 2012*

### Chapter One

*[1] U.S. Department of Education Website www2.ed.gov/about/offices/list/ocr/docs/t9interp.html*

### Chapter Two

*[1] Women hold 4% of D1A athletic director jobs-the maneater.com article by Kate Grumke*

*[2] Time for change in LHU athletic department is at hand – The Express October 28, 2009 by Austin Shanfelter and Jerry Swope*

*[3] Ibid.*

### Chapter Three

*[1] Commonwealth of PA court documents*

*[2] Lock Haven U. athletic department faces four pending lawsuits by John Beauge Penn Live .com 1/13/2010*

*[3] Obituary from The Express May 18, 2012*

*[4] Rudy v. PASSHE et al. Justia.com Dockets and Filings*

*[5] Lawsuit haven should gain lawyer for mascot by Lindsey Hewitt in The Express 5/3/2012*

*[6] Miller, Taylor, Bonomo named in lawsuit. From Staff Reports - The Express November 19, 2009*

*[7] Ibid.*

*[8] Ibid.*

*[9] Ibid.*

*[10] Ibid.*

*[11] PLOW Presentment written as evidence for a review of LHU Athletics by former NCAA executives Judith Sweet and Ronald Strattan*

*[12] Justia.com John Wilson, Jr. v. Lock Haven Univ, et al*

*[13] Discrimination alleged in latest lawsuit vs. LHU - The Express - January 6, 2010 No byline*

*[14] Justia.com John Wilson, Jr. v. Lock Haven Univ, et al*

*[15] Judge: LHU men's basketball coach failed to establish discrimination- February 1, 2011 The Express by John Beauge – Special to the Express*

*[16] Former Lock Haven University basketball coach loses lawsuit. The Express no byline April 13, 2011*

*[17] Domenique Wilson Sentenced to 70-196 Years in State Prison by Jim Runkle Lock Haven.com June 8, 2010*

*[18] Jury: Wilson guilty of brutally raping college students by Scott Johnson LockHaven.com (The Express) March 3, 2010*

*[19] Domenique Wilson Sentenced to 70-196 Years in State Prison by Jim Runkle Lock Haven.com June 8, 2010*

*[20] Ex-Basketball Player Gets 230 Years for Rapes by Teresa Masterson nbcphiladelphia.com - March 10, 2011*

**Chapter Four**

*[1] Sharon Taylor v. Preserve The Legacy of Wrestling et. al – In the Court of Common Pleas of Clinton County, Pennsylvania Civil Action-Law December 16, 2009*

*[2] Eastern Wrestling League Archives as compiled by Allen Brown and displayed on ewlwrestling.com*

*[3] Lock Haven University web site – lhup.edu/news_releases*

*[4] Ron Bowes Entering HOF – The Express website LockHaven.com. Nov 11, 2011, No byline*

*[5] ZoomInfo.com profile of Ronald Bowes*

*[6] Eastern Wrestling League Archives as compiled by Allen Brown and Bruce Closson and displayed on ewlwrestling.com*

*[7] Sharon Taylor v. Preserve The Legacy of Wrestling et. al.– In the Court of Common Pleas of Clinton County, Pennsylvania Civil Action-Law December 16, 2009*

*[8] Ibid.*

*[9] Ibid.*

*[10] In the Court of Common Pleas of Clinton County, Pennsylvania Sharon Taylor v PLOW et. al. – Motion for Summary Judgment of Defendant Todd Bartley*

*[11] Quoted in the motion from Taylor's Brief*

*[12] In the Court of Common Pleas of Clinton County, Pa Civil Action Law – Defendants PLOW, Austin Shanfelter, Neil turner and Thane Turner's Reply Brief in Support of Motion For Summary Judgment*

*[13] The Locker Room Show June 9, 2009*

*[14] The Locker Room June 16, 2009*

*[15] Brief of Plaintiff Sharon Taylor in Opposition to Motion For Summary Judgment filed by Defendant Todd Bartley –filed April 14, 2011 in the Court of Common Pleas of Clinton County Pennsylvania*

*[16] Ibid.*

*[17] Ibid.*

*[18] Court documents: Opinion and Order handed down by the Court of Common Pleas of Clinton County, Pennsylvania as displayed on LockHaven.com*

*[19] Ibid.*

*[20] Ibid.*

*[21] Ibid.*

## Chapter Five

*[1] Oyez.org – Oyez Project of the Chicago-Kent School of Law*

*[2] Ibid.*

*[3] Ibid.*

*[4] Donna Lopiano by Jon Show - Street and Smith Sport Business Journal March 22, 2010*

*[5] TakeBackTheNight.org – History page*

## Chapter Six

*None*

## Chapter Seven

*[1] No action taken on 'emeriti' status for Sharon Taylor by Scott Johnson, Lock Haven Express May 18, 2013*

*[2] Sense of shame by Gayatri Devi Lock Haven Express May 22, 2013*

*[3] Ibid.*

*[4] Unbelievable non-action, by Dr. Betty B. Schantz, Emeriti Lock Haven. Lock Haven Express May 25, 2013*

*[5] Ibid.*

*[6] Ibid.*

*[7] Sharon Taylor deserves LHU "emeriti" status by Mark J. Temons-Williamsport. Lock Haven Express Yourself May 23, 2013*

*[8] Ibid.*

*[9] Lock Haven Trustees Remain Silent on former AD's Status by Ellen J. Staurowsky, Ed.D - CollegeSportsBusinessNews.com May 23,2013*

*[10] Petition: Give Sharon Taylor emeriti status. Staff Reports Lock Haven Express August 5, 2013*

*[11] Ibid.*

## Chapter Eight

*[1] A fitting tribute to Dr. Craig Dean Willis – The Express June 11, 2013 no byline*

*[2] Ibid.*

## Chapter Nine

*[1] Job posting on HigherEdJobs.com for an opening at Alcorn State University 12/3/2012*

*[2] Court Filing: Diane Milutinovich v. Board of Trustees of the California State University; John Welty; Jeannine Raymond; Scott*

*Johnson, et al. Third amended Complaint Superior Court of California, County of Fresno*

*[3] Title-IXBlog.com August 2, 2008*

*[4] 'Hard time' for Vivas during tenure at Fresno State, USA Today 5/13/2008 by Jill Lieber Steeg*

*[4a] Duke Journal of Gender Law and Policy Volume 17:1 p.12*

*[5] A Civil Action by Jonathan Harr 1996 Vintage Books*

*[6] Turmoil in Fresno-Firing of Johnson-Klein becomes lightning rod, by Ron Kroichick, SFGate.Com march 9, 2005*

*[7] Fresno State Fires Stacy Johnson-Klein, Bulldog Playbook on FresnoState.scout.com March2, 2005*

*[8] FreeRepublic.com Trial Notes*

*[9] Ibid.*

*[10] Sigel and Yee Daily Journal of Verdicts and Outcomes on sigelyee.com*

*[11] Ibid.*

*[12] Sports Culture Creates leeway and Landmines Regarding Sexual Harassment by Paul Steinbach in March 2008 Athletic Business website*

*[13] Favia v. Indiana University of Pennsylvania. Amended Memorandum Opinion as displayed on Leagle.com*

*[14] Ibid.*

*[15] Ibid.*

*[16] Duke Journal of Gender Law and Policy Volume 17:1 p.12*

*[17] Court Filing Kathleen A. Bull vs. Board of Trustees of Ball State University, Jo Ann M. Gora, Thomas Collins, Patrick A. Quinn - U.S. District Court Southern District of Indiana*

*[18] Ibid.*

*[19] Ibid.*

*[20] Ibid.*

*[21] Ibid.*

*[22] American Association of University Women website –Resources Section - www.aauw.org/resource/bull-v-board-of-trustees-of-ball-state-university*

*[23] Heinz Bio on the Valdosta State web site -www.vstateblazers.com*

*[24] Court Document – Complaint For Damages and Request for Jury Trial - Melissa Heinz v. Winthrop University; Anthony DiGregorio; Thomas Hickman; and Richard Posipanko. United States District Court For the District of South Carolina*

*[25] Ibid.*

*[26] Ibid.*

*[27] Ibid.*

*[28] Ibid.*

*[29] USA Today Online – Winthrop fires women's soccer coach after 7 years – No byline 12/1/2009*

*[30] Court Document – Complaint For Damages and Request for Jury Trial - Melissa Heinz v. Winthrop University; Anthony DiGregorio; Thomas Hickman; and Richard Posipanko. United States District Court For the District of South Carolina*

*[31] Ibid.*

*[32] Lawsuit by Former Women's Soccer Team Settled 2/15/2012 www.winthrop.edu/news-events*

## Chapter Ten

[1] US District court, Middle District of Florida – First amended Complaint Jury Trail Demand. Jaye Flood and Holly Vaughn, Plaintiffs v. Board of Trustees Florida Gulf Coast University et. al. Defendants

[2] Ibid.

[3] Mercersburg Academy web site

[4] US District court, Middle District of Florida – First amended Complaint Jury Trail Demand. Jaye Flood and Holly Vaughn, Plaintiffs v. Board of Trustees Florida Gulf Coast University et. al., Defendants

[5] Ibid.

[6] Inquiry: FGCU officials tried to fire coach a year ago by Brad Kane Naples.News.Com 2/8/2008

[7] Ibid.

[8] US District court, Middle District of Florida – First amended Complaint Jury Trial Demand. Jaye Flood and Holly Vaughn, Plaintiffs v. Board of Trustees Florida Gulf Coast University et. al. Defendants

[9] Inquiry: FGCU officials tried to fire coach a year ago by Brad Kane Naples.News.Com 2/8/2008

[10] Sidelined: Title IX Retaliation Cases and Women's Leadership in College Athletics by Erin E. Buzuvis, Scholarship.Law.Duke.edu

[10a) Ibid.

[11] SPIKED: FGCU volleyball coach fired for having inappropriate relationship with student. 1/22/2012 NaplesPress.com. No byline but staff writer Kathleen Cullinan contributed to the report

[12] Ibid.

[13] Flood/Vaughn v. FGCU Settlement Agreement

[14] Ibid.

[15] Ibid.

[16] Ibid.

[17] Ibid.

[18] FGCU, former coaches reach $3.4M settlement by Dana Caldwell & Tom Hanson 10/15, 2008 Naples News

[19] Ibid.

[20] Ibid.]

[21] Ibid.]

[22] ClaytonSateSports .Com

[23] Former FGCU AD Carl McAloose introduced as new Edison athletic director by Dana Caldwell Naples.com posted 2/17/2014

[24] Former FGCU attorney adds second discrimination lawsuit against university by Brad Kane Naples News 5/14/2008

[25] Ibid.

[26] Gender Bias Alleged—Again—at Florida Gulf Coast by Kate Maternowski 6/8/ 2009 Inside Higher Ed website

[27] Ibid.

[28] Bonnie Lee Yegidis v. Board of Trustees Florida Gulf Coast University. United States District court Middle District of Florida

[29] Gender Bias Alleged—Again—at Florida Gulf Coast by Kate Maternowski 6/8/ 2009 Inside Higher Ed website

[30] Excerpt from Executive Summary of Florida Gulf Coast University Gender Equity Assessment p. 3

**Chapter Eleven**

*[1] College Sports' L-Word by Debra Blum Chronicle of Education - March 9, 1994*

*[2] [As quoted from page 20 of Strong Women, Deep Closets: Lesbians and Homophobia in Sport, by reviewer Julia Ronnback in her article Effective Cure Against Ignorance - idrottsforum.org/reviews]*

*[3] Duke Journal of Gender Law & Policy Volume 17:1 2010*

*[4] Dugan v. Oregon State University - http://www.aauw.org/resource/dugan-voregon- state-university*

*[5] SDSU, ex-swim coach reach $1.45 million settlement by Brent Schrotenboer Union-Tribune Sept. 26, 2008*

*[6] Resources section of AAU web site - aauw.org/resource/handler-v-novasoutheastern- university*

*[7] Case: Sulpizio v. San Diego mesa College – National Center for Lesbian rights website - nclrights.org/cases-and-policy/cases-and-advocacy/sulpizio-v-san-diegomesa- college*

*[8] Ibid.*

*[9] University of Tennessee-Martin Sued by Former Volleyball Coach Title IX Blog May 30, 2008*

*[10] Surina Dixon wins lawsuit vs. TSU ESPN W. August 12, 2011*

*[11] Burch, et al, v. Regents of California, et al. AAUW Resources website aauw.org/resource/burch-et-al-v-regents-of-the-university-of-california-et-al/ updated 12/07*

*[12] Ibid.*

*[13] Title IX Blog website title-ix.blogspot.com/2008/11/former-iowa-state-coachwins- 287k*

*[14] UC to pay ex-coach millions in bias suit. Los Angeles Times July 20, 2007 by Richard C. Paddock*

## Chapter Twelve

*[1] Donna Lopiano by Jon Snow. Street and Smith Sport Business Journal March 22, 20120*

*[2] Women's Law Project website - womenslawproject.org*

*[3] BruceBaumgartner.com*

*[4] The stronger Women Get, the More Men Like football1994 Harcourt Brace by Mariah Burton Nelson*

*[5] Ibid.*

*[6] From a poster created by Mary Stanley quoting from Jill Ruckelshaus' speech to the 1977 California Convention of the National Women's Political Caucus in San Jose*

## Chapter Thirteen

*[1] Virginia (Ginny) Hunt (Montana State University.) was elected "President-elect in Jan. 1982, but never rose to the presidency*

*[2] Female Athletes: More to Lose Than Just Their Organization by Candace Lyle Hogan. The New York Times 1/25/1981*

*[3] Ibid.*

*[4] Ibid.*

## Appendix B

*[1] New York Times, June 1975*

*[2] It was determined that, in athletics cases, because claims of discrimination involve teams separated by gender, all findings of discrimination are seen as intentional as a matter of law and, thus, are subject to monetary damages.*

*[3] Breaking Down Barriers: A Legal Guide to Title IX, published by the National Women's Law Center, 1994*

Made in the USA
San Bernardino, CA
27 December 2016